KASHMIR
RETURN TO DEMOCRACY

KASHMIR
RETURN TO DEMOCRACY

By

DEV. P. KUMAR

SIDDHI BOOKS
IMPRINT OF
COSMO PUBLICATIONS
1996 INDIA

ISBN 81-7020-755-X

First Published 1996

Manufactured in India

Published by :
MRS. RANI KAPOOR
for SIDDHI BOOKS
Imprint of COSMO PUBLICATIONS
For GENESIS PUBLISHING (P) LTD.
24-B, ANSARI ROAD, DARYA GANJ,
NEW DELHI-110002, INDIA.

Lasertypeset by:
AD Computers

Printed at:
Mehra Offset Press

To
Dear Baneesh, Shalini
and
Laabanya Ramaul

Preface

I wrote "Kashmir-Pakistan's Proxy War" about two years ago. The present book was being written in a wider scope even as the election dates in Jammu and Kashmir were being put off every six months. That explains why I had to bring in the Lok Sabha elections in the first chapter.

The disturbances in the State, which are the handiwork of Pakistan, are growing less and less every day and is now very much in control. The question now is will insurgency and terrorism be finally over and peace descend on Kashmir.

I would never have been able to do the job had it not been the tireless assistance and helping hand my wife, Bindi, gave me in mobilizing the materials and in composition of ideas.

I am most grateful to the help and cooperation extended by Mr. Ram Mohan Rao, information advisor to the Government of Kashmir, who gave much of his valuable time to this book.

August 30, 1996 — D. P. Kumar

Contents

Chapter 1

Return to Democracy

It is the people of Jammu and Kashmir who have won over the proxy war waged by Pakistan—at least the first round of it—the Lok Sabha (lower House of Parliament) elections in Jammu and Kashmir were held in the month of May, 1996. The polls were conducted successfully and in the most free and fair manner. Pakistan had been saying that it would not allow elections to be held in Kashmir and went all out to see that India failed to revive the democratic process in the State. With this aim in view, Pakistan had launched a proxy war for the last seven years. But the people of the State, even in the political atmosphere with insurgency and terrorism reigning in the State sponsored by Pakistan, disproved Pakistani thesis. The State has now faced the elections to form their State Assembly. The crucial point now is, whether a successful Assembly election will give lie to the thesis created all these years by Pakistan and its subservient groups in Jammu and Kashmir.

It was no ordinary election that was held by India in May and September, 1996, in Jammu and Kashmir. It was the most challenging election held in India and unlike the situation in Assam, "where militants or the ULFA had to be tackled, in Kashmir it was a neighbouring and powerful country, Pakistan, that is involved."

"After seven years of militancy and insurgency and two unsuccessful efforts of reviving the political process in the State recently, the completion of a peaceful election for the Lok Sabha has sent the message loud and clear that pro-Pakistani outfits, particularly the Hizbul Mujahideen's writ of not allowing elections does not run any longer", according to a top officer of the Jammu and Kashmir State government. The Hurriyat had also threatened that nothing would move in the State from May onwards elections are held, but all services to supply food, water and power have been maintained.

Rao decides to have Elections

It was towards the end of the then Prime Minister, P.V. Narasimha Rao's term of office that an announcement was made to have the Lok Sabha election from Jammu and Kashmir state, simultaneously with the general election in the country. The Assembly Elections, regarded as more vital, it was stated, would be held later, if all went well with the polling (for the Lok Sabha), first in Ladakh and Jammu on May 7. The elections for Anantnag and Baramullah would take place, later on May 23, and to Srinagar and Udhampur constituencies on May 30, it was announced. The time gap was allowed to make adequate arrangements for posting of military and para-military personnel to ensure a fair and free poll and to save people from terrorist attacks.

It was regarded as a major decision by the Narasimha Rao Government to have the elections in Jammu and Kashmir after long seven years, during which the State witnessed the most harrowing time of terrorism and insurgency. The Chief Election Commissioner, T. N. Seshan, announced to newspersons on May 18 in New Delhi that all necessary arrangements had been made to ensure a fair and free poll and every possible contingency had been taken care of. The elections to the Lok Sabha would take place in time, before the term of President's rule was over in July 17 for the Assembly elections, a further period of President's rule would be asked for in Parliament.

During his five-year rule, P. V. Narasimha Rao for the first time, visited Jammu, to declare that "despite Pakistan's conspiracies", elections in Jammu and Kashmir would be taken to their logical conclusion. Elections to the State Assembly would take place after the Lok Sabha elections. Rao declared "Pakistan cannot take over Kashmir by proxy war, though it might continue with its ill intentions to impoverish Kashmiris and cause damage to the economy through proxy war. But this war will also fail as had happend with the three earlier direct wars that Pakistan fought on Kashmir." He declared that Article 370 of the Constitution which granted special status to Jammu and Kashmir "is an inseparable part of the Constitution," meaning it would be retained.

The Kashmir Electorate

Until some time ago India had been thinking for having a poll in Kashmir for its legislative assembly, but with the general election of 1996 approaching in the month of May, the Government of India decided that Jammu and Kashmir would also go for Lok Sabha poll in the State, to pull it out of quagmire it had fallen into for seven years—ever since the 1989 elections—and give the people the courage to face the Assembly elections later. The Election Commission which had been making efforts for a long time to hold the elections in the State also agreed with the idea. It was thus decided that Jammu and Kashmir would go to poll for the Lok Sabha poll along with rest of the country, and so it did. The schedule for Lok Sabha poll fixed for Jammu and Kashmir was: May 7, Ladakh and Jammu; May 23, Baramullah and Anantnag and May 30 Srinagar and Udhampur.

The Kashmir electorate was also apparently keen to vote. Despite non-participation by some political parties, there was tremendous enthusiasm among the 44 lakh electorate in the six Lok Sabha Constituencies in Jammu and Kashmir. This number included the nearly 200,000 Kashmiri voters, who had left the State and were living mostly in camps in Jammu, Delhi and other parts of the country for the last six years ever since they had to leave the State under threat of terrorists. There were 158 candidates in the field and 5 of them were women and even some militants. As many as 88 of them wanted to fight as Independents. It was almost double the number of candidates (some 90) who had filed nominations during the last elections seven years ago. Although campaigning was yet to begin, people were brimming with enthusiasm, hoping that revival of the democratic process would end the seven-year old turmoil. Officials said that the increase in filing of nominations by people in the State, including some "reformed militants" proved that people were giving up militancy and were prepared to participate in the electoral process. "This is a rebuff to Pakistan which had declared that it would not allow elections to take place in Jammu and Kashmir", according to a senior official. There was, however, a lingering fear that militants might try to disrupt the polls and senior police officers said they could not rule out stray incidents, but would maintain security. Many Government officials were reluctant to be on poll duty in the Valley, as a result of which several hundred Urdu-knowing officials had to be brought to the Valley from outside the State. Some additional para-military forces had also to be airlifted to maintain security and allow elections to go peacefully. The State Governor-General, K. V. Krishna Rao said at a Press Conference that Pakistan was trying to scuttle the poll process in the State. The administration had reports that there had been some infiltration attempts from across the border. The Government would make available 500 companies of para-military forces in Baramullah and Anantnag constituencies in the Kashmir Valley who would be later shifted to Srinagar and Doda-Udhampur constituencies.

On the other hand, some political parties announced their non-participation in the polls. The most important party in the State, the National Conference, stated that ground realities were not conducive for the elections. It, however, did not link its demand for greater autonomy for the State with the elections, and said the two were separate issues. The All Kashmir Hurriyat Conference, a conglomeration of some fundamentalist parties in the Valley, also announced the boycott of the poll. Despite this, the Ikhwan-ul-Muslimoon's political wing, the Awami League, fielded independent candidates (as the Awami League had not yet been recognised by the Election Commissioner). The Centre accorded Z-category security for the Jammu and Kashmir candidates to prevent attacks against them by militants.

Countdown Begins

The countdown for the most prestigious parliamentary constituency of Srinagar began amidst full poll preparation by the Government and rocket attacks by militants. Militants tried prove their prowess and disruptive potential by firing rockets targeting hotels, housing polling staff and security personnel. Two of the rockets exploded in the Shankarcharya hills. The State Governor-Gen., Krishna Rao declared that he would not allow any force to disrupt the polls. Srinagar was the most crucial area for militants and terrorists to prevail over. Srinagar was therefore given the maximum protection by the authorities. In Srinagar, slogans such as "we want freedom" were still being heard. Srinagar had witnessed massacres beginning with Gowkadal in January, 1990 to Hanyar in August, 1993. Moreover, militants still entrenched the downtown localities, continued to have their influence on the willing and unwilling populace of downtown. Officials realised that it was Srinagar which has represented Kashmir in the past and it was destined to represent it in future. As the campaigning progressed, the Government feared Pakistani bid to kill candidates and took necessary steps. Pakistan's stakes had been heightened in Kashmir since the late eighties and if elections were held smoothly, it would lose face both with the Kashmiris and its own nationals back home. That is why Pakistan had been drumming up support in the Islamic world, especially in the Organisation of Islamic Conference (OIC) on Kashmir. Elections in Kashmir would see Islamabad losing its top slot in the OIC and blunt its criticism of India on Kashmir in the international fora.*

Pak throws in Last Gauntlet

On the eve of poll, Pakistan threw its last gauntlet to

* "Government fears Pak bid to kill candidates" by Arun Joshi, *Hindustan Times*, April 9, 1996

prevent the polling in Kashmir. Breaking the restraints of all diplomatic privileges, on April 28, Pakistan's High Commissioner in India, Riaz Khokhar, accused the Indian Government "of intending to rig the forthcoming polls in Kashmir." In an interview given to the India Abroad News Service, he declared "All elections (in Kashmir) in the past have been rigged. The present elections will be rigged." Debunking the electoral process in the State as a "Complete fraud" which would "Complicate matters further" between Pakistan and India. Khokhar questioned the credibility of the poll exercise when "you have 600,000 troops in place and you cordon it (the State) off and bring people at gun point and not even allow international observers." (The charge that India has put in 600,000 troops in Kashmir, made earlier by the Pakistani President himself, has been contradicted several times before).

"It would be a lot easier and would save the Government of India a lot of money...if it were to stuff the ballot boxes in Delhi and announce any results it wants to announce", Khokhar remarked contemptuously.

During his four years in India, Khokhar had earlier too crossed the mark of diplomacy and indulged in making comments not consistent with the position he holds. He was promptly summoned to the Foreign Office and told by the Foreign Secretary, Salman Haider that the tone and content of the interview given by the High Commissioner had "outraged" the Indian public opinion. His observations were "unacceptable, provocative and amounted to an interference in India's internal affairs.

"We are in no need of advice from outside, least of all Pakistan, on how to conduct elections". Haider told Khokhar. He said that the problem in Jammu and Kashmir was essentially that of "Interference and armed intervention from Pakistan". Haider rejected the charge of rigging of elections, past or present. International community, he said , had not been deceived by Pakistani propaganda on this score and Pakistan's own strategy of fomenting violence had been exposed.

While most political party leaders' reaction was in tune with the Foreign Secretary's observations that his remarks were not in keeping with the status of a foreign representative in India, majority of them wanted Khokhar to be declared *persona non grata* and be asked to leave the country for his outburst. Those favouring the High Commissioner's expulsion were the Bharatiya Janata Party, Janata Dal, Janata Party and Samata Party. The Congress Party felt that Khokhar's remarks were in bad taste and violated all norms that govern international relations between sovereign nations. India did not proceed in the matter.

On April 4, India accused Pakistan of doing its utmost to thwart the election process in Jammu and Kashmir for "it wishes to continue the relentless and ruthless proxy war against this country." Reacting to the statement issued by the OIC contact group in New York, India's official spokesman explained that it would not help restoration of normalcy and peace in the State if the group permits itself to be used by Pakistan to issue inaccurate and provocative statements. The Organisation of Islamic Conference continues to be used by Pakistan to purvey anti-India propaganda, the statement said.

Only days before the poll, Pakistani Prime Minister, Benazir Bhutto urged on the new Prime Minister, Atal Behari Vajpayee, to put off the polls in Jammu and Kashmir and to reduce tensions between two neighbouring rivals over the Kashmir issue. She told reporters at the northern town of Gilgit (in occupied Kashmir) that Vajpayee should put off the remaining parliamentary elections in the "India-ruled Kashmir, talk to the umbrella All Party Hurriyat Conference of separatist groups fighting Indian rule and put on the agenda the future of Kashmir in talks with Pakistan."

U.S. Gesture for First Time

But just on the eve of the poll, the USA lent a helping hand to India by releasing a report on global terrorism, from which the US itself had meanwhile begun to suffer. It was an annual report in which the US government stated that Pakistan was officially supporting militancy and fomenting violence through a bombing campaign in Kashmir, which was in other words to chastise Pakistan offcially. The US State Department said there were credible reports of official Pakistani support for militants fighting in Kashmir, including for the groups that claimed responsibility for the bombing on India's Republic Day celebrations and the attack which killed an AFP correspondent in Srinagar in 1995.

Although the terrorism report the previous year too had accused Pakistan of backing militancy in Kashmir, the report this time mentioned specific instances and the groups Islamabad was backing. "There continued to be credible reports in 1995 of official Pakistani support to militants fighting in Kashmir, including Pakistani, Afghan and Arab Nationals, some of whom engage in terrorism",according to the report entitled 'Patterns of Global Terrorism 1995' released in Washington DC on April 30, 1996.

The report said one Pakistan-backed group, Harkat-ul-Ansar is believed to be linked to Al-Faran, the group that claimed responsibility for the kidnapping in July of tourists, including two US citizens. Other Pakistan-backed groups claimed responsibility for numerous bombings in Kashmir, including one on foreign journalists. The report said bombings, claimed by Kashmiri groups, occurred throughout the year, including explosions in a stadium in Kashmir during Republic Day festivities in 1995.

While noting that Pakistan was also a victim of terrorist related violence, the report said Islamabad claimed that Afghanistan and India were supporting terrorism in Pakistan. But significantly, the report did not make any mention of "credible evidence" to back Pakistan's claim, as it did in the case of Islamabad's subversive activities in Kashmir.

In an overview of global terrorism, the report reiterated the US belief in a strict counter-terrorist policy.

Contest and Results

Prior to the poll, more than one thousand public rallies were organised by the candidates in the fray in all the six constituencies of the State. Attendance at these rallies were quite good though their critics said that much of the audience was orchestrated by security forces. These charges were vehemently denied by all the political parties, including the Awami League, which was the popular outfit of the new party participating in the poll, the Ikhwan-ul-Muslimoor poll.

It is the traditional parties that continued to be favourites with the electorate in Jammu and Kashmir when elections were held to the six Parliamentary seats in the State. The six seats were shared by the national parties, for the National Conference did not contest the elections and its absence was felt by a majority of the electorate during the election.

The Congress Party, which secured some 570,800 votes constituting 26.16 per cent of the polled votes in the State, won four seats—Baramullah, Srinagar, Ladakh and Jammu, while the Bharatiya Janata Party (BJP) secured 407,560 votes constituting 18.68 per cent votes. the BJP could win only the Udhampur seat. The Janata Dal got 365.874 votes, constituting 16.77 per cent of the total votes polled and bagged Anantnag seat, while another candidate, Farooq Ahmed Indrabi lost to the Congress candidate by just 16 votes in Srinagar constituency.

Bahujan Samaj Party (BSP) and Congress Party (Tiwari) which joined the fray for the first time got 123.401 and 17.279 votes respectively. There were 83 independent candidates, who together secured 491, 274 votes in the six parliamentary constituencies, constituting 22.52 per cent. No independent candidate was, however, successful in the elections though one of them came second in the tally of votes polled in Baramulla constituency.

While the traditional political parties thus remained relevant in the situation despite apprehension in some quarters, independent candidates were also able to secure a sizeable number of votes in the elections.

In Ladakh Parliamentary constituency, the total votes as recorded by the Election Commission were 106,347. The Congress candidate, P. Namgyal, a former Union Minister, polled 54,592 votes as against Qamar Ali Akhoon (Independent) who secured 44,457 votes. The BJP nominee Ms. Saplez Angnoo secured only 5,728 votes. Qamar Ali Akhoon, a National Conference rebel contested as an Independent. The BJP nominee lost her deposit in the three cornered contest in the cold desert constituency.

The Jammu Lok Sabha seat was won by Mangat Ram Sharma, who polled 195,166 votes defeating his nearest BJP rival, Vaid Vishnu Datt by a margin of 47,672 votes. The BJP candidate polled 147,494 votes. Because of dissidence in the Congress and hectic campaigning by the BJP, observers had predicted that the Congress would lose the seat this time. But Sharma defied all the calculations and romped home with a comfortable win at the end.

Another blow to a Congress dissident came with the victory of the Pradesh Congress Committee President, Ghulam Rassol Kar in Baramullah constituency over his nearest rival, Ghulam Nabi Mir (Independent) by a margin of nearly 65,000 votes.

Congress Wins in Srinagar

In the prestigious Srinagar Parliamentary constituency, the Congress nominee won the election. In the keenly-contested electoral fight, the Congress candidate, Gulam Mohammad Mir Magani, defeated his nearest Janata Dal rival, Farooq Ahmed Andrabi, by a margin of 1,549 votes. While the Congress candidate secured 55,503 votes, the Janata Dal Candidate got only 53,904 votes. A BJP candidate was also in the fray.

In Anantnag, the total votes polled were 357,858 out of which 27,003 votes were declared invalid. The Janata Dal candidate, Mohd. Maqbool Dar secured 117,221 votes as against the nearest Congress rival, Taj Mohi-ud-Din who secured 57,173 votes.

The response in Udhampur constituency was beyond expectations as the BJP candidate, Chaman Lal Gupta there secured 166,206 votes, while his nearest Congress rival,

Janak Raj Gupta secured 96,151 votes, thereby showing a winning margin of 70,055 votes in favour of the BJP candidate. Both contested from Jammu last time and D. D. Thakur of Janata Dal was placed third, in a fray of 40 candidates.

Political observers saw Anantnag, Baramullah, Srinagar and Udhampur as prestigious Parliamentary constituencies in the State where the elections were well-fought because of the massive turnout of voters.

The victory of the Congress in four of the six constituencies spelt gain of three seats for the Congress as compared to 1989 elections when it bagged only two. In 1989, it had won Jammu and Udhampur seats only. The most surprising win for the Congress this time was in Jammu where the party candidate had the better or his BJP rival.

The overwhelming voters' participation in the Lok Sabha elections in Kashmir nailed the persistent propaganda made in Pakistan that the poll in the State would either not be held or would be rigged. It was seen, however, that even in an atmosphere that was created to fill the people of Kashmir with fears, they have opted to reject militancy and vote for strengthening the democratic political process in the State.

Political observers saw that large-scale participation of the people—the polling percentage averaged 49 per cent in the State—conclusively proved that the people of Jammu and Kashmir have won the proxy war waged by Pakistan and opted for restoration of democratic institutions such as Parliament and State Assembly in place of militancy that had during the past seven years completely weakened the functioning of the State's civil administration and affected economic growth in Jammu and Kashmir. The successful election in Jammu and Kashmir has totally exposed the Pak propaganda that people in the State would reject the call for elections. Long before the electoral exercise, cynics had opined that the initiative for elections to the six Lok Sabha seats—Srinagar, Jammu, Anantnag, Baramullah, Udhampur and Ladakh—would be totally rejected by the electorate of the State and if at all the people opted for elections there were chances of large-scale rigging. The participation of the people in the electoral exercise has totally disproved this whimsical view.*

Anantnag and Baramullah

Despite a 'bandh' call by militants and threats given by terrorists and also stray cases of bomb blasts, an estimated 50 per cent of the 1.47 million electorate in Baramullah and Anantnag constituencies exercised their franchies. It was by and large peaceful polling in the Kashmir Valley held after a gap of seven years of militancy. Men and Women formed long queues outside the 2,111 polling centres in the two constituencies—undeterred by firing from across the border and ignoring the threats held out by militants and boycott calls given by the All Party Hurriyat Conference (APHC). The impressive turnout satisfied not only the Election Commission, but also the political parties contesting the polls.

The voter turnout in Anantnag sand Baramullah were as below:

	1996	*1989*
Anantnag	43%	5.07%
Baramullah	35%	5.48%

The turnout was more than eight times of what it was in the 1989 elections in Anantnag, when barely five per cent votes were cast.

The moderate to heavy turnout in the elections in Baramullah and Anantnag belied earlier fears of a total washout of the electoral exercise in the strife-torn Kashmir Valley. It was seven long years since elections were held in the troubled border State and even in the 1989 polls, barely 5 per cent votes were cast in Baramullah and Anantnag. In sharp contrast, almost eight to ten times that number of votes were cast this time, a turnout which is larger than in some other States, such as Gujarat in the general elections

* "Poll proves Pak has lost its proxy war" by A. R. Wig, *Hindustan Times*,June 7, 1996.

in the country. Polling was also largely peaceful in the Valley despite stray demonstrations, bandhs and bomb-blasts as well as firing by Pakistanis along the Line of Control. According to the Chief Electoral Officer, Jalil Ahmed Khan, the highest percentage of voting was recorded in Uri segment of Baramullah Constituency. Three blasts rocked the apple township of Sopore as life remained crippled in the Valley for the fourth day, in the five-day 'bandh' call given by APHC and some militant outfits.

The final phase of the Lok Sabha elections in Jammu and Kashmir concluded amid stray violence and anti-election rallies. Though militants had threatened to unleash large-scale violence, the turnout was commendable —37% in Srinagar and 55% in Udhampur. The Chief Secretary of the State, Ashok Kumar, said the good turnout was a reflection of "the people's desire for peace and restoration of democracy in the strife-torn Valley". The BJP leader, Atal Behari Vajpayee, congratulated the people of the State for turning out in large numbers to cast their votes. "It was a befitting reply from ordinary Kashmiris to all those who wanted to disrupt the democratic process in the State".

Change in Mood of Political Parties

There was a major change in the mood of the political parties and the people after the successful conclusion of the elections. The Governor-General, Krishna Rao, who had been working patiently in the last four years to bring about this change, stated: "Now that the Parliamentary Elections in Jammu and Kashmir have been completed, the State Government thinks that it has a clear mandate to hold the Assembly polls...Next time (at the time of holding the Assembly polls) we won't be confronting so many problems since the message has gone home that the Government can weather all challenges." The mood of political parties has also changed and there were reasons to think that the National Conference might be regretting its decision of not participating in the poll, he stated.

It was clear from the way the Kashmiris had voted in the elections that they had not punished the migrant. The results of the elections in three Parliamentary constituencies of Kashmir did demolish many common notions about the relationship between a candidate and the electorate. The voters of Anantnag, for example, had never seen BJP candidate, Sarla Taploo, but she took everyone unwares by securing 39,960 votes and ending up as the second runner-up in a 16-cornered contest. Apart from the 7,000 Kashmiri Hindu migrants even the nearly 33,000 Kashmiri Muslims are believed to have voted for her. The BJP's only aim was to won the migrant voter in Jammu and Delhi.

The wife of slain Kashmir BJP chief, Tika Lal Taploo, Sarla, had returned to Kashmir just for a day to file her nomination. The Taploo family had migrated from Kashmir in 1990 after Tika Lal Taploo was killed by militants. She reached Srinagar a day before filing her nomination papers, stayed overnight at a heavily-guarded guest-house and left for Anantnag the next day in a cavalcade of bullet-proof vehicles, and then for Jammu. BJP candidates, R. N. Vaishnavi (from Srinagar) and M. N. Kaul (from Baramulla) have similarly performed very well...The BJP is anathema to Kashmiri Muslims for its rigid stand on Kashmir, and in most elections (in the past) the party did not even field its candidates. In the past, even the Kashmiri Hindus have voted against the party.

Two reasons are being cited for the BJP's performance. Some observers believe that the militants have deliberately asked their supporters to vote for this hard-line party so that they can discredit the electoral process by dubbing it as a farce. Some, however, give the credit to poll officials. Another notion proved wrong was that contact between a candidate and the electorate is crucial for his chances. Mohammad Maqbool Dar. Janata Dal candidate from Anantnag who got a landslide victory, had been a migrant for six years.*

APHC and Others Marginalised

The All Party Hurriyat Conference and other organisations not only did not participate in the poll, but had given a

* Aasha Khosa, *Indian Express,* June 8, 1996.

call to boycott it. By ignoring such calls and voting in the largest numbers, the people of Kashmir sent out a number of messages. The most significant of these was that they were feeling fed up with living under the shadow of the gun. They were yearning for a return to civilian rule. This could mean the first major breakthrough in ending the ongoing impasse in Kashmir. It is clear that even the National Conference, the largest party in Jammu and Kashmir, which has ruled the State for long, had apparently misjudged the public mood by not participating in the poll. It must have been out of touch with the reality on the ground. And it is clear hat in realising this fact, it decided to enter the arena during the State Assembly elections held in September. The APHC leaders are still keeping off the polls. Its predicament will be awful. Unless the APHC leaders are determined to bring about their own marginalisation, they should find an entry point to get into the political process.

The implications of the success of Jammu and Kashmir elections were tremendous. "Defying fear, nearly 2.1 million people voted, with participation ranging from 35 to 55 per cent in the Valley and Doda. Contrast this with 1989 when under five per cent dared cast their ballots in Anantnag and Baramullah. The cynic will say that the people were overawed by the security presence. But this was no less in the recent Israeli elections, and in the last general elections in Pakistan. If the security personnel asked people to vote and escorted them to the polling stations, they did not compel them to vote in any particular manner. Thus 7.5 per cent of the ballots were invalidated in Srinagar, or about three times the norm. If T. N. Seshan said that the poll was 'relatively fair', he presumably implied that larger numbers would probably have turned out to exercise their franchise had they not feared reprisals."*

For the National Conference, it had now no option but to enter the arena during the he Assembly Elections in

* "Polls in J & K—From Fear to Hope" by B. G. Verghese, *Indian Express*, June 19, 1996.

September.The APHC leaders must also think of their future role and they would have to think if they should not join the political process that has been started with the holding of Parliamentary elections in the State. After seven years of militancy and insurgency, the completion of a peaceful election has sent the message loud and clear that the pro-Pakistani outfits, particularly the Hizbul Mujahideen's writ of not allowing elections does not run any longer. Besides, it has shown to the people that the All Party Hurriyat Conference is a divided house and is in a very bad condition, said the Chief Secretary. Ashok Kumar. "The APHC" leadership can't stand on its two legs. There is no idealism in them, no guts. They are not people who are prepared to sacrifice...The election is one more nail in the coffin of militancy or the Hurriyat's movement in the State... The Hurriyat had threatened that nothing will move in the State from May onwards, but all the services such as supply of food, water and power have been maintained."*

Deve Gowda's Efforts to Resolve Militants' Issues

After assuming Prime Ministership, H.D. Deve-Gowda formally opened a channel of communication with the former Kashmiri militants by meeting the leaders of the Forum for Permanent Resolution of Jammu and Kashmir. Three top militant leaders. Babar Badar, Bilal Lodhi and Imran Rahi met the Prime Minister, along with their close associates, Ghulam Mohi-ud-din Lone. Shabir Ahmed Wani, Abu Abid and Ghulam Mohammad Chaman. The Meeting marked the resumption of the dialogue that had been initiated by former Home Minister, S. B. Chavan in March. Soon after Deve Gowda told the Lok Sabha that Assembly elections in Jammu and Kashmir would be held before the first week of October this year. The exact dates for the poll would be announced by the Election Commission in consultation with the Centre. Deve Gowda, at the same time, moved a statutory resolution

* "India wins proxy war against Pakistan" by Sabina Inderjit, *Times of India*, May 29, 1996.

on extension of President's rule in the State for six months from July 18, 1996. On the question of autonomy, demanding which Dr. Farooq Abdullah, National Conference leader, had not participated in the Lok Sabha polls, Deve Gowda made it clear that this issue would be decided after holding discussions with an elected government in the State—which meant after the Assembly polls—and after all opposition parties had agreed to this. Deve Gowda pointed out that his United Front's 'Common Minimum Programme' had already made this clear. However, on June 11, the National Conference concluded a two-day meeting of its Executive Commitee, saying that the party would not put any pre-condition for participation in the Assembly elections, declaring that "We will decide (about participation in the polls) only after the election dates are announced." Dr. Farooq Abdullah welcomed the new United Front Government's assurance on restoration of maximum autonomy to the strife-torn state and said the NC called for its speedy implementation. Dr. Abdullah told reporters that his party would try to grant autonomy to all the three regions—Jammu, Ladakh and Kashmir—and ensure fulfillment of cultural aspirations of the people belonging to different ethnic groups.

Benazir's Gestures

Soon after the Jammu and Kashmir election results were announced and H. D. Deve Gowda became the Prime Minister of the United Front Government—ushering a new regime in India—Pakistani Prime Minister, Benazir Bhutto, drastically changed the Pak attitude and seized the chance to offer an olive branch to her new Indian counterpart for resumption of Indo-Pak talks. In a congratulatory message to the Indian Prime Minister, she expressed the hope that the two countries would be able to resolve their differences justly, "given mutual respect and a firm adherence" to the internationally-established principles. Bhutto's message was markedly for more positive and cooperative then 'let us wait and see' policy that had been adopted after the BJP formed Government a fortnight ago. With Gowda now in the saddle, it appeared that the Pakistan foreign office was feeling far more comfortable, and even guardedly optimistic, about the possibility of improving relations. Suggesting that the two countries could put their acrimonious pasts behind them for the sake for their people, Bhutto went on to reiterate her Government's offer of talks to India, provided it entailed discussion on the core issue of Jammu and Kashmir. In this connection, she also pointed to the manifesto of the Janata Dal, an ally of the ruling coalition, which promises discussions with Pakistan on the issue. India's External Affairs Minister, I. K. Gujral promptly responded by saying that the "latest unconditional offer for resumption of bilateral talks would be helpful". "Our response will be helpful. We are willing to discuss everything on earth with our neighbours", Gujral said. The Prime Minister, Deve Gowda, also suggested revival of the Indo-Pak Foreign Secretary-level talks as a step in the direction of the two countries joining in "a wide-ranging and comprehensive dialogue."

In his first address to the nation, on June 16, Deve Gowda stated that the election to Parliament from Jammu and Kashmir was a triumph for "our democratic polity and it showed the maturity of the people in rejecting militancy and militants, including those inspired and abetted from across the border." "Building up on these positive developments, we shall complete the task of restoration of normalcy and popular government in Jammu and Kashmir", the Prime Minister asserted.

U.S. Plan for Talks between India and Pakistan

The United States, which had always taken the side of Pakistan on the Kashmir issue expressed its concern over the "unresolved Kashmir dispute". The U.S. said so, for the first time, after the Jammu and Kashmir Parliamentary elections had been announced and Pakistani Prime Minister, Benazir Bhutto wrote a letter to the Indian Prime Minister saying "for the sake of our people and as civilised nations, let us sit across the table for a search for lasting peace". The U.S. welcomed the prospect of resuming talks, stalled in January, 1994, between India and Pakistan.

Prime Minister, Deve Gowda" said U.S. President, Bill Clinton. Clinton said in his letter written around mid-July that his administration had been making a constant plea to both India and Pakistan to return to the negotiating table. "We have offered to facilitate such talks should both parties desire our help", he stated. Clinton pointed out that the U.S. Embassy in New Delhi was in frequent contact with the major Kashmiri political groups and with Indian officials involved in Kashmir. "Through these channels we are working to reduce human rights violations, allow greater access by international organisations to Kashmir and encourage political dialogue in Kashmir that would lead to the restoration of a credible democratic process", Clinton stated. He shared Congressman, Nick Joe Rahall's view (to whom he wrote all this in a letter) that "the Kashmir dispute if left unresolved poses a threat to peace and stability in South Asia." "I believe the only way to obtain a solution is through direct negotiations that take into account the views of the people of Kashmir" Clinton observed restating his administration's known position.

However, a little before, on June 8, the U.S. had also indicated that Pakistan was responsible for the terrorist activities in Kashmir, including the abduction of American tourist Donald Hutchings and other foreigners and the killing of a Norwegian hostage by the Al-Faran group. It was for the first time that the U.S. came out on this issue, nearly a year since six foreigners had been abducted and four of them are still untraceable—probably killed by their tormentors. The Norwegian was killed by the Al-Faran because he had 'protested' and another U.S. citizen succeeded in escaping their clutches.

The State Department spokesman, Nicholas Burns, said on June 6, "We have made this a big issue in our relationship with both countries (India and Pakistan), and we are willing to do whatever we can to get these people out. We have worked with the Government of India and the Government of Pakistan at the highest levels through our ambassadors —Ambassador Wisner in New Delhi and Ambassador Simonsin Islamabad... The Indian Government is in charge of the search operation and any negotiations that are underway with the Al-Faran group... We are giving the Indian Government all the support that we can."

It was in response to *Los Angeles Times* article (saying that the Clinton Administration has done very little to help American citizens when they are kidnapped around the world, including Kashmir) that Burns disclosed that the U.S. had taken this up as a big issue not only with New Delhi but also Pakistan, which has admitted that it is giving political, diplomatic and moral support to the terrorists operating in Kashmir. The State department in its annual global terrorism report, has been repeating each year for the last few years that there are credible reports of official Pakistani support to Kashmiri militants. It is this official report that is now providing the basis for making the Hutchings kidnapping a big issue with Islamabad.*

New Economic Packages

Soon after the announcement of the Assembly elections, Prime Minister, Deve Gowda, unveiled in Parliament the new economic packages for Jammu and Kashmir in two installments. On July 23, he said the Government would take up work on the 290-km. railway line from Udhampur to Baramullah as a national project. A special allocation of Rs. 50 crores was being made this year for the project which was estimated to cost Rs. 2500 crores in total. The Prime Minister, emphasising that terrorism had been reduced considerably in the Valley, said that the package was important in view of the fact that massive unemployment of youth in the State had been a contributory factor to the growth of militancy there. In addition to providing employment in the State, on completion, the rail communications would help the mobility of people from the State to the rest of the country for employment, education, trade and other purposes. The survey work from Udhampur to Banihal had been completed and survey work upto Baramullah would be over by March, 1997. The Government would provide Rs. 200 crores for this phase of the work. With adequate funding, the entire line

**Indian Express,* June 9, 1996.

upto Baramullah could be completed in 8-10 years.

The Jammu-Kashmir national highway, the only surface link between the Kashmir Valley and Jammu, is at present beset with problems of frequent blockades as a result of landslides and snow avalanches. To provide a dependable alternative link between the two regions of the State, the Government would take up the Bhughal Road Project under the Centrally-sponsored scheme of "roads of economic importance." The project spread over a length of 85 km. is estimated to cost Rs. 77.40 crore (1994-95 costs). The project cost would be shared between the Centre and the State in the ratio of 50:50. The road would generate considerable employment potential along the entire stretch passing through backward areas of the State. When completed, the road, apart from generating economic activities, would help mitigate the sense of isolation of the people of Kashmir.

Work on the Dulhasti Hydro Electric Project (3 × 130 mw) came to a halt in 1992 with the withdrawal of the French civil contractors. An amendment to the overall agreement with the French consortium was finalised in July 1995. Tenders for the balance civil work has been obtained and a decision is expected to be made shortly by the National Hydro-Power Corporation to award the contract. The government will ensure that the civil works are commenced at the earliest. Another major Hydro-Electric Project, the Uri Hydro-Electric Project (4 × 120 mw), is under construction in the State. The work on this is going on according to schedule and the first unit is likely to be commissioned this year to provide the much-needed relief to the power-starved state.

Unveiling in Parliament the second economic package for the State on August 2, the Prime Minister said the Government had written off loans of thousands of small-scale industrialists, sanctioned more money for migrant camps and given the State Rs. 352 crore as special central plan assistance to balance its budget. The "second economic package", Gowda said, was not an attempt to curry favour or influence voters. It was aimed at helping the "suffering masses" in Kashmir. The package included waiving of outstanding loans given to people upto Rs. 50,000 with interest, a special Central Plan assistance of Rs. 352 crore and development of infrastructure for tourism.

The State Government has identified 31,000 borrowers from small-scale trade and industry, transport, hotel and houseboat businesses who had taken loans of Rs. 181.87 crore. The interest on these loans had reached Rs. 212.79 crores, as there had been no payments. The waiving of the loans would enable the small borrowers to apply for fresh loans. As regards the borrowers above Rs. 50,000, an inter-Ministerial committee was being constituted to look into the questions of moratorium and rescheduling of repayments and other reliefs like reduction in interest rates. There are 27,000 migrant families from the Valley living in camps in Jammu. The facilities at the 13 camps were required to be upgraded. Government would provide an additional sum of Rs. 6.6 crores to provide the additional facilities, the Prime Minister announced.

Assembly Elections

Election to the crucial Assembly elections were then announced by the Election Commission. The poll is to begin on September 7,1996 and will be completed by September 30. Polling in the second and third phase is to be held on September 14 and September 21. The Election Commission will make a formal announcement about the Assembly elections soon after the receipt of a communication from the Governor-Gen., K. V. Krishna Rao.

G.V.G. Krishnamurthy, Election Commissioner, stated that of the 87 Assembly seats in Jammu and Kashmir, special security arrangements would have to be made for 46 constituencies in the militancy-affected Valley in the wake of fresh reports that Pakistan-backed militants were planning to disrupt the poll process. Extra security would also have to be provided for candidates, election officials and polling booths in the Udhampur-Doda which falls under the Jammu region, having 37 seats. Ladakh area has four Assembly constituencies.

At present, the Valley has an electorate of over 21 lakh

spread over 3,843 polling stations, while Jammu has more than 20 lakh votes in 2,766 polling booths and Ladakh has an electorate of over 1.3 lakh in 425 polling stations. Like in the Lok Sabha elections, special arrangements would be made for nearly 2 lakh Kashmiri migrant voters to exercise their franchise through postal ballot.

Krishnamurthy stressed that the unprecedented turnout during the Parliamentary elections in Jammu and Kashmir clearly showed that the people there had unequivocally accepted the fact that they are part of India, belying Pakistani propaganda to the contrary.

Will there be an End of Kashmir Problem?

The Indo-Pakistani conflict over Jammu and Kashmir has presumably been the longest confrontation in modern times. As it has frequently been pointed out, the French and the Germans, who fought the bloodiest battles ever in the first half of the century have become partners in the European community. There is even no travel and economic restrictions between them now. The pathetic war in Vietnam has also come to an end. So has the racial confrontation in South Africa. The Indo-Pak conflict over Kashmir is going on for nearly half a century, and the question that troubles the mind is whether the conflict, which has been three full-fledged wars and now the proxy war, will go into the twenty first century.

Fortunately, there are signs in Kashmir today that show that Pakistan has learnt the lesson of six-and-half years of a futile proxy war which has done tremendous harm to Kashmir and its people and Pakistan is coming to the realization that it cannot be carried on any more. Pakistan had recruited some young Kashmiris to give itself the false image of the deliverer. This falsehood is coming to an end.

The people of Kashmir have realized the wrong path that some of them, particularly of the younger generation, had taken and are now eager to return to the safety of their homes, forsaking the guns and Kalashnikovs. There are signs on the horizon that they are fast returning to the right path.

Reading the situation correctly, the Government of India decided to plunge into elections after long years of Pakistani proxy war in which Pakistan was harassing India by using the latest weapons picked up from the Afghan war and with terrorists picked up from all possible sources—Afghans, Kuwaitis and volunteers from Middle Eastern countries to aid them, and of course, some Kashmiri youngmen who Pakistan had trained and equipped.

At first, it was the Assembly election which was still being though of, but just before the Lok Sabha election in the rest of the country in May this year, the Government thought of having a rehearsal, before setting in full-fledged Assembly poll—to go for parliamentary elections form Jammu and Kashmir later. This, it was thought would open up the field for a full selection to the Jammu and Kashmir Assembly. It was a right decision.

In the most successful Lok Sabha polles held in Jammu and Kashmir and perhaps the most fair and free poll ever held, inspite of years of insurgency and terrorism raging in Kashmir—more than 50 per cent votes exercised their right in the most peaceful poll and the people demonstrated their will to return to the path of democracy—after nearly six-and-a half years of Pakistani proxy war to take them away from that faith.

The results were heartening of the six constituencies that went for poll in the Lok Sabha election form Jammu and Kashmir, four went to the Congress Party, and one each to the Janata Dal and the Bharatiya Janata Party. The most important party of Jammu and Kashmir, the National Conference, did not contest. But it is expected that the NC is going to be in the Assembly poll dates for which have now been fixed. It is going to be a very interesting contest, and thereafter, things are probably going to settle down, as they did in Punjab after long years of terrorism.

It is as yet too early to say how the situation will shape up in future. For, if Pakistan continues to be intransigent and there is every reason to think that Pakistan cannot give up its fight over Kashmir because its very existence depends on keeping up a confrontation with India, it will continue with the dispute one way on the other. After all, it is recorded history how even Benazir Bhutto's father, the late Zulfiqar Ali Bhutto, first duped Indira Gandhi into signing the Simla Agreement in the way he wanted it and then went back on it soon after the return to his country.

One is not looking forward to a repetition of that chapter. However, Benazir Bhutto, the present Prime Minister of Pakistan, on assumption of power by the new United Front Government by H.D. Deve Gowda, sent him a message of congratulations, expressing hopes of beginning talks with India again. Recently, Bhutto has said substantive discussions with India could only begin after the Assembly elections in Kashmir were "out of the way". In an interview to a newspaper in Dubai, Bhutto stated that the talks (between the two countries) would wait till polls were over "in order to avoid sending wrong signals to the people there." Her view was that the Assembly elections in Kashmir would not change anything in the troubled State.

Chapter 2

The Simla Agreement in Ruins: Pakistan's Perfidy

The Simla Agreement (see appendix-vi) between India's then Prime Minister, Indira Gandhi and Pakistan's President, Zulfiqar Ali Bhutto was signed on July 2,1972, after the third Indo-Pakistan war, that ended in the birth of Bangladesh and also India capturing parts of Jammu and Kashmir. The Agreement provided for a 'Line of Control' dividing Kashmir being gradually endowed with the 'characteristics of an international border', which, if adhered to by Pakistan, would have meant a division of the present Kashmir, more or less on the lines that the State is divided between India and Pakistan, and thus lead to a solution of the Kashmir problem that has now vitiated the atmosphere between the two countries.

However, soon after signing the Agreement, Zulfiqar Ali Bhutto visited Lahore and virtually repudiated the Agreement, saying Pakistan was ready to go to "a thousand years war" with India, thus virtually bringing to an end a solemn Agreement that he had signed at Simla. For nearly 18 years thereafter, Pakistan held its hands, but in 1989 it launched its proxy war in Jammu and Kashmir, carrying on depredation and destruction all around in the State in its bid to frighten the people and also the Government to submission. The proxy war is still on.

Meanwhile, P.N. Dhar, a former Secretary to the late Prime Minister, Indira Gandhi, who played a leading role in the Simla talks held between Mrs. Gandhi and Zulfiqar Ali Bhutto, wrote two major pieces in the *Times of India* of April 4,1995, making startling disclosures to the effect that Bhutto had agreed to the Line of Control (LoC) in Kashmir as the *de facto* border under the Simla Agreement.

P.N. Dhar's disclosures, made a good 23 years after the conclusion of the Simla Agreement signed by Indira Gandhi and Zulfiqar Ali Bhutto, were well-timed in the sense that Zulfiqar's daughter, Benazir was about to make a trip to the United States to discuss the Kashmir problem with the U.S. leaders. (Her meeting with the U.S. President, Bill Clinton brought her new US arms aid worth $390 million and the US ignoring Pakistan's nuclear capability). Dhar wanted to point out to the world and the US leaders how by the Simla Agreement, Pakistan had agreed to the border of Kashmir as the *de facto* borderundere the Simla Agreement—from the 'Line of Control' or 'actual line of control' which it was until then.

Dhar made the disclosure while he was the Chairman of the Indian Institute of Economic Growth. He belongs to the class of bureaucrats who do not speak, nor has he ever attempted an autobiography, particularly to throw light on the crucial period between June 28 and July 3,1972, the period of the Simla talks of which he was the key player. He was among those who had played an important role in communicating messages, drafting, redrafting and correcting various clauses of the Simla Accord and had been privy to the secret talks held between Indian and Pakistani delegations.

Dhar's articles are full of incontrovertible facts of the situation prevailing then—at the time of signing of the Simla Agreement—and trying to show how Pakistan has been in the wrong in ignoring the Simla Agreement, which was like a word of honour pledged by the then Prime Minister of Pakistan, Zulfiqar Ali Bhutto.

Pakistan, on the other hand has been harping and fruitlessly, on the UN Resolutions on Kashmir even now. The Simla Agreement made a reference to the principles and purposes of the Charter and not to any UN resolution. In fact, the Simla Agreement was a recognition by both sides of the principle of settling bilateral disputes bilaterally, peacefully and without side interference. In any case, the resolutions of the UN have become a treaty is applicable as long as things are as they were all the time of signing the treaty. "If Pakistan backs out of the Simla Agreement, it will be creating a situation which it may have to regret later...India extends its hands of friendship to Pakistan as one civilized nation to another, as one who has historical and ancient links with the other, as one who has inherited the same legacy of history and is cherishing it. It is for Pakistan to grasp this hand of friendship or not. A time will come when both India and Pakistan will have to come together in peace and friendship as two sovereign neighbours and chalk out a path of mutual cooperation for their mutual benefit. Why not do so now?" Indian leaders have pointed out.

No instance of territory conquered Returned to Defeated Country

Pakistan calls itself an Islamic State, but it cannot force the concept of a religious state on India by calling it Hindu India. India is not a Hindu State, but a multi-lingual and multi-religious country where there are 10 million Buddhists, 12 million Sikhs, 5 million Christians and 130 million Muslims in a population of about 900 million. They enjoy equal rights and special safeguards under the Constitution. India does not accept the concept of religion as a basis of statehood for itself. It would be better both for India and Pakistan to try to settle their mutual differences bilaterally, peacefully and without outside intervention, as was accepted by both sides in the Simla Agreement signed on July 2,1972 "Why is it, then, that Pakistan has turned down all efforts made by India to settle differences bilaterally and peacefully? This may be due to their internal difficulties, rivalries and jealousies. Partly, it may be due to the mistaken belief that by internationalising bilateral problems they are going to get a better bargain", it has been pointed out.

T.N. Kaul who was Prime Minister, Indira Gandhi's Secretary at the Simla talks, asked Madame Benazir Bhutto, who was present at Simla with her late illustrious father, Zulfiqar Ali Bhutto: "Is there any instance in recent history where territory conquered has been returned to the defeated country within months of cessation of war? Is there any instance in recent history where 93,000 prisoners of war have been returned to vanquished nation unconditionally and within months of the cease-fire? I am mentioning these points to emphasise that internationalisation of bilateral problems, so far as our sub-continent is concerned, has only made more difficult to resolve.*

This was the essence of the Simla Agreement where a reference was made to a final settlement of the Jammu and Kashmir question. T.N. Kaul said: "I recall asking President Bhutto across the conference table at Simla, "Sir, when you were the Foreign Minister of Pakistan at the Tashkent Conference in 1966, you said that Kashmir was the basic cause of all our differences. Today, you are the President of Pakistan. Are you willing to agree to a peaceful, bilateral and final settlement of the Kashmir question? He replied, "You are right, Mr. Kaul. I did say that at Tashkent. But I did not represent a defeated country then. Today, I do. But as soon as I get back to Pakistan, I will prepare the ground for it. Unfortunately, President Bhutto was not able to fulfil his promise because of internal pressure particularly from Pakistan's military intelligence."

Kaul went on: "Pakistan has been harping on the UN resolutions on Kashmir. The Simla Agreement made a reference to the principles and purposes of the charter and not to any UN resolution. In fact, the Simla Agreement was a recognition by both sides of the principle of settling bilateral

---

*T.N. Kaul, "The Kashmir Question", *The Observer*, March 4, 1995.

disputes bilaterally, peacefully and without outside interference. In any case, the so-called resolution of the UN on Kashmir have become out of date. There is a principle of international law which says that a treaty is applicable as long as things are as they were at the time of signing of the treaty. We cannot wait for Pakistan to internationalize it. If Pakistan backs out of the Simla Agreement, it will be creating a situation which it may have to regret later."

Pakistan virtually repudiating Simla Agreement

Despite the three-part article written by Abdul Sattar, former Pakistani Minister of Foreign Affairs, writing a rejoinder to P.N. Dhar, seeking to controvert what P.N. Dhar had said in his article, it is clear that he (Sattar) was merely trying to repudiate the Agreement, which in fact Bhutto had done long ago while back in Lahore, soon after the Simla Agreement.

It is clear that Pakistan has gone back on the Agreement and that the Simla Agreement has no validity for it any more. If this is the situation, which it really is, it is questionable whether it is worthwhile for any Indian leader to go into any agreement with Pakistan in future to resolve any problem. Since the decade is ending, and along with it the century, thus prolonging any agreement with Pakistan or the signing of any future agreement, it is worthwhile to ask if India should enter into any agreement with Pakistan—looking at the fate of the Simla Agreement.

The only saving grace in this probably in Indira Gandhi at much later date—when she was no longer in power and was in the Opposition and in political wilderness—had denied the existence of an informal understanding with Bhutto during the crucial Simla talks. Bhutto was later going through imprisonment by the Zia-ul-Haq government. That might be the reason why he refused to acknowledge an informal agreement reached between him and Mrs. Gandhi, for it would have given an additional handle to Zia-ul-Haq "to slap accusations of high treason apart from the murder" charge.

The following are some of the articles in this connection:

LoC as border : Bhutto's deal with Mrs. Gandhi: P. N. Dhar

The overriding consideration for India at the Simla Conference was to put an end to its adversarial relations with Pakistan and to forge an instrument that would help to build a structure of durable peace between the two countries. But to translate the idea into negotiable points was no easy task for D.P. Dhar and Aziz Ahmed, the emissaries appointed by the two governments to prepare the ground for the conference. They met in April 1972 at Muree and after three days of hard bargaining produced two documents: an agenda for the conference and an agreed set of principles that should guide the negotiations at Simla.

The principles were meant to generate an appropriate ethos for the Summit meeting between Prime Minister, Indira Gandhi and President, Zulfiqar Ali Bhutto. Recognising 'the need for establishment of durable peace' and 'ending of military conflict' and 'the desirability of diverting resources towards development', the principles demanded willingness to think afresh and cast aside the shackles of past policies.

In pursuance of this, the Indian side took note of the traditional Pakistani view that there could be no enduring peace and stability in the sub-continent unless the Kashmir problem was settled and decided to persuade Pakistan to address the issue. At first, Pakistan resisted discussion on this subject. Its priorities were determined by the events related to the emergence of Bangladesh as a sovereign state. Bhutto was especially concerned with the return of the territories and prisoners of war taken by India during the military conflict of 1971.

Gradual Move : On Kashmir, Pakistan strongly felt that it would be more feasible to first try and settle other, less emotionally charged disputes step-by-step and to take up the Kashmir question later. This approach, they believed, would generate a friendly atmosphere and a favourable public opinion for acceptance of a solution of the problem which would necessarily have to be a compromise.

India though willing to take up the issues of occupied territories and prisoners of war, was keen, in addition, to solve long-term problems, Kashmir in particular. India itself had advocated the step-by-step approach in the past but this had not yielded the desired results. This time, India was determined that the Simla Conference should not turn into a replica of the Tashkent Conference which addressed the immediate problems created by the war of 1965 without tackling the basic reasons that gave rise to it. To break this impasse, Bhutto agreed to negotiate on long-term problems, his code name for Kashmir, provided that the solution, if arrived at, was implemented gradually, in a piecemeal manner and in step with improvement in overall Indo-Pak relations.

To understand the political climate prevalent in the sub-continent in July 1972 when the Simla Conference was held, it is necessary to recall the events that altered some basic perceptions the Pakistan leadership held dear.

The emergence of Bangladesh as a sovereign state had brought out sharply the inadequacy of religion as the sole basis of nationality. It also repudiated the two-nation theory and struck a deadly blow to Pakistan's claim, implicit as well as explicit, that it spoke on behalf of the Muslims of the sub-continent. Bhutto was acutely conscious of this fundamental change of context and he stated this frankly in his preliminary conversation with Mrs. Gandhi.

Personal Position : Furthermore, Bhutto said that he was convinced by the events of 1971 that Pakistan could not acquire Kashmir by military intervention. "Kashmir troubles me a lot", Bhutto said. He did not want its dark shadow looming over Indo-Pak relations. He wanted his countrymen to get over the trauma of the emergence of its eastern wing as a separate independent state as quickly as possible and concentrate on making the residual Pakistan a prosperous country. Therefore, Bhutto was personally inclined to accept the *status-quo* as a permanent solution of the Kashmir problem. However, he had several constraints in this regard which he spelt out as follows:

(*a*) His political enemies at home and, especially, the army bosses would denounce him surrendering what many in Pakistan considered their vital national interest.

This would endanger the democratic set-up which had emerged after 14 years of army rule. In this context, Bhutto repeatedly talked about his fear of what he called the Lahore lobby, though he never clearly explained what it was.

(b) He was anxious to carry the support of all political elements in Pakistan in favour of any agreement that emerged at Simla. He wanted all members of the delegation, representing the entire political spectrum of Pakistan, to support and be committed to the outcome of the conference. He said that there should be no dissenters in his delegation when he left Simla.

Bhutto was very keen to have the support of Aziz Ahmed who led the Pakistan negotiating team. Ahmed was the senior-most civil servant of Pakistan and carried great weight in the ranks of its civil service. He had also a reputation for being a hard-liner. Ahmed's support would, according to Bhutto, secure him the support of the bureaucracy which constituted a very powerful segment of the Pakistan political elite. Aziz Ahmed was against the enlargement of the agenda to include Kashmir. But he yielded ground when the Indian side explained that it was not insisting on an immediate and formal acceptance of the *status-quo* which they believed could be looked upon as the imposition of harsh terms by the victor in war. The Indian side felt that such a move might nurture a revanchist ideology in Pakistan. They reminded themselves of the consequence of the Treaty of Versatiles and were against doing anything which could be the basis of another war.

The Indian side, therefore, put their proposal in a low key and in an indirect manner by proposing that the name of the line dividing India and Pakistan in Jammu and Kashmir be changed from the 'cease-fire line' to the 'Line of Control'. Aziz Ahmed objected to this. He pointed out, quite rightly, that the proposed change of terminology would mean a change in the status of the line. Aziz Ahmed put forth this view vehemently and stated that he was not prepared to accept the change in the nomenclature of the line.

But this change was the core of the Indian solution to the Kashmir problem: the *de facto* line of control was to be graduated to the level of the *de jure* border. Since no agreement was reached on this point, negotiations were called off and the curtain came down on five days of hectic talks which had begun with great hopes throughout the sub-continent. This was the afternoon of July 2 and the Pakistan delegation was scheduled to leave the next morning. Soon the word spread that the conference had failed Mediamen rushed to announce the failure.

Troops Withdrawal: In the midst of this developing gloom, Bhutto asked to see Mrs. Gandhi and a meeting was fixed for 6 p.m. at the Retreat where she was staying. When Bhutto came to see Mrs. Gandhi, he met P.N. Haksar and me briefly and said, "You officials give up too easily". Mrs. Gandhi and Bhutto met for an hour while Haksar and I waited in the adjoining room.

Emerging from the meeting, Bhutto looked very pleased and said that "we have settled the matter and decided to give you some work to do before dinner." After he left, Mrs. Gandhi briefed us on what transpired. At their meeting, Mrs. Gandhi, told Bhutto that she was sympathetic to his concerns and that she would have to appear to be dictating terms to a defeated adversary. She agreed to the earliest possible withdrawal of troops from occupied territories in the interest of an over-all Agreement. (*Times of India*, April 4, 1985).

Kashmir — The Simla Solution: P. N. Dhar

Mrs. Gandhi elaborated the merits of the Indian proposal in the following terms: it was the only feasible solution. An important feature of the proposal was that neither country was gaining or losing territory on account of the war. It also did not involve any transfer of population from one side to the other. Kashmiris as an ethnic community were left undivided on the Indian side. The line of control was, therefore, an ethnic and linguistic frontier. In fact in 1947, at the time of the partition, it was also an ideological frontier, being the limit of the political influence of Sheikh Mohammad

Abdullah and his National Conference Party. True, there were some anomalies in this otherwise nearly etched picture but, these, Mrs. Gandhi pointed out, could be removed by mutual consent.

Bhutto responded with feeling and apparent sincerity. After long and agonising reflection, Bhutto said, he had come to the conclusion that the Indian proposal was the only feasible one. But he could not agree to incorporating it in the Agreement for the reasons he had stated earlier. He would, however, work towards its implementation in practice and over time. Mrs. Gandhi herself was worried that a formal withdrawal of the Indian claim on Pak-occupied could create political trouble for her. She agreed that the solution should not be recorded in the Agreement for reasons advanced by Bhutto, but it should be gradually implemented as he had suggested.

Secret Clauses: It was also agreed that the understanding would not be a written one. The insertion of secret clauses in the Agreement was considered inconsistent with the desire to build a structure of durable peace. It was decided, however, that the Agreement would be worded in a manner that would facilitate the implementation of the understanding. This resulted in some last-minute negotiations which were carried on during the return banquet of the President of Pakistan on the eve of his departure for his country.

Thus, several clauses included in the Agreement had to be drafted and re-drafted in a way that would provide the context in which the Agreement was to be read and implemented. The most important of these was sub-clause 4(ii), which says: "In Jammu and Kashmir, the line of control resulting from the cease-fire of December 17,1971 shall be respected by both sides without prejudice to the recognised position of either side. Neither side shall seek to alter it unilaterally, irrespective of mutual differences and legal interpretations. Both sides futher undertake to refrain from the threat or the use of force in violation of this line". The phrase "without prejudice to the recognised position of either. side was a concession to Bhutto to save him from his domestic critics. But to prevent the abuse of this concession and to lay the foundation for a future settlement of the Kashmir issue, the second and third sentences had to be incorporated and the sub-clause is, therefore, to be read as a whole.

And this is how it was interpreted by observers who followed the negotiations closely. Peter Hazelhurst. The *London Times* correspondent, writing under the title 'Concessions at Simla Summit bring hope for deal on Kashmir', described the Agreement "as a historic breakthrough in the protracted efforts to resolve the differences between the estranged Asian neighbours during the past 25 years." Interpreting sub-clause 4(ii) referred to above, he wrote, "Apparently this will mean that Pakistan has agreed to settle the Kashmir issue bilaterally with India and President, Bhutto of Pakistan will not raise the dispute in the United Nations if he keeps to the spirit of the Agreement. This would appear to be an important concession to Mrs. Gandhi, the Indian Prime Minister, who has advocated bilateralism as the means of settling Kashmir and other disputes with Pakistan.... The Agreement also stipulates that both parties have agreed to recognise the cease fire line in Kashmir as it stood at the conclusion of the war in December, and convert it into a line of peace." (*The Times* , London, July 4, 1972).

Bhutto agreed not only to change the cease-fire line into a line of control, for which he had earlier proposed the term 'line of peace', but alos agreed that line would be gradually endowed with the "characteristics of an international border" (his words). The transition was to take place in the following manner: After the resumption of traffic between India and Pakistan across the international border had gined momentum, movement of traffic would be allowed at specified pints across the line of control. At these points of entry, immigration control and customs clearance offices would be established. Furthermore, Pakistan-occupied Kashmir would set up its branches there and later the area would be taken over by the administration. India would make proforma protests in a low key. (This is what actually happened in 1974 when Bhutto constitutionally made a PoK a province of Pakistan without much protest from India).

It was thought that the gradual use of the LoC as a *de*

facto frontier, public opinion on both sides would be reconciled to its permanence. In the meanwhile, the opening of trade and commerce and cooperation between India and Pakistan would result in casting tensions between the two countries. When Mrs. Gandhi, after recounting their points of agreement, finally asked Bhutto, "Is this the understanding on which we will proceed?" He replied, "Absolutely, *Aap mujh par bharosa keejiye* ".

One of Bhutto's aides, who was very close to the Americans, briefed Mr. James P. Sterba, *The New York Times* correspondent fully on the understanding that his boss had reached with Mrs. Gandhi. In his news analysis, which appeared within hours of the signing of the Agreement, Mr. Sterba, after referring to the inflexible positions of the two governments on the Kashmir problem, wrote, "President Bhutto, Pakistan's first civilian leader in 14 years, came to Simla ready to compromise. According to sources close to him, he was willing to forsake the Indian—held two-thirds of Kashmir that contains four-fifths of the population and the prized valley called the vale, and agree that a cease-fire line—to be negotiated—would gradually become that border between the two countries. The key word is 'gradually'. President Bhutto wants a softening of the cease-fire line—and a secret agreement with Mrs. Gandhi that a formally recognised border would emerge after a few years, during which he would condition his people to it without riots and an overthrow of his government." (The Simla Agreement—Behind the Progress Reports there is the possibility of a Seçret Agreement, *The New York Times* , July 3, 1972).

Crucial Point : This was the understanding between the leaders of the two countries and this was the Simla solution of the Kashmir problem. The Agreement that was signed at Simla in the first hour of July 3, 1972 was the launching pad for the implementation of the Simla solution. Some Pakistanis maintain that the recent events in Kashmir have overtaken the Agreement while Indians insist that the dispute should be resolved through bilateral negotiations as stipulated under it. This debate misses the crucial point that the Simla Agreement provided not only a mechanism for the solution of the Kashmir problem but it also envisaged the solution itself.

The Simla solution seemed the only way in which the political leadership of the two countries could resolve their conflicting claims over Kashmir. It is still the only way that remains open to them. To be sure, aspirations of the Valley Muslims need to be satisfied. The Indira-Abdullah Accord which was an answer to this question has come unstuck, due largely to the growth of Muslim fundamentalism and the massive intervention of Pakistan, in flagrant violation of Simla commitments. If Pakistan accepts the Simla solution, the Kashmir problem will be reduced to manageable proportions. It will simply become an internal problem, one of altering the existing Centre-State relations in a manner that will satisfy Kashmiri demand for more genuine autonomy. (*The Times of India*, April 4, 1985).

Bhutto had agreed to LoC as De Facto Border

Former Pakistani Prime Minister, Zulfiqar Ali Bhutto had agreed to the 'Line of Control' dividing Kashmir being gradually endowed with the "characteristics of an international border," according to a senior member of the Indian delegation to the Simla talks, Mr. P.N. Dhar. "The Simla Agreement provided not only a mechanism for the solution of the Kashmir problem, but it also envisaged the solution itself", says Mr. Dhar.

While some US newspapers had reported such a "secret agreement" between Bhutto and Gandhi, this was never authenticated by either side. Breaking silence for the first time, Mr. Dhar, who served Mrs. Gandhi as a Secretary in the Prime Minister's Office in the 1970s, told *The Times of India* that "Bhutto agreed not only to change the cease-fire line into a line of control, for which he had earlier proposed the term 'line of peace', but also agreed that the line would be endowed with the "characteristics of an international border."

Mr. Dhar's revelations are contained in an essay written for *The Times of India*, published on the editorial page of this edition. Stating that what he has now revealed does not in any way contravene the provisions of the Official Secrets Act, Mr. Dhar said this essay world be followed up with a more detailed account of what Mr. Bhutto had agreed to but that would be made public "only after I am no more."

Mr. Dhar recalls that "it was agreed (between Mr. Bhutto and Mrs. Gandhi) that the understanding would not be a written one. The insertion of secret clauses in the agreement was considered to be inconsistent with the desire to build a structure of durable peace. It was decided, however, that the agreement would be worded in a manner that would facilitate the implementation of the understanding."

In particular, Mr. Dhar draws attention to sub-clause 4(ii) of the agreement which says: "In Jammu and Kashmir, the line of control resulting from the cease-fire of December 17, 1971 shall be respected by both sides without prejudice to the recognised position of either side. Neither side shall seek to alter it unilaterally, irrespective of mutual differences and legal interpretations. Both sides further undertake to refrain from the threat or the use of force in violation of this line."

Says Mr. Dhar: "The phrase" without prejudice to the recognised position of either side "was a concession to Bhutto to save him from his domestic critics. But to prevent the abuse of this concession and to lay the foundation for a future settlement of the Kashmir issue, the second and third sentences had to be incorporated and the sub-clause is, therefore, to be read as a whole."

"Mr. Bhutto had agreed" recalls Mr. Dhar, that "after the resumption of traffic between India and Pakistan across the international border had gained momentum, movement of traffic would be allowed at specified points across the line of control. At these points of entry immigration control and customs clearance offices would be established. Furthermore, Pakistan-occupied Kashmir would be incorporated into Pakistan. To begin with Bhutto's party would set up its branches there and later the area would be taken over by the administration. India would make proforma protests in a low key."

It was thought that with the gradual use of the LoC as a *de facto* frontier, public opinion on both sides would get reconciled to its permanence. Meanwhile, the opening of trade and commerce and cooperation between India and Pakistan would result in easing tensions between the two countries. When Mrs. Gandhi, after recounting their points of agreement, finally asked Bhutto: "Is this the understanding on which we will proceed?" He replied: "Absolutely, *Aap mujh par bharosa keejiye* " (you may depend on me.) (Sanjaya Baru, *The Times of India*, April 4,1995).

Dhar's disclosure Well-timed?

The startling disclosure by P.N. Dhar, a former Secretary to the late Prime Minister, Mrs. Indira Gandhi, that her counterpart in Pakistan, Mr. Zulfiqar Ali Bhutto, had agreed to the Line of Control (LoC) in Kashmir as the *de-facto* border under the Simla Agreement has come at a time when the present Prime Minister of Pakistan, Mrs. Benazir Bhutto, is set to leave for Washington to discuss the Kashmir problem with the US leaders.

Mr. Dhar who is now Chairman of the Institute of Economic Growth, belongs to the old school of Bureaucrats who not speak. Then even do not write their autobiographies to make a fast buck. During the crucial period between June 28 and July 3,1972, he was among those who had played important role in communicating messages, drafting, redrafting and correcting various clauses of the Simla Accord and had been privy to the secret talks held between the Indian and Pakistani delegations.

It is for the first time that a person associated closely with the signing of the accord has chosen to say that the agreement provided not only mechanism for the solution of the Kashmir problem but also envisaged the solution itself. The solution, in a nutshell, was that Mr. Bhutto's party would declare occupied Kashmir as one of the provinces so that the autonomy of PoK is eliminated, increase trade and communication between the two countries by setting up more border movement and take several other steps so that gradually "the *de-facto* line of control could be converted as the *de-jure* line of control at a later date."

Mr. Dhar, who was his head of the Indian delegation, got a sudden heart attack when talks were in progress and was admitted to Snowdon Hospital in Simla. Mr. P.N. Haksar, Principal Secretary to the late Prime Minister, Indira Gandhi who closely associated with the talks. The then Cabinet Committee on Political Affairs (CCPA) of Mrs. Indira Gandhi comprising Dr. Swaran Singh, Mr. Jagjivan Ram and Mr. Fakhruddin Ali Ahmed was also camping at the site for consultation and approval in the event of any mutually accepted formulae emerging from the talks.

Mr. Zulfiqar Ali Bhutto, apart from being assisted by Mr. Aziz Ahmed, a senior civil servant of Pakistan, had brought his young daughter, Miss Benazir Bhutto at the crucial talks had a warm effect in the cool atmosphere and even when the talks had virtually broken down and everybody was picking up, it was her visit to the hospital and meeting Mr. Dhar that clinched the Agreement.

But surprisingly, none from the Indian side and the Pakistan delegation, ever spoke of the secret clause. Mr. Dhar has said that there was indeed no secret clause. But he quoted a sub-clause 4(ii) of the accord to assert that this was indeed the understanding.

The timing Mr. Dhar chosen to break his 23-year old silence has baffled diplomatic circles to some extent. One view is that since Mrs. Benazir Bhutto, who was an unofficial party to the signing of the agreement, is visiting the USA and will be discussing the Kashmir issue, hence, Mr. Dhar is reminding her of the commitment made to India by her late father and also informing her that it was she who had accompanied her late father.

One of the most crucial aspects of the accord was that it was a bilateral agreement. This was for the first time that the venue of this dispute was not settled in Tashkent as in 1965 or in any other world capital. The very fact that Mr. Bhutto had agreed to travel to Simla to discuss the Kashmir issue and related matters was a feather in the cap of the Indian Prime Minister. She had proved to the then masters of the world that a problem had been settled bilaterally and there was no need for any international mediation. Mr. Dhar's politely reminding Mrs. Bhutto, who inherited the legacy of her late father, that she should not internatinalize the issue and honour the commitment made by her country. (*The Tribune*, Chandigarh, April 5, 1995).

Chapter 3

Pakistan's Proxy War Against Kashmir

The beginning of 1986 saw a mushrooming growth of Muslim organisations including Ummat-e-Islami, Tahafuz-ul-Islam, Muslim Employees Front, Islamic Students' League all of which came under a conglomerate, Muslim United Front (MUF), Jammu and Kashmir. Jamaat-e-Islami quickly joined it leading to an Islamic upsurge. The National Conference (Farooq) and Congress (I) join hands (in November, 1986) to meet the challenge while maintaining their separate identity to check the coming in of Muslim fundamentalism in the Kashmir Valley. The years 1990-1994 (April) saw political and democratic activity paralysed under fear of the gun, growth of fundamentalist and secessionist groups. The formation of Tehrik-e-Hurriat Kashmir (TEHK) at the instance of Pakistan as a political conglomerate of secessionist for leading the militant 'movement' in Jammu and Kashmir was in February, 1990—because the decision to form another broad-based political platform as TEHK had become moribund due to domination of the Jamaat-e-Islami in it in December, 1992. Then was launched the Kul Jamaat Hurriyat Conference as the joint political platform of secessionist groups.

It was in fact the Pakistani President, General Zia-ul-Haq who had launched the proxy war against India—after Pakistan found that in a frontal war, such as in 1965 or in 1971, it was making no headway. The proxy-war began surreptitiously. The first batch of Pak-trained youth was arrested in September, 1986, and the first Pak-trained militant, Aijaz Dar, was killed in an encounter on September 18 of that year. Then was formed the Jammu and Kashmir Muslim Conference on January 16, 1989 and Quit Kashmir Movement was launched by the Jammu and Kashmir Liberation Front on May 11. Some 72 subversive prisoners were released by the State government as a goodwill gesture on July 12, but the next day three Central Reserved Police Force personnel were killed in Srinagar, as the first organised attack on para-military forces by militants. On August 7, the Block President of the National Conference (Farooq) was done away with—the first political killing by militants. Dr. Rubaiya Sayeed, daughter of the then Union Home Minister, Mufti Mohammad Sayeed, was abducted on December 8 and she was released by the JKLF militants in exchange of five hardcore militants on December 13, 1989.

Terrorist Activities Continue

Through the subsequent years, the activities of terrorists continued. On February 5, 1990, there was an attempt by Pak nationals to violate the international border at Suchetgarh, Jammu. Secessionist leaders S.A.S. Gillani, A.G. Lone, Professor Abdul Ghani, Maulvi Abbas Ansari and Qazi Nissar were arrested between February and April and there was another attempt by a Pak mob to violate the border at Keran (Kupwara) on March 28. Then was Mirwaiz Maulvi Farooq assassinated by Hizb-ul-Mujahideen militants on May 21.

Militant outfits sponsored a three-day strike by Muslim State Government Employees in the Kashmir Valley on July 23. Yasin Malik, 'Commander-in-Chief' of the JKLF and other top JKLF militant leaders were arrested at Srinagar on August 6. Between September 15 and November 25, militant outfits sponsored a 72-day strike by State Government employees in Kashmir Valley.

The militants caused an explosion on January 24, 1992, at the Jammu and Kashmir Police headquarters in Srinagar, causing serious injuries to the Director General (Police) and other Security Forces personnel. Then on April 1 were the five detained leaders, S.A.S. Gillani, Dr. Qazi Nissar, A.G. Lone, Prof. Abdul Gani Bhatt and Maulana Abbas Ansari released and a decision was made at a meeting of secessionist overground parties on December 27-28, to form the Kul Jamait Hurriyat Conference.

Major Encounter at Sopore

There was a major encounter and arson at Sopore on January 6, 1993. On March 2 and 3, two close relations of the Pradesh Congress chief, Ghulam Rassol Kar were killed by militants to sabotage any effort aimed at initiating political process. A close relation of the Union Minister, Ghulam Nabi Azad, was also shot at. On March 14, the Jamaat-e-Islami leader, S.A.S. Gillani was abducted by JKLF militants and Dr. Abdul Ahad Guru, a senior JKLF leader was kidnapped and killed by Hizbul Mujahideen militants on April 1. Then, between April 22 and 27, Jammu and Kashmir Policemen observed a strike over the killing of Constable Riaz Ahmed during Army search operation. The striking policemen held demonstrations raising anti-India and pro-Azadi slogans. The Army disarmed the striking policemen to end the strike. On May 7, Prof. Abdul Gani (Muslim Conference), S.A.S. Gillani (Jammu and Kashmir Jamaat-e-Islami) and Mian Abdul Qayum (TEHK) were prevented from leaving the country to attend the ISI-sponsored meeting at Jeddah. In September, 1993, the Kul Jamaat Hurriyat Conference was formally launched from the pulpits of Hazratbal Shrine. On September 21, the Maqdoomi Sahib mosque was set ablaze by militants. On October 15, Hazratbal Shrine was occupied by the armed militants forcing the Security Forces to lay siege around the Shrine, and a week later, 39 persons were killed in Security Forces firing at Bijbehara, Anantnag. Militants surrendered at Hazratbal Shrine after a month's occupation of the mosque on November 17.

On March 29, 1994, there was a blast by terrorist at

Badami Bagh Cantonment, killing 13 Army officers including a major general. A delegation of the Hurriyat Conference visited Delhi to consult politicians and intellectuals of different opinions to find a peaceful solution of the Kashmir issue between April 11 and 14, 1994.

Since 1989, both the Security Forces and civilians have suffered the highest casualties in 1994 and the number of abductions has been the largest. The rulers also know that in January, 1995, alone there were 157 attacks on the Security Forces. They have seen the dangerous signals emerging from such events as bomb blasts at the Jammu Republic Day parade, detonation of powerful landmines in December, 1994 near Mendher which killed 11 Army personnel at the spot, and a series of explosions around Akhnoor in the first week of February, 1995. Then from March beginning onwards there was the most devastating hold-up by Afghans and Pakistanis of the Chrar-e-Sharif for nearly two and half months, leading to the burning of the mosque and almost the entire town bringing the blackest mark on the name of India's defence and para-military forces.

In these years, the foreign terrorists and local militants killed thousands of people, SF personnel, Government officials, top political leaders and politicians, members of the judiciary and the Press and even foreign tourists. Many terrorists and local militants also got killed in the process. There were also a large number of kidnappings by militants and destruction of property by militants, playing havoc in the State in all these years of proxy war.

Pakistan Sponsored Terrorism

1992 was a significant year to Pakistan-sponsored terrorism in Jammu and Kashmir, Pakistan decided to finance the induction of trained, battle-hardened Muslim terrorists from various countries into Kashmir—"Jehad" was their objective.

This became necessary as by the end of 1992 various militant organisations—trained, armed and sustained by the Pakistan Inter-Services Intelligence (ISI) and the Pakistan Army—which were operating in the Kashmir Valley were disillusioned with the aims of proxy war.

Thus, when in October-November, 1992, it was suggested by some functionaries of secessionist organisations to the Pakistan ISI and some important members of Markaz Dawat-ul-Arshad (a Lahore based international fundamentalist and terrorist organisation) that trained Muslim mercenaries to Kashmir should be despatched, the proposal was well received and the Pakistan ISI promised to provide the requisite financial assistance. The Markaz Dawat-ul-Arshad had already recruited and trained a large number of Muslim youth from various countries for "Jehad" in Afghanistan and other regions.

As it happened, after the fall of the Najibullah Government in Afghanistan a number of battle-trained, well-armed Mujahideen were available. They were at a loose end and were causing trouble in Pakistan. They could he diverted to Jammu and Kashmir and used for "Jehad" there they could infuse new fervour into the terrorist groups operating in the Kashmir Valley and step-up terrorism.

Pakistan launched upon a systematic propaganda that Muslim mercenaries had gone to Kashmir to "help their brethren" in conducting "Jehad." The foreign mercenaries were also required to train the newly recruited Kashmir youth who had been lured or bribed or intimidated in launching upon a career of terrorism. But, the infiltration of the foreign mercenaries across the Line of Control was not easy. The Indian Security Forces maintained a constant vigil and had sharpened their vigilance.

Nevertheless, considering the vast mountains and thickly forested terrain through which the Line of Control runs, it was possible for the foreign mercenaries to infiltrate into the Kashmir Valley. This commenced after the melting of snows in 1993. The pro-Pakistan terrorist groups like the Hizbul Mujahideen, Al Barq and Al-Jehad as also the Pan-Islamic Harkat-ul-Jehad-e-Islami and the 'Harkat-ul-Mujahideen' (which combined in 1993 to form the Harkat-ul-Ansar) were mainly responsible for inducting Muslim foreign mercenaries into the Kashmir Valley. The Harkat-ul-Ansar came in the limelight when they kidnapped two British tourists in June 1994.

Many Mercenary Cadres

By the end of 1993 an estimated 800 of these mercenaries mainly from Afghanistan, Pakistan and Pakistan-occupied Kashmir as also a few from Lebanon, Sudan, Algeria, Baharain, Jordan, Saudi Arabia, Kazhakistan, Egypt, Yemen, etc. had arrived in the Kashmir Valley. They had accelerated violence and launched upon intensified terrorism, killings, looting, murders, mayhem, kidnappings and rapes. Some of these mercenaries had specialised in the preparation of IEDs, laying of anti-personnel tank mines, laying ambushes, operating wireless sets, sophisticated and heavy weapons. They were employed in these specialised tasks to augment terrorism.

Pakistan had set-up a clandestine radio station, "Sada-e-Hurriat" to convey its directives to militants groups, pro-Pakistan secessionist parties and foreign mercenaries engaged in terrorist activities. In addition, propaganda broadcasts were made to boost the morale of the militants and terrorists.

The infiltration of foreign mercenaries has continued in 1994. The Markaz Dawat-ul-Arshad which has a large number of well-trained Muslim mercenaries operating under its control, has been sending mercenaries who have been at a loose end after the Afghan war to Kashmir. They are provided full material and logistic support by the Pakistan ISI.

Trained cadres have been working with Al Barq on a contract basis. The Pan-Islamic Harkat-ul-Ansar and the pro-Pakistan Hizb-ul-Mujahideen, Muslim Mujahideen and Al Barq have also recruited a number of well-trained and experienced mercenaries who had fought in the Afghan war. They were pushed into Kashmir as and when possible in 1994.

ISI Infiltration in Doda

Besides the Kashmir Valley, alien mercenaries have also been sent to the Jammu region, particularly to the Doda district. They have launched heinous terrorist attacks on the Security Forces, the minority community of Hindus and the alleged "informers." what is more, Pakistan ISI has been infiltrating Pakistan criminals for short-term assignment like blowing up passenger buses or planting bombs in religious places and shopping centres to create maximum panic, destroy life and property and, above all, to communalise the rioting in the region. The militants—working alone or in groups have been briefed by their Pakistan masters to attack Hindu leaders and Hindu places of worship. The objective is to cause a chain reaction and create bad blood between the communities.

To facilitate the entry of these terrorists and mercenaries into India, Pakistan is misusing its diplomatic missions in New Delhi, Kathmandu (Nepal) and Dhaka (Bangladesh). The Pakistani agencies have been providing funds, fake travel documents and other facilities to the terrorists and mercenaries who are routed through Nepal and Bangladesh. They take advantage of the land contiguity and the Indo-Nepal and the India-Bangladesh borders.

Not much fervour for 'Jehad' among Kashmiris

But, a number of these foreign mercenaries who were recruited for "Jehad" and infiltrated into Kashmir are a disillusioned lot. They have confessed that they have not found much fervour for "Jehad" among the Kashmiris. In fact, the local population has not co-operated with them; it has been hostile to them. This is because the common people have suffered owing to the increased activities of the Security Forces, who have had to step up action against the terrorists, innocent civilians and their families got caught in the cross-firing.

In addition, foreign mercenaries were misbehaving with Kashmiri women, forcibly marrying them or raping them. They added fuel to the fire and the local resentment has been mounting. A few cases of AIDS were reported from amongst the women who had been subjected to sexual assaults. This added to the scare among the people who had been forced to harbour the foreign mercenaries. No wonder, by the end of 1993, some of these foreign mercenaries left

Kashmir complaining of lack of cooperation from the local public.

It has been estimated that about 1200 foreign mercenaries, half of them Afghans and a number of them drawn from Pakistan and Pakistan-occupied Kashmir (PoK), have been operating in the Kashmir Valley and the Doda district of the Jammu region. Since 1991, 49 foreign mercenaries were arrested in Jammu and Kashmir for their involvement in various militant activities. Also 187 of the mercenaries died in various encounters.

Hazratbal Crisis

The Hazratbal crisis was sparked off late in the evening on October 15, 1993 when troops of the Border Security Force cordoned the Shrine, after receipt of information by the Government of Jammu and Kashmir that the locks to the room in which the Holy Relic—a strand of the beard of Prophet Mohammed—had been placed had been cut open and replaced.

The trouble, which culminated in the crisis had been brewing for a long time. The Hazratbal Shrine has been a special place of reverence and worship for most Kashmiris for a long time; it was also being used as a political platform by the National Conference leaders for over four decades.

Various militant group had all the time been trying to get control of the Shrine. Prominent among them have been the Jammu and Kashmir Liberation Front, the Hizbul Mujahideen, and the Al Umar Mujahideen. There was a marked increase in their activities since April 21. On that day the Security Forces had cordoned off an area in the Dhobi Mohalla, adjacent to the Shrine. The militants ran into Hazratbal. The Security Forces had decided to call off their operation when the militants started firing at the Security Forces from inside it. The Security Forces felt that returning the fire might damage the Shrine. From then onwards, the militants organisations started functioning from within Hazratbal with impunity.

In the recent past, the terrorist organisations had been

trying to rouse the passions of the people on religious grounds. Their effort was to move the people of Kashmir away from the liberal Sufi traditions and instil in them fundamentalist practices. Pakistan has also been trying to motivate the Afghan mercenaries to come to Kashmir by telling them that Islam was in danger in the State and many places of worship had been damaged.

More than ten attacks had been mounted against Moslem Shrines in the Valley since September 21, 1993. On the night of September 21, militants set ablaze the Maqdoomi Saheb Mosque in Srinagar city, damaging the Mosque and its "Hamam". There was a call for the people to demonstrate against the Government, but the people did not believe in the accusations. Four days later, on September 25, an attempt was made to set ablaze the Naqshband Mosque in Srinagar city. The Jammu and Kashmir Police guards on duty foiled the attempt.

On September 27, the Kangan Mosque in Srinagar district was sought to be damaged by the militants, who set fire to three houses close to it. The timely arrival of the Fire Brigade prevented the fire from spreading. On October 10, they tried to set ablaze the Asar-e-Sharief Mosque in downtown area. The JKP guards on duty fired in the air and the militants ran away.

Thus, when the State Government received information that the locks of the room in which the Holy Relic was kept were broken, and fresh locks put, they could not take any risk. They decided to cordon off the Shrine and ask the militants inside to come out. The experience that the State had gone through between December 27,1963 when the Holy Relic had vanished and was replaced equally mysteriously on January 3, 1964 had not been forgotten.

On the first day of the cordon,—the Army replaced the BSF on November 16—the militants tried to get away by setting fire to the barracks adjacent to the Hazratbal, hoping that in the ensuing confusion they would be able to run away. But the Army had brought fire tenders, and the fire in the barracks was soon put down. The people residing in the nearby localities like the Dhobi Mohalla were evacuated.

On October 17, when the Inspector General of Kashmir Police, A.K. Suri, went to the Shrine and tried to engage the militants in a conversation, he was told that they would not hesitate to blow up the complex if the Security Forces tried to storm the Hazratbal. As if to reinforce the threat a rocket was fired in the direction of the Shrine that night which fell short of it by a few hundred meters.

Bijbehara

Srinagar itself saw sporadic demonstrations on Friday, October 22. The sizeable among them gathered at Fateh Kadal, which was dispersed and in the process, three persons lost their lives. But the worst incident occurred on that day at Bijbehara in Anantnag district where the Border Security Force had to fire on a violent demonstration taken out in the town in protest against the Security Forces surrounding the Hazratbal Shrine. There was Section 144 of Cr.P.C. in operation. One of the BSF jawans lost his nerve and fired, with the result that a cross-fire broke out and 30 persons were killed and more than 40 injured. The death toll later mounted to over 45, with more persons succumbing to their injuries.

The Government instituted an inquiry. The BSF unit stationed in Bijbehara was replaced the next day.

Food provided at Hazratbal

Meanwhile, the hostages in the Shrine were suffering the pangs of hunger. The State Government asked them to come out from inside the Shrine and take food in the verandah. But they were not allowed to do so by the militants. The talks were not progressing. On Sunday, Wajahat Habibullah again established contact with the militant leaders and as a one time exception food was allowed to be taken inside.

The State Government associated two prominent local leaders, Maulvi Abbas Ansari and Prof. Abdul Gani in the talks with the militants. Despite both these negotiators having the blessings of the Kul Jamaat Hurriyat Conference, they received threats in the local media. It was at this juncture that Ms. Robin Raphael, the U.S. Assistant Secretary of State, made a statement questioning the status of accession of Jammu and Kashmir to India, though a subsequent US Government statement pointed out that there had been no change in its attitude and that it would look forward to a solution of the problem under the Simla Agreement. There was also a directive of the Jammu and Kashmir High Court that the Government should not put any impediment on the despatch of food by the Jammu and Kashmir Muslim Auqaf Trust to the inmates of the Shrine. The food was sent on Saturday, October 30.

The pressure inside the Shrine was obviously mounting. On October 27 two people, including a dumb boy, were released from Hazratbal. On October 31, the only woman left in the Shrine came out. The pressure mounted further. On November 1, scuffles were reported among the militants inside the Shrine. The discussions among the constituent units reached no conclusion.

The talks received a setback when Lt. General (retd.), M.A. Zaki, the Security Advisor to the Governor and Wajahat Habibullah, Commissioner for Srinagar were injured in a road accident on November 4. The State Government nominated the Additional Chief Secretary (Home), Mahmood-ur-Rehman as its representative. Lt. Gen. D.D. Saklani took over as Governor's Security Advisor in place of Lt. Gen. Zaki. Mahmood-ur-Rehman indicated to the inmates that if they wanted to have food they would have to come out near the gate. They refused the first day but could not resist hunger the next day. On Sunday, November 14, two persons ran out of the Shrine. The trickle had started and indications were that many would follow.

The official representative, Mohmood-ur-Rehman and the militants had a long talk on Monday, November 15. An agreement was arrived at and around 2.30 in the morning the process of coming out of the Shrine started. The militants handed over the weapons, came out of Hazratbal, and subjected themselves to the Rule of Law. Not a shot was fired by the Army, which had maintained a vigil around the Shrine for thirty-one days.

Chrar-e-Sharief set on Fire by Mercenaries

In the first week of March 1995, a heavy presence of terrorists belonging to the pro-Pakistan militant groups, Hizbul Mujahideen and Harkat-ul-Ansar, was noticed in the vicinity of 15th century shrine of the Sufi Saint, Sayeed Noor-ud-Din Wali at Chrar-e-Shrief, some 30 km. from Srinagar. The groups were led by one, Mast Gul, and predominantly consisted of foreign mercenaries, who had already killed two BSF personnel.

The terrorists were armed with LMGs, UMGs, Rocket launchers and other weapons. They set up a number of bunkers around the Shrine and nearby places. The reports of their having planted mines around the Shrine were also received during the same period. The terrorists told the villagers that they would leave the town after the Id-ul-Zuha on March 3, when the weather would also improve. But the terrorists were storing weapons, eatables and drinking water which made it evident that they had no intention to leave the place even after the Id-ul-Zuha. The security forces put up check-posts and observation posts around the Chrar-e-Sharief town to prevent the militants from bringing weapons and ammunition from outside on March 7.

By the time it was becoming evident that the foreign mercenaries wanted to desecrate and destroy the most revered of the Shrines of Kashmir which was also a symbol of Sufism and communal harmony. Mast Gul and his foreign mercenary associates had on numerous occasions threatened to destroy the Shrine despite loud protests by the local militants and occasionally by the residents of Chrar-e-Shrief. They would often fire towards security force pickets which forced the people of Chrar-e-Sharief to leave the township from the second week of March.

The State Government on March 14, while reiterating that it had no intention to carry out any operation in the shrine, asked the militants to vacate the town. An assurance was given that if all the foreign militants gathered outside the town, the administration was prepared to send them back to Pakistan across the Line of Control unharmed. The appeal was rejected by the militants.

Simultaneously some leaders of All Party Hurriyat Conference and media persons started going to Chrar-e-Sharief and meeting Mast Gul and others. The Hurriyat leaders did not realise that wide coverage in the local press about their meeting only encouraged Mast Gul to take steps to negate all efforts by the Government to get the Shrine vacated. The administration enforced Section 144 of Cr.P.C. with effect from March 19,1995, prohibiting people other than the natives of Chrar-e-Sharief and adjoining areas from going into the township.

All through April, the militants kept on firing towards Security Force pickets and more and more migration resulted from this. Towards the end of April less than 1,000 natives were left in the town out of a total population of about 10,000. Occasional in-fighting amongst the foreign mercenaries and local militants continued to take place with the former insisting on damaging the Shrine and the latter opposing it.

During April, the Government once again made its intention very clear of providing a safe passage to foreign mercenaries through Suchetgarh border, provided they surrendered before the Security Forces.

In a desperate bid to destroy the shrine as well as to make good their escape during the ensuing confusion, the militants set on fire the residential houses at Baba Mohalla on May 8, at 11 p.m. The fire spread to adjacent houses in the township. The fire-fighting operations by 16 fire tenders were hampered by the firing of rockets and PRG by militants on security forces from within Chrar-e-Sharief town. After six hours, fire brigade personnel and police were able to bring the fire under control. However, fire again erupted in some areas around 6.45 a.m. on May 9, which was also put out by that evening. The Holy Shrine as well as the adjacent mosque was saved. About 1000 structures including 800 houses and 200 shops were gutted in the fire set up by the militants, sometime before the fire was noticed, foreign mercenaries led by Mast Gul had heated exchanges with local militants and one of the local militants who had vehemently opposed any damage to the Holy Shrine was hanged to death.

The Advisor (Home), and other senior officers visited Chrar-e-Sharief on the morning of May 9 and 10 to take stock of the situation and launch relief operations. The Government announced *ex-gratia* relief of Rs. 5000/- per family, free ration for two months and provision of blankets, utensils and other essentials to those who suffered in the fire. The Indian Red Cross Society offered blankets, medicines and utensils to the fire sufferers.

Mast.Gul had earlier sent a message to his masters in Pakistan mentioning about the oath he had taken to escape alive or else burn the entire Chrar-e-Sharief. After the houses were set on fire he confirmed his action on the wireless and got compliments from his mentors from across the border.

The Governor of the State, General (retd.),K.V. Krishna Rao while expressing deep concern on May 8 over the attempt of the militants to desecrate and destroy the holy Shrine and damage the township, reiterated the Government's promise of safe passage to foreign mercenaries provided they laid down the arms.

While the State Government was busy in organising relief operations and taking steps to assuage the feelings of the residents of Chrar-e-Sharief whose houses and property was damaged by the act of the militants, the foreign mercenaries set on fire the Holy Shrine, the adjacent Khankah and the green mosque at 2.30 a.m. on May 11. They set ablaze other residential houses of the town also and fired towards the Fire service personnel to prevent them from going ahead with any fire fighting operation. Simultaneously heavy fire from militants was directed towards Security Forces. The Shrine and the adjoining Mosque were reduced to ashes on the holy day of Id. Curfew was clamped in the towns of Srinagar, Baramulla, Ananatnag, Sopore, Chadoora, Bedgam as a precautionary measure when fundamentalist groups attempted to whip up communal frenzy by calling on people from mosque to the now almost burnt town from sporadic clashes. Some temples were destroyed in Bedgam and other districts.

The Shrine was burnt by Pakistani and Pakistan-trained mercenaries as a score of militants were killed in gun-battles when troops foiled the mercenaries' bid to escape. Six security men had been injured in the fighting; two died. A spokesman for the Al Fateh group, who styled himself as a 'general', claimed 32 militants were killed of these, 10 belonged to his force, 7 to Harkat-ul-Ansar and 5 to Hizbul Mujahideen.

The Shrine was the most important symbol of Kashmiriyat and Kashmiri Sufism in which an overwhelming majority of Hindus and Muslims of the Valley have believed for the last seven centuries, Sheikh Nooruddin Noorani was also known as Nund Rishi. He was honoured as Alamdar-e-Kashmir, and was called "Param Guru" by Hindus in the hallowed days of harmony among the communities in Kashmir. The Sheikh was contemporary of Lal Ded, a highly respected Hindu spiritual priestes who also espoused the secular spirit.

At Chrar-e-Sharief, it was known as early as in February, that the Shrine was being used as a sanctum by armed militants, including foreign mercenaries. A wait and see policy was followed in the hope that the situation would defuse itself, as had happened at the Hazratbal Shrine in the previous year. But one's memory goes back to a similar situation which arose in the holy mosque in Mecca some

Terrorist Violence in J & K

	Total Incidents	*Attacks on SF*	*Attacks on other s*	*Explosion and Arson*	*Other Incidents*
1988	390	6	1	142	241
1989	2154	49	73	840	1192
1990	3905	1098	485	1810	512
1991	3122	1999	321	611	191
1992	4971	3413	507	744	307
1993	4457	2573	539	900	445
1994	6895	2675	1594	1774	852
1995	6819	2570	1836	1633	780
Total	32713	14289	5356	8454	4520

years ago, when armed terrorists entered it. The Saudi Arabian authorities had no qualms about dealing with them by armed action.

Killings in Terrorist Violence

	1988	*1989*	*1990*	*1991*	*1992*	*1993*	*1994*	*1995*	*Total*
Total Killed	31	92	1177	1393	1909	2567	2867	2768	12801
SF Personnel	1	13	132	185	177	216	199	234	1157
Govt. Officials	1	3	62	57	36	34	26	46	265
Top Political leaders	–	–	1	–	–.	2	6	–	1
Politicians	–	3	24	10	4	8	6	12	67
Judiciary	–	3	1	1	–	1	–	2	8
Pressman	–	–	2	1	1	1	2	2	9
Hindus	–	6	177	45	67	87	95	99	576
Muslims	28	64	573	456	706	841	858	983	4507
Sikhs	–	–	6	12	10	7	5	2	42
Others	–	–	16	12	35	40	73	55	231
Militants	1	–	183	614	873	1330	1596	1332	5929
Foreign Tourist	–	–	–	1	–	–	1	1	3

Kidnappings by Militants

	1989	*1990*	*1991*	*1992*	*1993*	*1994*	*1995*	*Total*
Incidents	2	57	100	124	181	332	395	1232
Persons Abducted	2	70	159	183	269	368	549	1599
Foreigners*	-	-	12	.	-	2	6	20
Women	-	8	8	13	26	20	31	106
Politicians	-	33	53	26	4	3	3	122
Govt. Officers	-	21	27	43	37	36	55	219
SF Personnel	-	12	29	38	92	25	14	210
Killed	1	29	29	38	92	157	209	553
Released**	1	32	73	112	128	164	163	673

* Israelis-7, Swedish-2, Dutch-1, Japanese-1, French-1, British-4, Americans-2, German-1, and Norwegian -1.

**In most cases released after extortion, torture, exchange of Militants, Rape. (remaining untraced)

Criminal Acts Extortion and Lootings by Militants

Year	*Incidents*	*Amount Robbed (in Rupees)*
1990	23	2,26,91,200
1991	31	62,30,768
1992	39	64,86,563
1993	50	83,57,626
1994	149	548,46,532
1995	130	31,37,826
Total	422	10,27,50,415

* Only a small fraction of such cases is reported to the authorities due to fear.

Destruction of Property by Militants

Year	*Total Incidents*	*Govt. Bldg.*	*Educational Institutions*	*Hospitals*	*Private Houses*	*Bridges*	*Shops*
1988	128	4	4	–	19	1	–
1989	294	191	172	–	427	16	–
1990	646	501	129	–	1242	172	202
1991	391	45	24	–	819	24	83
1992	564	65	57	–	2312	28	200
1993	662	98	46	–	1110	34	400
1994	606	172	119	4	666	46	162
1995	688	127	133	2	1814	16	402
Total	3979	1203	684	6	8409	337	1449

Recovery of Weapons From Militants

Weapons/Explosive	*1988-90*	*1991*	*1992*	*1993*	*1994*	*1995*	*Total*
Rocket Launchers	141	140	174	95	31	36	617
Machine Guns	124	176	174	166	141	81	864
AK Series Rifles	1474	2602	3775	2424	2196	2055	14526

Contd...

Sniper Rifles	1	3	13	60	41	38	156
Pistols/Revolvers	858	946	808	801	941	965	5398
Grenades	2994	2236	2818	4798	2603	2870	18319
Rockets	370	329	267	174	395	170	1705
Rocket Boosters	156	203	144	99	66	24	692
Mines	1101	217	307	766	1049	634	4074
Guns	30	79	81	95	223	370	878
Explosives (Kg.)	1966	588	436	3275	1342	1484	9060
Bombs	708	72	228	376	56	126	1566
Grenades	-	-	1	10	56	. 27	94
Launchers Mortar	-	-	-	12	7	12	31
WT Sets	22	37	68	171	211	246	755

"You rise and we will do a Bangladesh here"

Actually, it is from 1987 onwards that Pakistan started taking in volunteers to launch the proxy war against India in Kashmir first, and later to infiltrate into Doda district of Jammu. They were taken to Pakistan and given training there. The pioneers in the military attacks were the Jammu and Kashmir Liberation Front, who have been there for a long time, presumably beginning with Maqbool Bhatt who assassinated an Indian diplomat, Ravindra Mhatre in Birmingham in the U.K. The JKLF was always pro-azadi, but the group got a boost by Pakistan in the mid-80s. Discontent in Kashmir became very useful for Pakistan—discontent in the form of a democratic government being dismissed, discontent which followed the dismissal of Dr. Farooq Abudullah. The Muslim United Front was already there. All this was exploited by Pakistan—combining the sentiments of these dissatisfied elements to help its proxy war. Its first message to the militant groups in Kashmir was that "You rise against India and we will do a Bangladesh here. We will give you arms. We will give you training" and what was understood in this message was "at the proper moment, we will also come to your aid—to make you independent."

The next was to send its own trained cadres to Kashmir, and also to help Hizbul Mujahideen to take over from the

JKLF, and to introduce trained cadres of Kashmiries. But doubts still remained in Pakistan's mind: would these pro-Pakistan elements play their game and help the State in coming over to Pakistan?

By 1992 end, the JKLF was converted into a toothless organization by Pakistan by reducing the assistance given to it. The favoured the pro-Pakistan Hizbul Mujahideen. Pakistan also simultaneously began to internationalize the issue. The strategy was that as far as the Muslim world was concerned, it was to convey a simple message: Kashmir is Muslim. India is Hindu and is keeping the place in subjugation. You must help liberate it. Its jehad for the Muslim world. A UN resolution gives the right of self-determination to the people there. India is not giving this right to the people in Kashmir and violating human rights.

Slowly, the Government of India was able to put its acts together and the situation improved. With this the administration and economy also improved. Kashmir's main economy depends on fruit-growing. This improved considerably and the administration saw to it that fruits grown in the State were sent out and sold at outlets in the metropolitan centres. By and large, the economy was restored except tourism and tourism-related work. In early 1994, the Prime Minister, who had taken charge of the Jammu and Kashmir portfolio, took personal interest in the question, sent his officers to the State to find out ways of giving a boost to the economy. More resources were provided. As of now, the economy of the State is doing well, except for tourism or tourism-related industries, such as hotels, houseboats, taxis etc.

Prime Minister's Effort to Remove Alienation

To remove alienation, certain means of fine-tuning of operations were undertaken. When General Krishna Rao went to Srinagar in March, 1993, as Governor he introduced the concept of unified headquarters. This helped in better coordination of the Army, the Border Security Force, the State Police and the Intelligence Agencies, the maximisation of benefits from all available forces. All this has helped and restored normally.

Effort to remove alienation by establishing a democratic government. This was given a concrete shape in 1994. The Government wanted to conduct elections in May-June, 1995. The electoral rolls were updated. The work of delinking of constituencies was completed. Elections were to be scheduled in June, 1995. It was at this stage that Pakistan sent its mercenaries who filled up the holy township of Chrar-e-Sharief and burnt the mosque. There was confusion in the valley and political parties were unsure whether elections should take place or not. The Election Commission decided to defer the holding of the elections. However, the Government of India planned elections again in December, 1995. But the poll could not take place, because of Dr. Farooq Abdullah's demand that the pre-1953 position must be restored to the State Government.

So far as proxy war is concerned, militancy was on the losing end. People want a change and they were not supporting Pakistan. The JKLF and Hizbul Mujahideen and their associates were gradually losing their motivation. Pakistan had already introduced some 2,500 mercenaries to act as terrorists. But the people of Kashmir were gradually giving them up and trying to find their own path to a better life.

Chapter 4

Regional Aspirations

LADAKH MADE AUTONOMOUS COUNCIL BEFORE POLL BUT JAMMU STAYS AS BEFORE

After years of struggle, Ladakhis, inhabitants of the high plateau in the north-west of Kashmir and adjacent to the Tibetan plateau, had their dreams partially fulfilled. The people of Ladakh, mainly Buddhist, had long been struggling to become a Union Territory, separated from Kashmir, but at last they were given an Autonomous Hill Development Council status—on the model of the Council that had been conceded in the other extreme border of the country, Darjeeling, in West Bengal.

This only partly met their long-cherished demand. Though still a part of Jammu and Kashmir, they have a Development Council of their own and there would be a separate allocation of funds for the region which Ladakhis will spend for development of their region. The Ladakhis enthusiastically welcomed the step taken by the Centre in September, 1995.

Thupstan Chhewang, the Congress Party leader in the 26-member Council was elected as the Chief Executive

Councillor.

The All-Party Hurriyat Conference on called the formation of the Leh Autonomous Council, as "politically motivated". Reacting Chhewang called the remarks "totally unjustified and unwarranted". "It exposes them thoroughly, as on the one hand they are demanding autonomy or some sort of 'azadi' for themselves, yet they are opposing autonomy for a region of the State", he said. Chhewang said that the threats of stopping essential supplies to Ladakh on the Hill Council issue by the Kashmiri leaders showed their communal bias against other regions and communities. "They have no reason to oppose it as the mechanism of self-rule for Leh has been under the Jammu and Kashmir Constitution", he remarked.

He said that the Ladakhis would oppose the grant of the pre-1953 status to the State (which was being demanded by the National Conference), as it would amount to subjugation of Jammu and Ladakh regions by Kashmir. "We have scaled down our demand from grant of Union Territory status for Ladakh to autonomous council only in the national interest and to preserve the unity and integrity of the State", he said.

The Ladakh Council has got going, and its impact is bound to be felt in the coming elections.

Leh People Awaiting Elections

On November 8, 1995, leaders of the Ladakh Autonomous Hill Development Council were in New Delhi. By the time, Prime Minister, P.V. Narasimha Rao, had offered to hold elections in Jammu and Kashmir, to be held after December 15, 1995, and were yet to be accepted by Dr. Farooq Abdullah, former Chief Minister and leader of the National Conference. Chhewang in his interview said despite the fact that sub-zero temperatures prevail throughout the day in Leh during the second week of December, Ldakhis had told the Election Commission that they were looking forward to the proposed Assembly Elections.

By the time the Congress (I)—dominated Ladakh Autonomous Council delegation was still in New Delhi, the Prime Minister's offer to resolve the Jammu and Kashmir problem had come from Ouagadougoi for 'greater autonomy' had come. The Chief Executive Councillor, told a Press Conference that Ladakh's four MLAs would oppose any move to implement the 1975 Accord once the Assembly was constituted. The Congress (I) politicians of the Jammu region were with their Ladakh colleagues in their opposition in enlarging the autonomy. "We will not compromise on this issue. No pre-1953, no 1975", Chhewang pronounced.

Both Thupstan and his colleague and former Union Minister, P. Namgyal, welcomed the Centre's decision to hold elections in the State. "We will ensure that elections are held peacefully and that there is a large turnout. We will not go in for any alliance with the National Conference, which has traditionally been the strongest party in the Valley. We will want to form Government on our own'", said Namgyal.

Formation of Ladakh Council Criticised

The Srinagar-based Hurriyat Conference which calls for the separation of Jammu and Kashmir from India and the establishment of what it describes as "Nizam-e-Mustafa" there, promptly criticised the constitution of the Leh Autonomous Hill Council (LAHC) in Ladakh. In addition, it had taken several steps in the last two months or so to put pressure on the powers—that be in New Delhi and Srinagar to restore the position as it existed in Leh before the formation of the Autonomous Hill Council.

The attitude of Dr. Farooq Abdullah's Valley-based National Conference which stands for a limited accession of the State in the Indian Union and of the dominant section of the Pradesh Congress led by Ghulam Rasool Kar to the new dispensation in Leh was no different. Almost all Kashmiri leaders of these parties had expressed their unhappiness over the setting up of the LAHC and interpreted it as a step that would hurt the setting up of the LAHC and interpreted it as a step that would hurt the Kashmiri psyche and ultimately lead to the disintegration of the State.

Even a cursory look at how the successive Kashmiri rulers managed things in the State between October 1947 and January 1990 would reveal that they were squarely responsible for strengthening the "forces of disintegration" in Leh as well as in Jammu. For Example, Sheikh Abdullah's Government did not permit the Registrar-General of India to hold the census in the State in 1951 along with the rest of the country much to the chagrin of the people of Jammu and Ladakh.

To enable Kashmir to establish its hegemony over the State's politics, administration and economy, Sheikh Abdullah secured for the Valley (having a land area of 15,853 sq. km. and less than 45 per cent of the State's population) as many as 43 seats in the 75- member Legislative Assembly. In other words, the people of Jammu and Ladakh, who constituted more than 55 per cent of the State's population and inhabited 1,22,994 sq. km. of the States total area of 1,33,847 sq. km. were left with no alternative except to elect 32 legislators.*

Not only this, the Government in Srinagar denied the people of Jammu their legitimate right to return legislators by whom they wanted themselves to be represented. It did so by rejecting wholesale the nomination papers of candidates seeking elections to the Assembly on the tickets of the Praja Parishad—the sole opposition party in the Sate. The results of this action were the boycott in Jammu of the first election to the Assembly and entry of no less than 28 nominees of Sheikh Abdullah to the legislature without facing the electorate.

Ladakh Hill Council—A New Chapter

The history of modern Ladakh can be considered as

* Now raised to 48 in the Valley, 37 in Jammu and 2 in Leh, making total of 87, against total of 76, as before.

the history of emergence and assertion of nationalism and integration with modern India. Nationalism remained a dominant ideological creed and became a rallying force among Ladakhis while fighting back the Pakistanis and the Chinese in 1962, 1965 and 1971, says Sonam Namgyal, formerly Deputy Minister form Ladakh, in the Centre.*

Till recently, the illiterate and tribal people of Ladakh were unaware of things happening in other parts of the country. But with mobility, they have become aware of their rights as citizens of India to share the fruits of economic growth. They realised the importance of being organized to help them in putting their demands and aspirations at the national level. The Ladakh Buddhist Association though formed during late '40s, received strength and support from the masses only recently. During the late '80s, under the leadership of the LBA, the seeds of autonomy and decentralisation were sown in the form of demanding Union Territory status for Ladakh. The LBA launched a powerful agitation for the redressal of its demands in 1989. However, time was not ripe, as the state of which Ladakh is part was in turmoil. The Central Government, sensing the mood in the Kashmir Valley, was reluctant to grant autonomy to make it an Autonomous State. But the Centre did hold talks on the issue in order to find a solution. The LBA along with the Ladakh Muslim Association kept not only their agitation and demands alive but also scalled them down in the larger national interest by demanding an Autonomous Hill Council status which was ultimately accepted in October 1993, though implemented later.

"With the announcement of a Hill Council, a new chapter has opened for the tribal people of this area. It means freedom for them from the clutches of political and economic centralisation at the levels of the State and the Center", says Sonam Namgyal. Now the time has come when the Ladakhis will decide who will govern them and what aspects of the area are to be developed for

*Sonam Namgyal, "Ladakh Moving Closer to India", *Indian Express*, June 9, 1995.

their betterment. With inadequate funds at Ladakh's disposal, however, an optimum utilisation of the scarce resources is necessary. Moreover, the allocations should go to those sectors of the economy where growth potential is high, like the small-scale and cottage industry of wool, wood and dry fruit processing. Commercialisation of the mineral wealth should be taken and the possibility of MNCs entering Ladakh should be explored. Ladakh has been on the tourist map of the world since 1974. Today tourism is an ever-increasing source of income not only for the country, but for this area. The area still lacks a five-star accommodation and a full-fledged airport.

Agitation Earlier for Union Territory

After going through much harassment and torture, the leaders of the Ladakh Action Committee also, like the people of Jammu, had all the time been feeling that they had no alternative but to resume their agitation for implementation of an agreement the LBA had arrived at with the Government of India. They had called off the agitation following a series of meetings with representatives of the government of India to redress their grievances. The agitation which shook the trans-Himalayan region in 1992 and 1993 was aimed at securing a Union Territory status for Ladakh region of Jammu and Kashmir. Being totally frustrated in their aim, they decided to mount the agitation again in October 1993. They had been demanding an end to what they called "Kashmiri domination exploitation" and a recognition of their distinct geographic, cultural and ethnic identity. The talks were again resumed in the beginning of 1995 and it was decided by the Indian Government representatives to give Ladakh a Hill Council status, but again no official announcement was made by the Government in view of the impending elections.

In the talks held in 1993 and again in 1994, the Government representatives stressed the imperative need for maintaining Jammu and Kashmir's integrity. The Government however agreed to the suggested alternative of a Hill Council on the model of Darjeeling Hill Council, in the other extreme part of the country. The group of Ladakhi leaders who were adamant on their demand for a Union Territory status was persuaded by the Action Committee leadership to give up their demand for a Union Territory and go along with the agreement.

However, the Ladakh Action Committee leaders did not find the Central Government representatives honouring the agreement. What apparently shocked them most was the meeting with the then Prime Minister, P.V. Narasimha Rao on February 17, 1994 when they found the only assurance forthcoming was that the case would be examined afresh and "further meetings" held.

On April 5, 1995, an all-woman rally was held at Leh and the yelling ladies *gheraoed* the Deputy Commissioner in his office for hours. The Ladakh Buddhist Association demanded that the Centre must fulfil its commitment and grant them at least an Autonomous Hill Council, *a la* Darjeeling, before elections are held in the Sate of Jammu and Kashmir.

On April 8, the All Ladakh Students Union conveyed to the Prime Minister its resolution that two of their members would immolated themselves if the Centre did not bring forth by May 23 the legislation for actually setting up the agreed Ladakh Autonomous Hill Council. On April 9, Rigzin Spalbar, member of the Coordinate Committee for the LAHC told the Press that they would boycott elections to the Jammu and Kashmir Assembly if the Hill Council was not constituted before the polls.

The Centre, sent the Home Secretary to Leh on April 14 with the solemn assurance that it would fulfill its commitment before the polls. While he was confabulating in a well-heated room, Leh, at the height of more than 9,000 feet, the LBA observed a complete hartal in protest against the Centre's continued neglect and prevarication. The Centre had lost its credibility in their eyes by, time and again, backtracking on its assurances primarily under pressure from Kashmiri leaders who argued that any grant of autonomy would hurt the Kashmiri psyche and would adversely affect the efforts at restoring order in that trouble-torn Valley.

Kargil Separated

It was way back in 1952 that the Ladakhis under their Head Lama, Kushak Bakula, first raised their voice, demanding an effective share in the politics and administration of the State, and declared that they would join Tibet in the event of the Center agreeing to Sheikh Abdullah's demand for greater autonomy for his State. However, events evolved in ways other than those expected by the Sheikh and Ladakh remained rather quiet as long as the Sate remained under stewardship of Bakshi Ghulam Mohammad. But soon after the Hazratbal agitation in the Valley, in early 1964, the Ladakhis launched their first organised struggle against 'Kashmiri domination' and demanded a NEFA-type Central administration. Similar agitations seeking autonomy were launched again in 1974 and 1982. The authorities responded with both sternness and palliatives that controlled the fire but kept the embers burning.

To face charges of regional imbalances both from Jammu and Ladakh, two well-publicized commissions were appointed in 1967 and 1979 under the Chairmanship of Justice Gajendragadkar and Sikri, respectively. They highlighted the grievances of the Ladakhis and the discriminations they were facing and recommended the setting up of a separate development board for ladakh, establishment of degree college at Leh, regular supply of power throughout the year in the extreme cold climate of Ladakh and inclusion of at least 1 Ladakhi in the State Cabinet. Not much was done on the lines recommended. On the contrary in 1978, the State Government split the sprawling district of Ladakh into an overwhelmingly Buddhist Leh and a Muslim-majority (mostly Shias) Kargil.

The Government managed to contain the agitation of 1982 organised by Thupstan Cheewang and P. Namgyal. But accumulation of grievances, developments in the

Darjeeling hills under Subhas Ghising, the appearance of militancy in the Valley just below the horizon and the distant rumblings of events in East Europe and Central Asia caused their anger to explode on October 15, 1989. They demanded for Ladakh the status of a Union Territory and in the agitation that followed three persons lost their lives. The then Home Minister, Buta Singh, flew into Leh and a tripartite agreement was signed on October 29, 1989, in the presence of the Home Minister and two State Government Ministers, Mangat Ram Sharma and Muhammad Shafi Uri. The LBA leadership agree to scale down their demand from Union Territory Status to an Autonomous Council discussions involving both the LBA and the Ladakh Muslim Association continued for three years to determine the parameters and inner content of the proposed set up.

Ladakh Neglected

Ladakh occupies a strategic position. On the other side of the Great Himalyas Ladakhis the western extension of the Tibetan plateau. Ladakhis speak Tibetan language and profess Buddhism and practice the same rituals Tibet was the sword of the Dogras, since 1840. Carved out of Tibet, politically, it remained an ignored part of their State and, therefore, of India till, first, the Pakistani raiders and, then the Chinese brought this region within the ken of our vision.

So neglected was Ladakh that no Maharaja and no Chief Minister of this State before Syed Mir Qasim, in the early '70s, ever cared to visit this grassless plateau. Still, many expect the Ladakhis to feel and behave like other Indians. They are devout Buddhists. Ladakhis resist Kashmiri domination.

The region is inhabited by a peace-loving people subscribing to the Buddhist faith of penance and 'ahimsa' (non-violence). Politically chicanery and intrigue, which frequently characterised the goings-on in the pre-Independence and post-Independence Jammu and Kashmir region, never polluted the atmosphere of this inaccessible region or the minds of its sparse population. The result was that under all the regimes in Jammu and Kashmir—whether of the Maharaja or the government of India—the Ladakhis never seemed to exist. They were ignored to such an extent that the entire region comprising vast stretches of Leh, Kargil, Drass and Nubra were not even accorded the basic status of a Division in the State's revenue and administrative set-up. The whole area constituted just a district of the Valley, ruled by officers from Kashmir or Jammu.

Afterwards even the unity of Kargil and Leh were broken, when Kargil was made a separate district on a "patently communal plane". The creation of a separate Muslim district of Kargil was the first step to inject the virus of communal thinking and divide the areas across the Zojila Pass that had never known any communal tensions or feelings of separatism. After this, whatever was proposed by the Ladakhis were opposed by the people of Kargil, largely comprising Shitie Muslims. "In an unprecedented move in 1991-92, Buddhists in the Leh region organised a total boycott of Kashmiri Muslims whom they charged with proselytisation activities in furtherance of the sinister Pakistani game of converting Buddhist areas into a Muslim-majority zone. In reaction, the Muslim fundamentalists in the Valley gave a call for banishment of Ladakhis from Kashmir where they used to eke out a living by selling Ladakhi woollens and trinkets along the Residency Road pavements in Srinagar. These pavement shopkeepers fled to Jammu or moved back to Leh and the bazars of Leh which were dominated almost wholly by Kashmiri traders in carpets, jewellry, wood-carvings and papier-mache, witnessed an almost total extinction of the Valley traders. Hotels and restaurants run by the prosperous Kashmiri Muslims in Leh were shut down, and almost the entire Kashmiri officialdom fled the towns of Leh, and the areas in and around Khalsi, Nubra and Zanskar."*

---

* *Indian Express*, 1995.

The seed of communalism sown in furtherance of a sectarian goal by a segment of the ruling class in Srinagar had thus not merely polluted the tranquil Buddhist atmosphere of Ladakh but shook to the roots the Ladakhis' centuries-old belief in 'ahimsa' and peaceful co-existence. The entire Ladakh region seemed to have turned violent. Buses and vehicle from Kashmir were stoned and their movement beyond Khalsi made impossible. Slogans of separatism rent the air and a traditionally peaceful population gave vent to the pent-up ire against what it regarded as alien domination and exploitation.

During the time of Bakshi Ghulam Mohammad or Gulam Mohammad Sadiq, the Buddhists were treated better, but subsequently Kashmiri officials would be posted to Ladakh, "almost for ever". There was no Sheikh Abdullah "to deftly win Buddhist loyalty by exempting their *Gumpa* (monastery) lands from the operation of the all-pervading 'Big Landed Estates Abolition Act' of 1949, and above all, no Jawaharlal Nehru who wisely made it a point to receive and see off the high priest of the Ladakhis, context of Kashmir issue,"* It is only now, after decades, that the Government of India is recognising the grievous neglect it has committed in handing the Ladakh problem.

"KASHMIRI PANDITS" TURNED OUT OF THE VALLEY

A New Situation Created

Since 1989, yet another dimension has been added to the Kashmir problem because of the rise of terrorism that Pakistan has injected into the valley. Almost simultaneously with the growth of terrorism in the Valley towards the end of 1989, terrorists launched the move for destruction and driving out the Kashmiri Pandits, in other words the Hindus living in the Valley towns. Almost half of them had already left Kashmir through the period

* P. Stobdan, "Overlooking Ladakhi Aspirations", *Indian Express*, March 15, 1995.

from 1947 onwards. General, Zia-ul-Haq's shrewd strategic battle plan succeeded in stampeding more than 3,00,000 Kashmiri Pandits from the Valley prior to waging a full-fledged proxy war.

The systematic attacks by terrorists on Kashmiri Pandits gave lie to secularism, that the Valley was practising for centuries. The aim of the terrorists was obviously to destroy the ties between Muslims and Hindus that prevailed for centuries, the ties which the National Conference, the Congress and other secular parties had prided themselves on and wanted to preserve for ever, and thus the terrorist objective to give the last push to secularism was achieved. It took Pakistan-trained and financed terrorists little time to throw out the Pandits from out of the Valley to achieve their aim of freeing the Valley from Hindu elements, and climaxing it all at the end of five years, to destroy the Chrar-e-Sharief, the crowning symbol of Muslim-Hindu unity and secularism.

It is another matter that even during the earlier years, an ill-wind was blowing against Kashmiri Pandits, numbering some 6,00,000 to about 7,00,000 in a population of Kashmir's three million people, with whom they had been ethnically, linguistically, culturally and in all respects one, and living like one community, sharing in each other's joys and sorrows and living like brothers and sisters. In the intervening years, from 1947 onwards, the Pandits had been, facing iniquities and injustice in the Valley, have been gradually moving to different parts of India, and getting domiciled and settled there. They felt it would be better to go out and look for opportunities elsewhere, in other parts of India, but now they faced a situation in which they had to flee their hearths and homes in order to save their lives. Facing extermination, they fled to Delhi, Chandigarh and other places in India, just to be able to save their lives. More than 3,00,000 of them, plus some 50,000 Muslims and Sikhs also fled the Valley in order to be able to save their lives.

Till July-end (of 1990), some 62,851 Kashmiri Pandit families migrated to Jammu, Delhi and Chandigarh and other different parts of the country, in the face of oppression and torture in Kashmir. The flight of the Kashmiri Pandits from the Valley was a tragic commentary on inter-community relations in the State, wrote Amit Baruah in his article in the *Frontline* magazine (dated September 29 and October 12, 1990).

Quoting from figures given in Parliament recently, he said that till July end, 48,894 migrant families were registered in the Jammu region and 11,438 in Delhi. The other figures were Uttar Pradesh (857), Rajasthan (61), Haryana (94), Maharashtra (39), Punjab (1,293), Chandigarh (216), Madhya Pradesh (75), Himachal Pradesh (66), and Gujarat (54).

Assuming an average of 5 per family, the total number of migrants of Kashmiri Pandits would be more than 3,14,000 people. In his "Fleeing Pandits" article, Baruah, however, spoke of a handful of Kashmiri Pandits he met on the Leh highway and few villages. In Srinagar, prominent citizens made efforts to persuade the minority Pandits not to leave. A small committee was formed for the purpose, but the efforts were unsuccessful.

Kashmir Diaspora—Fate of Pandits

The Kashmiris who left their homeland in order to save their lives in the oldest part of the year and shivering in their bones were called 'migrants' and not refugees. These people left their ancestral orchards, lands and houses to live in tattered tents and in abject poverty and often without food and this they did only because they were forced to do so because of threats of annihilation and even conversion. Written posters pasted on doors of Pandit houses, letters, threatening reports in local newspapers asking Pandits to leave the Valley or face bullets. Slogans such as "Kashmir Me Rehna Hoga, Allah Akbar Kahna Hoga" ("You must recite Allah Akbar, if you want to live in Kashmir"). Such threats supported by selective killings of Pandits and rapes resulted in the expulsion of the Pandit community from the Valley.

The fact cannot to ignored that Kashmiriyat is essentially the ethos of Hindus and Muslims of Kashmir which goes beyond chauvinism, religious or cultural. Urdu is as alien to a Kashmiri as Hindi or English. Sanskrit and Sharda are the languages and the scripts that have treated, nurtured and enriched Kashmiriyat for centuries.

'Panun Kashmir', or 'our own Kashmir', the name that the Pandits gave their motherland symoblised the heart-beat of every exiled Pandit who had been pushed to the wall by administrative apathy.*

The crisis in Kashmir was largely the result of gross incompetence of successive governments at the Centre because of which Pakistani aggression in the state continued even after 47 years. Besides, the favouring, of a small percentage of Sunni Muslims at the cost of the majority like the Shias, Gujjars, Ladakhis, Jammu people and Kashmiri Pandits created an elitist class which apparently found solace in the fundamentalism and the visions of an independent state.†

The terrorist tirade against Kashmiri Pandits went on for months during which their 'migration' continued. It led to a total collapse of Dr. Farooq Abullah's government, in the second half of 1989 when there were more than 1,600 violent incidents including 161 bomb blasts. In a letter H.N. Jattu, President of the All India Kashmiri Pandit Conference said, "It is wholly incorrect that I and other Kashmiri Pandits migrated from the Valley at the instance of Jagmohan, Governor of Jammu and Kashmir. The truth is exactly the opposite. Mr. Jagmohan, in fact, did his level best to stop migration which had begun much earlier, when innocent leaders of the Pandit community were being brutally murdered and the Government of Dr. Farooq Abdullah was taking no action whatsoever. Politician, Tikka Lal Taploo was shot dead on September

* K. L. Swaroop, "Pandit Hopes", Letter to the Editor, *Times of India*, January 20, 1994.

† R. P. Raina (Faridabad), "Fate of Pandits", Letter to the Editor, *Times of India*, January 27, 1994.

14, 1989, Judge, N.K. Ganjoo on November 4 and journalist, P.N. Bhatt on December 28.

"When Kashmiri Pandits were being regularly killed on the pretext that they were 'informers' and agents of the Central Government, I and some members of the All India Kashmiri Pandit Conference discussed the alarming situation.

"On February 28, my secretary, Ashok Kazi, was done to death in a savage manner. On the same evening, I was violently abused on the telephone. From that day onwards, members of my community came to the conclusion that we must leave the Valley to save our lives and the honour of our women..."

Kashmiri migrants camping in Jammu were completely disillusioned by the lack of any policy of the Central and State Governments regarding their rehabilitation. They were not only sore with the government but also with the politicians as nothing had been done for their rehabilitation. "If they are unhappy with the way Government and the political groups are treating them in Jammu and elsewhere, their voices have remained unheard", said a migrant official who shuttles between Jammu and Srinagar.

More than 2,50,000 Kashmiri minority members had fled the Valley in late 1989 and 1990. Most of them rushed to Jammu believing it to be safe for them. Moreover, they thought it was temporary phase. Little did they know that they would have to be away form their homeland for so long, for in the Valley, the situation remained unchanged.

In Jammu, the migrants were lodged in the camps at Jhiri, Nagrota, Shivpora, Sherkhania and other places. Some of them are in Udhampur and Kathua districts of Jammu. The filthy conditions at the camp sites, the punishing summer and related difficulties simply made their lives miserable. The migrants also feared a threat to their cultural ethos. The local people also feared that the migrants would "pollute" the Dogra culture and cause and economic crunch in the region including reducing job opportunities in the already discriminated Jammu. The ethnic tensions are gradually surfacing. The leaders of the migrants have appealed to the Central Government to shift them out of Jammu for their 'proper rehabilitation'. They felt that Jammu was a small place to accommodate such a large migrant population. The refugees were clamouring: "Nothing is being done for us. We are being treated not as human-beings, but as herds."*

Save Kashmiri Pandit Campaign Committee

The "Save Kashmiri Pandit Campaign Committee" in its 1991 appeal said: "Is it not an exhibition of heartlessness to impute motives for our decision of migrating from the land of anarchy and violence or to allege that the migrants left at the bidding of the authorities in Srinagar? Must we tell these partisans that nothing is more distasteful to a Kashmiri Pandit than even the remotest thought of leaving the land which he loves only as a son would love his mother? The brutal killings of such prominent Kashmiri Pandits as the poet Sarvanand Kaul and his young son Virender and engineer, B.K. Ganjoo, the Doordarshan Director, Lassa Kaul, Prof. K. Ganjoo and so on are further proof of this. The killings were calculated to frighten off thousands. Given all this can there be any doubt about the falsehood propagated about the migration of Kashmiri Pandits from the Valley?"

As Pandits like K.L. Swaroop wrote latter: "From the middle of the 14th century, despots have indulged in religious begotry *vis-a-vis* those of a different faith, of course with the exception of Zain-ul-Abidin (Badshah). The majority community ultimately became a miniscule minority, hounded out of its home. It is this unpleasant truth which 'Panun Kashmir' is trying to highlight. The composite culture of Hindus and Muslims in Kashmir as propounded by spiritual leaders like Lalleshwari, Sheikh Nooruddin, Reshi Mol Sahib, Zainshah Sahib etc. are

* *Hindustan Times*, July 13, 1991.

proof of the catholicity and tolerance of the Shaivite and Vedantic philosophers of Kashmir. We uphold it and shall continue to. This blend of Hinduism and Islam culminating in the 'rishi cult' of Kashmir is not palatable to the rigid and exclusivist ideologues of Jamat-e-Islami who are determined to annihilate the cultural legacy of Kashmir."

Never before has a Whole Community Fled

Never before in recent Indian history has almost a whole Community fled without systematic presecution, organised massacres or large-scale communal riots. Why did it happen, asks Amitabh Mattoo, in a letter to the *Times of India* (on March 9, 1994). He answers: It is true that in the last months of 1989 and the first months of 1990 there was a definite climate of insecurity brought about by two factors. First, some prominent Kashmiri Pandits were killed. Most mentioned as being killed were killed for reasons other than their being Hindu. For instance, N.K. Ganjoo was presiding officer of the special court which had sentenced Maqbool Bhat, the founder of the JKLF, to death. Second, wild rumours, together with sensational headlines (and irresponsible reporting) in local papers, did create the impression among some sections that a systematic genocide of Pandits would follow. These alone, however, were not sufficient reasons for people to leave everything and flee from a land where they had been rooted for centuries from occupations they were engaged in, from a whole lifestyle.... In many cases Muslim neighbours did in fact try and prevent their Pandit neighbours form leaving. In other cases, they protected their property for months......there is little doubt that the hundreds of thousands of Pandits would not have left if the State Administration had taken some remedial steps. No attempt was made to make them feel secure or even emphasise to them the long-term implications of their leaving. Even the first note issued by the State Government appealing to the Pandits not to leave, was on March 7, 1990. All evidence suggests that the maximum number of people left between end-January and end-

February 1990...."

There is no doubt that the crisis in Kashmir is largely the result of gross incompetence of successive governments at the Centre. Besides, the favouring of a small percentage of Sunni Muslims at the cost of the majority like the Shias, Gujjars, Ladakhis, Jammu people and Kashmiri Pandits created an elitist class which apparently finds solace in fundamentalism and the visions of an independent State.

Jagmohan had later to say that it spoke volumes about the Union Government that "it had created about 2,50,000 refugees in its own country. President Clinton found time to respond personally to an ordinary functionary of PoK/Pakistani propaganda machinery. It is a measure of India's failure that Mr. Clinton remains oblivious of the gross human rights violation of the Kashmiri Pandits."*

First Kashmiri Pandits Convention at Jammu

In December 1991 the Kashmiri Pandits held their first convention at Jammu, demanding a 'homeland', to be called 'Panun Kashmir' (or 'Our own Kashmir'), and declaring that Kashmiri Hindus were in their fourth year of exile "after Islamic religious fundamentalists in the Valley of Kashmir took to armed subversion and terrorism and drove us out of our centuries old habitat." At the convention was introduced the historic 'Homeland' resolution, and it was adopted by more than a thousand delegates of the 'exiled community', who flocked from all towns and cities where they had taken refuge. The operative part of the resolution demanded:

(*a*) Establishment of a 'Homeland' for the Kashmiri Hindus in the Kashmir Valley, comprising of the regions of the Valley to the East and North of river Jhelum.

(*b*) The Constitution of India be made applicable in

* Jagmohan, "False Propaganda about Pandits", *Times of India*, March 2, 1991.

letter and spirit in this 'Homeland', in order to ensure right to life, liberty, freedom of expression and faith, equality and rule of low.

(*c*) The 'Homeland' be placed under the Central administration with a Union Territory status, so that it evolves its own economic and political infrastructure.

(*d*) All the 7,00,000 Kashmiri Hindus, which includes those who have been driven out of Kashmir in the past and yearn to return to their homeland and those who were forced to leave on account of the terrorist violence in Kashmir, be settled in the 'Homland' on equitable basis with dignity and honour.

A 48-pages booklet was published with the 'wholehearted endorsement' of the Resolution which became the rallying point for all in the community, saying "Panun Kashmir has evolved into a movement symbolising the hopes, the urges and the aspirations of the community."

On the genesis of 'Homeland', their booklet said, "the Jammu and Kashmir State is a conglomeration of heterogeneous geographical regions inhabited by diverse but distinct ethnic, religious miles of the State, the Valley of Kashmir accounts for about 3,000 square miles. Nearly a third of the State was annexed by Pakistan during the invasion of 1947 after the partition of the sub-continent. Ladakh, the largest segment of the State is thinly populated, mostly by the people of the Buddhist faith, and the neighbouring Kargil by Muslims. The Jammu province has a predominant Hindu population with some of its districts evenly represented by both Hindu and Muslim communities. The Valley of Kashmir is predominantly Muslim with a small representation of Hindus and Sikhs. The Hindus of Kashmir Valley are essentially Kashmiri Pandits."

"The Kashmiri Hindus have a distinct identity dating to more than five thousand years in the Valley. They are Kashmiri speaking and followers of Hindu faith with a unique emphasis on Shaivism. They are essentially peace loving and non-violent, living in a bent of mind made them assimilate, absorb and integrate the essence of those faiths which people from outside brought into the Valley. The mingling of faiths gave birth to the Sufi-Rishi tradition which is a part of real Kashmiriyat."

"Ever since the advent of Islam in Kashmir in 1339 A.D., the Hindus, who are the original inhabitants of the Valley have from time to time faced tyrannies of the Muslim rulers in various forms who imposed heavy taxes, perpetrated the most barbaric methods of torture, brutalised and killed them in thousands, forced their females into marriage and males into conversion, desecrated and demolished their temples and built mosques over them and forced the remaining Hindus into exile.... Even after the accession of the State of Jammu and Kashmir to the secular and democratic India in 1947, the Hindus of the Valley have been leading a life of subjugation, denial and deprivation, of fear and uncertainty, of unequal opportunities, of compromise and religious constraints and of persecution of all forms at all levels resulting in its continuous emigration during these apparently peaceful periods. This steady flow of migration spurted especially during the invasion by Pakistan in 1947, Indo-Pak wars of 1965 and 1971, and during the Kashmiri Pandit agitation in 1967. The steady flow reached a crescendo during the communal frenzy of 1986."

'Naya Kashmir' Manifesto with bias for Muslim Majority

"The National Conference rode to the crest of power in the wake of the accession of the State of Jammu and Kashmir to India with its 'Naya Kashmir' Manifesto. On paper, it looked as a secular, progressive and democratic model hoping to shape the future of the State by providing a political and economic agenda for the amelioration of the lot of the common man. But in practice, it aimed at reorganisation of the State into a political system which had a favourable has for the Muslims majority.

"By the introduction of land reforms in the State, the Hindus were hit severely as it deprived them even of their small holdings. They were forced to seek migration to towns and outside the State to earn a living. Many enactments were passed in succession in the year 1965 like Abolition of Jagirdari Act, Big Landed Estates Abolition Act, Restitution of Mortgaged Property Act, Distressed Debtors Relief Act and, in 1976, the Agrarian Reforms Act. These Acts were all contrived to the detriment of the Hindu community and as a prelude to its destruction. Under the garb of communal amity, equality and the provision of opportunities for the suppressed and the down-trodden, the Government in utter disregard to the principle of universal right to equality of opportunity and protection against discrimination on the basis of religion, promoted the cause of the Muslim majority of the State.

"The rules for recruitment to the State Government Services were changed from time to time to suit the Muslim majority, as also the rules for admission to educational institutions for professional and higher education. As a result the Hindus (in other words, Kashmiri Pandits in Kashmir Valley) faced discrimination in admission to schools, professional institutions and universities, in government jobs, placements, transfers and promotions and discrimination in the distribution of loans and subsidies for setting up private enterprises."

"While in the rest of India there were safeguards for the protection of minority rights, in Kashmir it was the other way round.... The voice of the minority community got drowned in the cacophony of Islamic revivalism and fundamentalism as it lost even its feeble representation when the only constituency of Habba Kadal, which had a Hindu majority, was redefined to the total disadvantage of the Hindus, rendering them ineffective even from electing their representative to the State Legislature."

Rise of Armed Terrorism

The booklet added: "Armed militancy and terrorism has surfaced in the Valley from the year 1988-89 on a large scale with the connivance and support of Pakistan. Muslim youth of the Valley have been crossing the border in large numbers since 1984 and returning with sophisticated arms and ammunition after receiving training in sabotage and warfare. Their design has been to subvert democracy and secularism, establish an Islamic theocratic State and to secede from India. As a first step, the minority Hidus of the Valley became the first victims of this operation and they were gunned down indiscriminately, hanged or murdered by other brutal means. Torture, molestation and rape, threatening letters and telephone calls, posters and quit-notices posted on doors and warnings through newspapers for the whole community to leave the Valley within short and specified time, became the order of the day leading to a mass exodus of this community. More than a thousand members have been to death, and nearly three hundred thousand forced into exile."

"While the exodus of the minority Hindu community on all occasions prior to 1947 were at the behest of and because of the tyrannies of despotic rulers swayed by fits of communal frenzy, the present exodus of 1989-90 is unparalleled in the history of world democracies. This time a large segment of a community has taken up arms with the aim of subverting secularism, mortgaging religious pluralism, decimating a Hindu minority and forcing its exodus in order to establish an Islamic State with the final aim of seceding from its parent country. This has happened in the largest democracy, that is India, and the minority Hindu community has been helpless victim of a terrorism sponsored by the majority community of the Valley, with the connivance and support of the State administration and overlooked by the Central Government."

Exile

"The Kashmiri Hindus are now in their fourth year of exile. Called as 'migrants' by the administration, in fact, they are refugees in their own country due to the total failure of the Indian State to provide security and safety to them when they were ruthlessly persecuted, threatened, tortured and murdered by the terrorists.

"A distinct ethno-religious community, which is ancient and aboriginal to the Valley of Kashmir, is not only facing dispersal and disintegration but also total extinction.... The situation for the Kashmiri Pandits has reached such a pass that they have become the victims of the worst apartheid in their own country—India, which has been in the vanguard of the battle against apartheid. Even the white minority regime of South Africa would take comfort looking at the treatment given to the exiles from the Valley as they face apartheid in social, educational, legal and bureaucratic institutions of the State. Far from lending a healing touch to this wounded community, it is being treated like a pariah as it has been segregated in schools, colleges and other institutions and made to accept sub-human living conditions..."

The Delhi Declaration, 1993

Two years later, the 'Panun Kashmir' organized a two-day conference of the world Kashmiri Pandits in New Delhi, and adopted a Declaration nothing with grave concern "the perpetuation of genocide and effecting of ethnic cleansing of Hindus in Kashmir"; the imminent danger of cultural disintegration and social obliteration of this proud community which has a historical and cultural continuity of more than five thousand years in Kashmir; the indifferent attitude of human rights organisations towards gross violations of human rights of Kashmiri Hindus by armed terrorist groups; the apathy of the Indian Government towards victims of terrorism forced into mass exodus and living under sub-human conditions in refugee camps; the involvement of Pakistan and other Muslim fundamentalist States and organisations in engineering terrorism and subversion in India; the failure of the Indian Administrative and political system to deal with internal subversion and its failure to protect the limb, life, honour and fundamental rights of its citizens in

Jammu and Kashmir, the failure of the Indian Foreign Office to effectively project the reality of Kashmir in its true dimensions of minority-cleansing, genocide of Hindus and perpetuation of Islamic rule (Nizam-e-Mustafa) and the impunity with which the fundamentalists and subversive have operated in India and thrown the entire nation in the inferno of terrorism, insecurity and erosion of the authority of the State.

Adopting the 'Homeland' resolution, the World Conference said: "We shall intensify our struggle of the 'back home movement' and for fulfillment of our political goal of achieving Panun Kashmir as a Union Territory in the North-East of river Vitasta (Jhelum), which will guarantee the right of return to all those 7,00,000 Kashmiri Hindus who have been forced out of Kashmir on pain of death and conversion in the last six centuries. The uninhibited flow of the Constitution of India in letter and spirit will be made applicable in Panun Kashmir:"

— That a Task Force will be constituted by Dr. Agnishekhar, Convenor of Panun Kashmir, to work out the modalities of establishing a "World Parliament of Kashmiri Pandits" which shall incorporate representatives of all Kashmiri Pandit organisations which endorse the 'Homeland' concept of Panun Kashmir.

— We shall as per matter of our commitment to democracy immediately after achieving of Panun Kashmir as Union Territory, as envisaged in the resolution of *Margadarshan* (of December 28,1991) conduct free and fair elections.

— We shall continue to observe 14 September and 19 January as 'Martyrs Day' and 'Exodus Day' respectively, as the two most important days in Kashmiri Pandit history, for times to come.

— To safeguard against cultural disintegration and social obliteration and to secure the future of our youth and students, we shall—

(*a*) found the Sharda Peeth, our University in Exile which shall promote studies in Kashmiri language, art, culture, philosophy, literature, history, architecture, archaeology and anthropology. Besides, it may promote professional and other academic and research institutions to promote the cause of quality education and cultural unity of India in promotion of democratic values and the modern world order,

(*b*) set up Kashmiri Cultural Data Resource Base and bring out in the shortest possible time a Hand Book on Kashmiri Culture,

(*c*) set up a museum of Kashmiri Art and Cultural Heritage,

(*d*) make a documentary which will be a step towards definitive commentary on Kashmiri Pandits,

(*e*) adopt Devanagri as an alternative script for Kashmiri language, and

(*f*) strive to get restored our right to visit our most sacred placed of pilgrimage and worship, i.e., the shrine of Sharda Peeth which at present is under the illegal occupation of Pakistan in the Pok. This ancient shrine is the seat of Sharda culture which has developed and thrived during the last 5,000 years in Kashmir.

Minority-cleansing Genocide

The resolution endorsed that no solution to the Kashmir crisis would be acceptable to Kashmiri Pandits unless Panun Kashmir representatives were taken into confidence and made part of any process leading to a last solution.

The Conference noted with grave concern "the apathy of the Government" towards the migrants who were living under sub-human conditions in refugee camps for years. The community leaders criticised the Indian Foreign Office for its 'failure' to effectively project "the minority-cleansing genocide of Hindus and perpetuation of Islamic rule in the Valley. The Conference was attended by T.N. Kaul, former Ambassador to the United States, Arun Shourie, eminent journalist, A.P. Venkateshwaran, former Foreign Secretary, A.K. Ray, former Ambassador and J.P. Mukhi, advocate of the Supreme Court. Jagmohan, former Governor of Jammu and Kashmir also attended the Conference. Said T.N. Kaul: "Pakistan does not understand the diplomatic language. If it does not want to understand our words, we must use our force to defend ourselves." The problems faced by the community should be settled in a peaceful manner as the pride of the Kashmiri culture "does not lie in attacking other religions."

In an article he wrote soon after, styled "Of Panun Kashmir", T.N. Kaul said, "The manner in which the problems of Kashmiri Pandits, who are living as refugees in their own country, India, are tackled, will determine the success or failure of India's policy towards minorities and have an impact on similar problems in our neighbouring countries. Kashmir is a symbol and testing ground of the policy of democracy, humanism and secularism which was propagated by Mahatma Gandhi, Pandit Nehru, Sardar Patel, Maulana Azad and other leaders who inspired us during our struggle for freedom. The problem of Kashmir is not merely of the spirit of India's cultural synthesis and the right of human beings to live in their homes with dignity, security and in harmony among themselves and with others."

Indo-American Forum

The Indo-American Kashmir Forum the organisation that primarily represents the cause of Kashmiri Pandits, later blasted the State Department's 1995 human rights report for 'biased and subjective reporting.' The report highlighted the government's lapses and 'glossing over the crimes committed by criminals and terrorists in Kashmir.' "Nowhere is this inadequacy more apparent than in the reporting of events in Kashmir where Islamic militants, caught up in the global resurgence of their religious fervour, are battling the State under the guise of freedom

It accused the State Department of holding Islamic militants in Kashmir "to a higher level of esteem than the treatment they have received in the US and elsewhere." Drawing a contrast between the way Islamic militants are dealt with within the US and the State Department report, the Forum said, "While the report time and again mentions extra judicial lapses, it fails to mention terrorism evoked through 'jihad' in Kashmir, a seditious activity that is the basis for judicial prosecution in the World Trade Center bombing. What appears to be very relevant in justifying stern public and State action against the New York terrorists fails to get even a cursory mention in the Kashmir portion of the report."

Security Zone for J & K Hindus

On July 4, 1995, the then Union Home Minister, S.B. Chavan, expressed his willingness to consider setting up a special protected area or a security zone in the Kashmir Valley to enable the Hindu migrants to return. The Bharatiya Janata Party had voiced this demand earlier, but it had been rejected then. Even now, Chavan does not think that creating a security zone for migrants would serve any purpose, mainly because their homes were scattered all over the Valley. Even if there was a security zone, they would have to move about in the Valley, an aspect they could be fearful of.

But there is the need for the government to facilitate the return of the migrants to the Valley as it is a major aspect in bringing about normalisation there. To this end, Chavan said he is even willing to consider providing financial assistance to the migrants to return and rebuild their homes, damaged or destroyed by militants active since 1989.

Organisations of Kashmiri Pandits like Panun Kashmir do not, however, Think that their members can return to their homes in the Valley, as they expect a fresh bout of violence to take place to make them flee once again.*

---

* Subhash Kirpekar, "Security Zone for J. & K. Hindus Advocated", *Times of India*, New Delhi, July 5, 1995.

Criticism of the US

Soon after the Delhi Conference, Dr. Ajay Chrangoo, 'Panun Kashmir' spokesman, held a Press Conference demanding a homeland for Kashmiri Pandits, and criticising the United States for allegedly "siding with fundamentalist forces" in the Valley. He said that a recent letter written by the US President, Bill Clinton, to the Kashmiri Council leader, Ghulam Nabi Fai, "was a clear signal that the United States had once again chosen to cultivate forces of theo-fasism in order to further its strategic interests in the Indian sub-continent." He said the letter had hurt the sentiments of more than 3,00,000 displaced Kashmiri Pandits who were forced by the militants to leave the Valley. Dr. Chrangoo urged the government to start a comprehensive dialogue at the national level with representatives of all ethnic and local regional minorities in the State. For proper political process, Dogras of Jammu, Buddhists of Ladakh, Gujjars, Bakarwalls, Kashmiri Hindus, Shias and sections of Jammu and Kashmir whose expression of political aspiration falls within the framework of the Indian Constitution should be involved, he suggested.

Dr. Chrangoo said India was capable of solving the Kashmir problem unilaterally, withstanding external pressures. He said "There is no need to be panicky. India is a big country. It is competent enough to withstand any amount of pressure from outside and the Government can solve the Kashmir problem on its own provided it has the will to do so." He held that the government was undermining the Simla Agreement by holding talks with Pakistan which has already violated the Agreement by supplying arms and ammunition to the militants in the Valley.*

On March 24, 1994, the 'Panun Kashmir' again attacked the USA while holding a 'protest march' in front of the American Embassy in New Delhi. Hundreds of Kashmiri Pandit—men, women and children raised their voice against

---

* *Times of India*, January 11, 1994.

the statement of the Assistant Secretary of State, Robin Raphel for saying that Kashmiri Pandits had left the Valley because they were encouraged by Jagmohan, the then Governor of Jammu and Kashmir to do so. The 'Panun Kashmir' through a letter of protest demanded an apology from Ms. Raphel for her 'disinformation' and asked the U.S. Administration to come clean on their strategic interests in Kashmir.

India should take the genocide to U.N.

From 1947 onwards the Pandits of Kashmir have been discriminated against and persecuted and more than 5,000 Pandits have already been killed and another 3,00,000 made to flee, points out Jai Mangharam Mukhi, in a perceptive piece written in *The Statesman* newspaper. Under a U.N. Convention, India is obliged to form a tribunal for trial and punishment of the offenders, says the author, a legal expert.

He points out that Jawaharlal Nehru took pride in being known to the world as Pandit Nehru. The Pandits of Kashmir have a history dating back to the vedas, written thousands of years ago, their homeland, the Valley, is a place of pilgrimage for the Hindus. It is Lord Shiva's land and among the pilgrims were the great Shankaracharya himself and Swami Vivekananda.

Why is it that the world does not know of the genocide of the Kashmiri Pandits? asks Mukhi in his article. There were hardly a few thousand Pandits left in the Valley. From 1947, they have been marginalised, discriminated against, persecuted, humiliated, attacked, killed and driven out in a systematic manner. They were victims not of Partition (or division of India into India and Pakistan). What happened to them did not happen in Pakistan. It did not happen in the British times. It happened in independent India. "The dark days began with Sheikh Abdullah and Nehru,"* Mukhi told.

The writer goes back into the past. He recalls that in

* Jai Mangaram Mukhi, "Kashmiri Pandits—Marginalisation began in 1947", *The Statesman*, June 6, 1995.

the old days it was the Kashmiri Pandits led by Pandit Kripa Ram Dutt who came in a delegation to the Ninth Sikh Guru, Teg Bahadur, at Anandpur Sahib, and sought his help against the atrocities unleashed by Aurangzeb and his Governor, Iiftikhar Khan. There had been in earlier times untold tortures, killings and forcible conversions. This time it was too much. The Guru said: "Find someone in this land who is pure-hearted, renowned and respected. If he stands up for you, you shall be saved." At this his son Gobind Rai, then not yet in his teens, who was standing near, said to his father "who can they find better than you?"

And so Guru Tegh Bahadur came to Delhi to remonstrate with Aurangzeb, Aurangzeb asked him to convert to Islam or face death. He chose death. It was by decapitation at the site "where you have Sis Ganj at Chandni Chowk." Bhai Mati Das, Bhai Sati Das and Bhai Dayal Das were also martyred. It is said that in the dust storm that followed a disciple took his decapitated head to Anandpur. Young Gobind Rai resolved to avenge. He mastered Persian, Arabic, Sanskrit and learnt the martial arts. On a Baisakhi day, he became Gobind Singh and created the Khalsa Panth—to protect religion and righteousness.

Continued Mukhi in his narrative: "We must redeem ourselves by taking steps. We must restore the Kashmiri Pandits to their homeland, rehabilitate them with security and honour, restore their property, repair and rebuild their temples and shrines. We must make full and adequate reparation to them for the injuries and losses suffered by them and we must bring the perpetrators of genocide to punishment. Genocide is the systematic and deliberate extinction of people by murder, physical attack, intimidation or creation of conditions calculated to cause an exodus. There is no doubt that the Kashmiri Pandits are the victims of a genocide. The policies pursued since 1947 reached their culmination when atrocities began, shrines where descreted, homes were burnt, men, women and children were attacked. More than 5,000 were killed....

"There is the United Nations Convention on the Prevention and Punishment of the Crime of Genocide. This came into effect in 1951. As a party to the Convention, India was under international obligation to see that genocide did not take place under the aegis of the State government and the government of India. The Convention says that India as a party shall undertake to prevent genocide and to punish all persons responsible for acts of genocide. All persons responsible are to be punished, whether they are constitutionally-responsible rulers, public officials or private individuals. Under the Convention, India has to constitute a tribunal for trial and punishment. Any country which is a party to the convention can also call upon the U.N. to take appropriate action. Such a country can also move the International Court of Justice", the author suggests.

JAMMU: DEMAND FOR TRIFURCATION OF THE STATE

Jammu wants Separation from Kashmir

A demand is slowly rising for trifurcation of the Sate into Kashmir Valley, Jammu and Ladakh. The Government is not at all allowing the demand to come up, for what is thought to be the harmful impact that it would otherwise have for the solution of the Kashmir problem. It would help the Pakistani viewpoint if the demand is conceded. It would mean division of the State in three parts, one predominantly Muslim, one predominantly Hindu and the other predominantly Buddhist, thus giving a handle to Pakistan to demand more forcefully the Kashmir part and this is what India would avoid at all costs.

The demand for trifurcation of the State has come up particularly since 1989 when the pro-Independence (for Kashmir), Jammu and Kashmir Liberation Front introduced the gun culture in the State. In the Jammu part, it was argued, most of the Pandits (Hindu refugees) who were driven out of Kashmir were living in camps. They even lift their jobs in the Kashmir Valley and now only about 200 or so Pandits out of the 1,37,000 that worked in Srinagar Secretariat are left in the Valley. All other Pandits have left either to Jammu or Chandigarh or Delhi. They are demanding to be rehabilitated in the southern part of the Valley, but the Government does not think it to be feasible. Of course, the question will come up about their voting in the forthcoming elections. It looks likely that their votes, some 35,000 of them, which they used to cast formerly mainly in Zadibal and Habba Kadal constituencies, will now be cast when representatives of the Election Commission visit them in their camps, or they are allowed to vote by mail.

It is well-known that through these nearly 50 years, the people of Jammu (Hindu-dominated) and Ladakh (virtually all Buddhists), who together have lesser representation in the Jammu and Kashmir Legislature, have always objected to being lorded over by Srinagar, which even according to population, her larger representation in the Assembly than them. It is known that every time that either Sheikh Abdullah, Dr. Farooq Abdullah or Ghulam Mohammad Shah was thrown out of power, it is the votes of jammu or Ladakh that went against them.

Professor Hari Om, teaching Modern History in the University of Jammu, has contented that Jammu and Kashmir has never been an organic political entity since inception in March 1846 under the Amritsar Treaty. Till its accession to India in 1947, the Maharaja was the only link among the heterogenous regions of Jammu, Kashmir and Ladakh or the former State's other parts. With the end of the Princely rule, even this link disappeared. In normal circumstances, the ideal course after the accession would have been the reorganisation of the State into three separate States of Jammu, Kashmir and Ladakh. This did not happen.

Once the Centre made the decision to maintain the State as a single political entity, it was imperative for it to take note of the dissimilarities in culture, language geography, history and political perceptions of Jammu, Kashmir and Ladakh and evolve an administrative structure in which each region could grow freely. This was an issue of crucial importance in view of the well-known anti-Jammu political mindset of the Valley leadership as clearly seen during Muslim Conference—National Conference political struggles like the 1924 Scrap Amritsar Treaty Crusade and the 1946 Quit Kashmir Movement...What happened was that the State was given a special status through Article 370 of the Indian Constitution at the behest of Sheikh Abdullah, "who in no way represented the common zeal."

Armed with absolute political powers under Article 370 Kashmiri rulers followed policies which created a situation in which no one from Jammu or Ladakh could reside and serve in Kashmir or become the Chief Minister of the State. It was not a mere lapse on their part. This was part of a grand design to exact revenge against people from Jammu who wanted independence. However, the worst part of the whole situation was the unqualified support of the National Conference and the Congress legislators from Jammu for all that the Kashmiri leaders did to marginalise and 'subjugate' Jammu and Ladakh, according to Professor Hari Om.

The consequence of the policies which the Valley leaders pursued were allotment of 44 seats to Kashmir in the Legislative Assembly as against 30 seats to Jammu and a paltry 2 to Ladakh,* (the representation of Hindus and Buddhists in Jammu and Ladakh being far less in proportion to their population), wholesale transfer of people to Jammu and Ladakh from Kashmir, the appointment of thousands of Kashmiri Hindus in Jammu and Buddhists in Ladakh against vacancies caused by retirement, death or dismissal of the incumbents and additional requirements, closure of the agricultural and Ayurvedic colleges in Jammu and so on.

---

* The figures are now changed to 46 for Kashmir Valley, 37 for Jammu and 4 for Ladakh, as recommended by the Election Commission and included in the People's Representation Act for the purpose of coming elections.

Appointment of Commissions: Sweeping Changes Recommended

It was under these circumstances that the people of Jammu and Ladakh launched one struggle after the other in order to achieve their due in the State's political and economic processes. So strong and popular were their struggles, like the 1952-53 Praja Parishad movement, the 1966-67 student agitation and the 1979 Poonch revolt, that the government had no alternative but to appoint commissions to look into the people's complaints. The Gajendragadkar Commission (1967), the Sikri Commission (1979) and the Wazir Commission (1980) all acknowledged that the allegations made by the people of Jammu and Ladakh against the powers-that-be in Srinagar were genuine. These commissions also recommended a number of sweeping changes in the State's politico-administrative and economic structure in order to compensate for the losses sustained by the people of Jammu and Ladakh. Unfortunately, the Kashmir rulers took no notice of the recommendations which various commissions had made with a view to harmonising inter-regional relations. "But given the intense unrest in Jammu and Ladakh, the demand for reorganisation of the State was not examined afresh", Prof. Hari Om pleaded repeatedly.*

Kashmiri leaders, Dr. Farooq Abdullah (National Conference) and Ghulam Rassol Kar (Congress-I) vehemently opposed the clamour for the trifurcation of the present state into three Centrally-administered Union Territories of Jammu, Kashmir and Ladakh. "They allow the vested interests in Jammu and Ladakh to subvert the State's polity painstakingly built up by Sheikh Abdullah, who "considered religious and regional bias a crime and domination of one region over the other an abominable act." The upshot of their argument is that the State's polity based on the principle of justice and equity caters as

*Hari Om, "Redress Past Wrongs in Jammu and Ladakh", *Times of India*, January 12, 1995.

much to the needs of Jammuites and Ladakhis as to the Kashmiris and that the demand of the people of Jammu and Ladakh for the reorganisation of the State's polity is unjustifiable, which, if accepted, would hurt the Kashmiri psyche, it was explained.

Political Aspirations of three Regions not identical

One of the most important reasons for solution of the problems of the entire State—without considering that the three different regions call for different treatments—or that the solutions for the three regions of the State are identical or nearly identical, and that the contradictions among them, if any, can be easily reconciled is that the political perceptions of all the people in the State are identical or nearly identical. The fact remains that the problems of the three regions of the State are not identical, or even nearly identical, in terms of composition of their population, their geographical features. Their language, their history and almost everything else. The only point seems to be that the three parts once remained together in Maharaja Hari Singh's empire. It is a misguided notion that the political perceptions of all the people in the State are identical or nearly identical, and that the contradictions among them can be reconciled. This has turned out to be the principal factor why the deadlock in the State presumably cannot be broken.

The prime reason for this is that the political aspirations of the people of Jammu, Ladakh and Kashmir are different. The people of Jammu and Ladakh, constitute more than half of the State's population and inhabit nearly 90 per cent of the State's land area. Besides even in the Valley population, Muslims and Pandits are conflicting and mutually exclusive. The political demand of the people of Jammu also include Statehood within India, regional autonomy and a statutory development board with or without Article 370. On the other hand, the demands of the far-off Ladakhis range from a Union Territory status to an autonomous Hill Council invested with "full political, administrative and economic powers and without Article 370.*

As far as the displaced Pandits are concerned, their demands range from a separate homeland in the Valley with a Union Territory status to a security zone within Kashmir, reservation for Pandit minority in all spheres and at all levels and application of the Indian Constitution to the State in full. More importantly, even the Kashmiri Muslims are not a homogeneous lot. As a matter of fact, they are vertically divided into four groups demanding independence, merger with Pakistan, pre-1953 constitutional status (limited accession of the State to India) and full integration of the State with India.

That there exists a profound cleavage of opinion among the Kashmiri leaders with regard to the State's political future can be seen from the J&K. Pradesh Congress Committee (I) President, Ghulam Rasool Kar's outright repudiation of his close ally and the former Chief Minister and President of his close ally and the former Chief Minister and President of the National Conference, Dr. Farooq Abdullah's clamour for the pre-1953 position on the ground that the ongoing process of the State's integration with India just cannot be allowed to be reversed. This is also clear from the December 21, 1994 statement of the People's League supremo, Shabir Shah, made in the general body meeting of the Kul-Jamait Hurriyat Conference. It reads like this: "The Hurriyat Conference cannot claim to represent the entire State as it only has members from 6 of the 14 districts and there is no representation from Jammu and Ladakh. Moreover, one of its constituents, the JKLF, is not participating in its

---

* In the talks between the Ladakhi Association and the Government of India, the Government has already conceded a separate status for Ladakh, on the same lines as conceded for Darjeeling in West Bengal State. The decision to create a Development Council for Ladakh was taken twice, Once during Prime Ministership of Rajiv Gandhi and again during Prime Ministership of P. V. Narasimha Rao, but never was it implemented, obviously keeping in view Jammu and Kashmir's overall interests and fearing lest a division of the State's territorial integrity should case a harm for its solution.

activities for the past several months..." but these are just a few of several such statements which serve to demonstrate how much the Kashmiri leaders are divided in their political perceptions.

Reorganise to meet Political Aspirations

Asks Professor Hari Om: What then is the solution? Should we continue to devise solutions based on the assumptions that the Valley leaders represent the general will, and that accepting the implementing the political demands of a section of the Kashmiri leaders would be the same as meeting the political needs of the people of Jammu, Kashmir and Ladakh? Or, should we go in for the reorganisation of the State in order first to accommodate the political aspirations of the people of Jammu and Ladakh and then start parleys with the Kashmiri leaders of all shades of opinion to determine what could satisfy them and their constituencies? These are the only two options available with us and we have to choose one. The first option we simply cannot exercise because it has the potential of creating more problems than solving the existing ones. Clearly, we have to go for the second alternative.

Jammu on Militants' Top of Agenda

After four and a half years of their depredations, the terrorists eventually turned their sight to Jammu, where a third of its population is Muslim, spread over Rajouri, Poonch and Doda regions and even in the rural areas of Jammu. The Governor-General (Retd.), K.V. Krishna Rao, was himself under attack on the Republic Day on January 26, 1995 even as he was reading out his Republic Day speech. The Republic Day incident had been preceded by a series of terrorists' blasts in buses and Hindu localities in and around Jammu city. There were attempts to blow up trains, but a communal flare-up in Jammu would have best suited the terrorists' plans. Though there were a large number of Muslims in Doda district, events in Kashmir affected the two communities of Jammu differently. Indeed, after the incident, the anger of the people encouraged the Bharatiya Janata Party to demand a ban on the entry of dissident Kashmiri leaders to Jammu. Soon after the incident, the Jamat-e-Islami Chief, Syed Ali Shah Gilani, said in a post-prayer speech at Jama Masjid of Jammu that Muslims of Rajouri, Poonch and Doda "are fully with the secessionist movement of Kashmir."*

Writing on the subject soon after the incident, a known commentator, Amrik Singh, pointed out that Jammu's claim for autonomy should not be rejected out of hand as an 'unacceptable claim.' He said in an article, "There are hints thrown here which go to suggest that while ladakh might be treated as a separate territory, Jammu may be divided into two areas, Hindu-dominated and Muslim dominated. It is also suggested as a footnote that the Muslim-Dominated area can then be merged with the Valley and so on. What this proposal overlooks is the fact that ethnically-speaking, the Muslims in Jammu Division are very different from those in the Valley ....Altogether, the situation is difficult as well as dicey. One thing stands out clearly, however. There is no indigenous political insurgency in the Jammu Division unlike in the Valley. There is no reason why the situation in this region cannot be handled differently in political terms as also more competently in administrative terms. The present weakness of the situation is not owing to any political challenge, but is largely the outcome of administrative mishandling. If that be so, it should be much easier to bring it under control than to deal with the continuing disaffection in the Valley."†.

Prof. Hari Om, however, does not quite agree with Amrik Singh that the terrorists had made Jammu as their target only recently. He says in his article "Jammu, the ISI Target" (published in *The Hindu* on February 25, 1995) that the militants and their Pakistani sponsorors

* Balraj Puri, "The Battlefield Shifts to Jammu", *Hindustan Times*, March 23, 1995.

† Amrik Singh, "Mishandling of Jammu", *Hindustan Times*, March 17, 1995.

have put Jammu on top of their agenda since March 1994 when two highly significant developments took place at the Geneva U.N. Human Rights Commission Conference. One was the withdrawal by Islamabad of the resolution on the alleged human rights violations in Jammu and Kashmir owing to the able and effective diplomacy of the Minister of State for External Affairs, Salman Khurshid, and other Indian leader. The other was the role of the representatives of the European Union and certain non-Government organizations like the Panun Kashmir and the Friends of Kashmir. The debunked the Pakistani no holds-barred propaganda blitz that the entire population of the State wanted to break its connection with the 'aggressor' India and tried to prove with statistics that the secessionist violence in the State was confined to a few urban areas in the Valley, as also three to four towns in Doda district of Jammu region, and that all the troubles in Kashmir were the handiwork on a few Kashmiris.

"Best way to save Jammu is to split the State": Prof. Hari Om.

According to Prof. Hari Om, ever since the Geneva debacle the ISI and the Kashmiri militants have been seeking to establish their foothold in the vicinity of Jammu city and strengthen the network in the city itself set up earlier and provoke a communal clash through terrorism which could lead to a possible divide between the people of the two communities...The violent incidents in and around Jammu, during the last 10 months, including over 60 bomb blasts in sensitive public places and in passenger and school busses which left 43 innocent persons dead and about 300 wounded, show how ruthless and meticulous the Pakistan agents have been in executing their strategy. These and the January 26 bomb blasts in Jammu's heavily-guarded Maulana Azad Stadium, which killed 9 persons and injured not less than 120, including school children and Governor's Adviser, Goswami, and in which the Governor-General (Retd.), K.V. Krishna Rao, had a narrow escape are nothing but a part of conspiracy the ISI and the Kashmiri separatists have hatched to destabilise Jammu and facilitate the State's merger with Pakistan. From what has happened in Jammu earlier and on January 26 under the very nose of the governor, it is clear that the situation in the city of temples is alarming. But what is even more alarming is the fact that the ISI agents and their sympathisers have infiltrated the crucial police and intelligence agencies and other vital departments, thus rendering the region's administrative aparatus a meaningless sham. In other words, the region's administration has become undependable and vulnerable with the militants having the advantage of choosing their time, venue and target, both VIP and soft.

Feeling insecure, a vast majority of the people accused the authorities in New Delhi and the Governor of downright inaction and demanding that the subversives within and outside the administration be "crushed with a heavy hand" so that the impending wider conflict is averted and peace restored in Jammu region. The best way to save Jammu and counter the Pakistani onslaught is to split the State, which came into being in March 1846, by a quirk of history into being Jammu and Kashmir and declare Jammu into a full-fledged State...The restructuring of the present State should be followed by elections to a legislature for Jammu and the installation of a genuinely-elected Government. This will enable the regions's government to evolve an effective policy against the infiltration of Pakistani elements and arms smuggling. The administration will then be in a position to weed out the sympathisers of the militants... The Kashmir Valley's politicians including Farooq Abdullah, Ghulam Rasool Kar and Mufti Mohammad Sayeed should spent more time there (in Kashmir) to win over the alienated Kashmiris. Their frequent visits to stay in Jammu would not help restore normality in the bleeding Valley. Such a move on their part would surely have a positive impact on the people's psyche, the Writer suggested.*

* Hari Om, "Jammu the ISI Target". *Hindu*, February 25, 1995.

Chapter 5

Pakistan's Complicity and US Role

From around the second half of 1989, Pakistan launched in Kashmir its Proxy War forcing India to a new type of warfare, unlike the ones in 1947-48, 1965 and 1971 in which Pakistan did not succeed in achieving its aims. Pakistan had found from its forty years of experience that until the Kashmiris were motivated and made to join the confrontation, it could not proceed an inch forward in its ambition to grab the State, which it had been nourishing for so long. After the 1971 attack, Pakistan kept quiet for a long time, seeking its way to promote rebellion among the youth of Kashmir to strike a new path. Pakistan succeeded in recruiting some youngmen of Kashmir and giving them training and arms, to return to their homeland and fight its war to start with in the guise of a liberation movement. From the second half of 1989, till date, these youngmen have been recruited in thousands and given training and sophisticated arms. The commandos came in innumerable groups, and wrecked havoc, killing their own people. It was somewhat later that Pakistanis and Afgans brought with them some "Mujahids" from Sudan, Kuwait, Saudi Arabia and Gulf countries. These latter were merely mercenaries and their aim was merely to loot and plunder, to subjugate the people and the Indian armed forces and the security forces.

Unprecedented Resolution passed in Indian Parliament

A firm response was required by India in 1994. The Indian Parliament adopted an unprecedented resolution, passed unanimously, asking Pakistan to vacate the areas of Jammu and Kashmir which it had occupied through aggression. The two Houses of Parliament pledged themselves in the statutory resolution that all attempts to interfere in the internal affairs of India would be met resolutely. They affirmed on behalf of the people that India has the will and capacity to firmly counter all designs against its unity, sovereignty and territorial integrity. "The State of Jammu and Kashmir has been, is and shall be integral part of India and any attempt to separate it from the rest of the country will be resisted by all necessary means", the resolution declared.

It was a historic moment, as only once before, at the time of the Chinese troops coming across. The Himalayas, had Jawaharlal Nehru had Parliament adopt a similar unanimous resolution to urge the nation stand up against the onslaught.

The resolution, moved by the Speaker of the Lok Sabha and the Chairman of the Rajya Sabha was a unique feature, declaring India's determination to get Pakistan vacate the occupied areas of Jammu and Kashmir, and came in close sequence to President, Shankar Dayal Sharma's stern observations at the joints sitting of the two Houses the day before, stating "we shall foil any attempt to destabilise Jammu and Kashmir either from across the border or from any other quarter." It showed the nation had reached the limit of its tolerance.

The resolution called upon Pakistan to stop forthwith its support to terrorism that was in violation of the Simla Agreement and the internationally accepted norms of inter-State conduct.

The Resolution

It said the House noted with deep concern Pakistan's

role in imparting training to the terrorists in camps located in Pakistan and Pakistan-occupied Kashmir, the supply of weapons and funds, assistance in infiltration of trained militants, including foreign mercenaries into Jammu and Kashmir with the avowed purpose of creating disorder, disharmony and subversion;

- Reiterates that the militants trained in Pakistan are indulging in murder, loot and other heinous crimes against the people, taking them hostage and creating an atmosphere of terror;
- Condemns strongly the continued support and encouragement Pakistan is extending to subversive and terrorist activities in the Indian State of Jammu and Kashmir;
- Calls upon Pakistan to stop forthwith its support to terrorism, which is in violation of Simla Agreement and the internationally-accepted norms of inter-State conduct and in the root cause of tension between the two countries;
- Reiterates that the Indian political and democratic structures and the Constitution provide for firm guarantees for the promotion and protection of human rights of all its citizens;
- Regards Pakistan's anti-India campaign of calumny and falsehood as unacceptable and deplorable; and

On behalf of the people of India, firmly declares that:

(*a*) The State of Jammu and Kashmir has been, is and shall an integral part of Indan and any attempts to separate it from the rest of the country will be resisted by all necessary means;

(*b*) India has the will and capacity to firmly counter all designs against its unity, sovereignty and territorial integrity, and demands that:

(*c*) Pakistan must vacate the areas of the Indian State of Jammu and Kashmir which they have occupied through aggression; and resolves that:

(*d*) All attempts to interfere in the internal affairs of

India will be met resolutely.

During the debate the statutory resolution, the former Union Home Minister, S.B. Chavan, launched a broadside against the United States, "for it is clear by now that it is from that country that Pakistan is getting all its inspiration and encouragement." He accused the United States of meddling in Kashmir. He questioned the *locus standi* of President, Bill Clinton and his administration to challenge the accession of Jammu and Kashmir to India. In the Rajya Sabha, while speaking on the same subject, Chavan used even stronger language. He challenged the US "to disprove my charge that it (the US) has a dubious role in Kashmir." "How can they question the instrument of accession and describe Kashmir as a disputed area? We cannot put up with any kind of bullying. No force in the world can say that Jammu and Kashmir is not a part of India."

Chavan levelled a far more grave charge against the US. "It seems clear to me", he said "that they (the US) are interested in Jammu and Kashmir. They are neither interested in helping Pakistan nor India. They will like to help themselves." He expressed his strong suspicion about the US motivation in hard-hitting words: "We on our part have to be on guard. We have to discuss with them frankly and try to find out what exactly are their intentions," he said.

The resolution was extraordinary and had extraordinary features, apparently lending weight to it of the nation's undivided support.

Diplomatic Victory for India at Geneva

India won a diplomatic victory in the face of heavy odds at the United Nations Human Rights Commission at Geneva in the beginning of 1994. Pakistan withdrew its controversial resolution on alleged human rights violations. The Pakistani move came after more than 20 countries appealed to its delegation not to press for a vote on the resolution. The Pakistanis evidently realized that there was no prospect of the resolution being carried.

Iran led the way when its delegate rose, just before

voting was scheduled to begin, to appeal to Pakistan not to press for action on the motion. The Iranian move was immediately supported by China.

Thereafter, delegate after delegate of developing countries such as Maxico, Brazil, Syria and Indonesia similarly appealed to Pakistan to withdraw the resolution. They all pointed out that the Pakistani move was having the effect of splitting the developing world and that every effort had to be made to prevent such polarisation. On behalf of the developed countries, Australia and Canada spoke in a similar vein urging Pakistan to withdraw the resolution. The European Union countries did not speak, but their opposition to the passage of the resolution had been clearly made to the Pakistani delegation.

India's Minister of State for External Affairs, Salman Khurshid said "this has vindicated our stand that Kashmir is a bilateral issue and should not be raised in international fora."

Satish Chandra, India's Ambassador to Switzerland, described the event as "an excellent development from our point of view." He said "This marks the failure of six weeks of intensive diplomatic activity by Pakistan which had sent emissaries to all 53 member countries of UNHRC to canvass support for its attempt to embarrass India." Pakistan showed sign of nervousness when it presented a revised draft of the resolution after finding itself totally isolated on this issue. It made a tactical retreat on the eve of the crucial voting on the resolution. It dropped the demand for sending a UN fact-finding mission to Jammu and Kashmir to investigate and report on the human rights situation there to the General Assembly. It was willing to drop this portion and replace it with a new paragraph seeking that "the Commission calls upon the Indian Government to ensure the promotion of and protection of human rights in Jammu and Kashmir.

Kashmir is Disputed Territory: Robin Raphel

The sharp reaction of Chavan against the U.S. meddling in Kashmir was a reaction to the statement made by the Assistant Under Secretary of State for South Asia, Ms. Robin

Raphel. Having herself served in Pakistan and lost her husband the then Ambassador in Pakistan, in the plane-crash that took Zia-ul Haq's life, Raphel is regarded, among the few in the US foreign policy establishment familiar with South Asia. Ms. Raphel during a background briefing on October 28, 1993 in Washington stated at the briefing that the United States did not admit that Kashmir's accession to India in 1947 necessarily meant that "Kashmir is forevermore an integral part of India." She just elaborated what the American authorities had been telling the Government of India for quite some time before this, that in Washingtons view, the entire Sate of Jammu and Kashmir is a "disputed" territory. Another State Department officer, John Mallot, had made a similar statement in New Delhi six months before. It is self-evident that if somebody brands an entire State as disputed territory, then it amounts to a refusal to acknowledge the accession of that State into the Indian Union. Why did she have to conduct such a background briefing for South Asian reporters in Washington particularly at this point of time when the Kashmir crisis was almost touch-and-go over the Hazratbal incident, when at another level there were preparations for the resumption of dialogue between India and Pakistan? Ms. Raphel made the statement during the sensitive period when India was trying to get the militants out of the Hazratbal Shrine.

Promptly after Robin Raphel's controversial remarks, not only did the Hurriyat Conference leadership as well as the militants inside the Hazratbal Shrine abruptly withdrew from the negotiation process, but militants inside the Shrine made it clear that only a total capitulation by the Government to all their demands would make them leave the Shrine voluntarily.*

Soon after she became Pakistan's ambassador in the US, Dr. Malheea Lodhi asked the US to play an active role in Jammu and Kashmir. As is the custom in the USA, she sized hold of an opportunity to address the faculty members of the

* "Robin Raphel's remarks can only worsen the situation" by Ajay Bose, *Pioneer*, November 3, 1994.

University of Richmond in Virginia, and made a lengthy speech calling upon the US to seize the unique position in the unipolar world and play a "pro-active role" in the Kashmir dispute. She said in her lengthy speech that unless the "core problem of Kashmir" was solved, it would be "impossible either for Pakistan or India to end the arms race."

Kashmir is Disputed Territory: Benazir Bhutto

Benazir Bhutto was to pay a visit to the US somewhat later, but in an interview to the *New York Times* in May, 1994, she expressed the apprehension that Pakistan might lose a plebiscite on Kashmir, "if the option of independence was given to the people of Kashmir." Pakistan would not agree to an independent Kashmir, she said categorically, adding that the question of an independent Kashmir was a ploy to divide the Kashmir vote.

Bhutto calimed that Kashmir "is not part of India". When the "*New York Times* said it was not Pakistan's either, she replied: "Well, it is a disputed territory, in which the people have to determine whether they wish to accede to India or Pakistan."

Even in the beginning of 1995, the Clinton Administration had begun blaming the Pressler Law as an obstacle to Washington's counter-terrorism efforts in Pakistan and was saying that Islamabad was "in the forefront of nations" that were working to combat terrorism. The State Department spokes-person, Christine Shelly, asked to comment on Prime Minister, Benazir Bhutto's plea for US assistance to help crack down on terrorist groups that used Pakistan as a base for their operations, said that because of the Pressler Law, Washington was precluded from providing Islamabad the wherewithal to fight terrorism.

Indian officials in Washington, who for years have been providing the US with evidence that Pakistan continues to foment the insurgency in Kashmir and conduct training camps for terrorist groups, some of which are directly supervised by the Pakistani Intelligence, said that Bhutto's recent remarks vindicated their assertion. One senior Indian Intelligence source said "after years of denying that there were terrorist training camps in Pakistan, she (Benazir Bhutto) is not only admitting the presence of these camps, but she is also begging for US assistance."

At the same time, Pakistani President, Farooq Lehgari, said on March 23, 1995, in a speech on Pakistan Day, that Pakistan would buy the most modern weaponry available to defend against arch-rival India.

Pakistan spends close to one-third of its entire budget on the military and most of that is geared toward a possible conflict with India, said an Associated Press report at the same time. It further said: The two countries have fought three wars in the past half century and have huge numbers of troops facing off along a cease-fire line in the disputed Himalayan State of Kashmir.

US will not Mediate on Kashmir: Tarnoff

Right on the eve of the Pakistani Prime Minister, Bhutto's official visit to the US, where she was planning to seek Washington's mediation on the Kashmir issue, the US Under Secretary for Political Affairs in the State Department, Peter Tarnoff ruled out mediation between India and Pakistan on the Kashmir issue, saying there could not be a "made in USA solution." Delivering a talk on "India as an emerging global power" organised by the United Services Institute in New Delhi, Tarnoff said, India and Pakistan would have to resolve the contentious issue on their own and even be prepared to make sacrifices wherever required. The first time Tarnoff ruled out US mediation on the Kashmir issue was when he was asked whether the United States would support any attempt to convert the Line of Control into the international border as was reported to have been accepted by the late Pakistani Prime Minister, Z.A. Bhutto. The second time was when Tarnoff was asked why Washington was not allowing New Delhi to develop nuclear and missile capabilities and to resolve the Kashmir issue on its own if it indeed wanted to see India emerge as a global power. Replying to the first question, Tarnoff said: "The United States was concerned that India and Pakistan have had a history of antagonism. But encouraged by recent events in other parts of the world, we feel it is possible for historic reconciliation. We hope that the two sides will continue to look for ways and means to resolve the issues"

Benazir visits United States

Pakistani Prime Minister, Benazir Bhutto then launched on a nine-day trip to the United States from April 12 for several objectives, Kashmir being the most important among them. During her talks with President, Clinton which were friendly, Bhutto pleaded with the US to mediate Kashmir talks, but did not get an encouraging response. At the conclusion of the visit, the two leaders issued a joint statement which said Jammu and Kashmir remained the "primary source" of tension in the region and they agreed on the need for substantive Indo-Pak dialogue to resolve the issue, taking into account the wishes of the people of the State. In the statement, the Pakistan Premier reiterated that Islamabad was amenable to US or other international mediatory efforts on Kashmir.

An agency report at the end of the visit said that, the Americans, true to form, maintained Kashmir was a disputed territory. But they suggested that India and Pakistan solve the dispute bilaterally, and merely recorded Bhutto's request for US mediation.

The joint statement recognised Pakistan as a key player in promoting peace and stability in South and Central Asia and spoke of upcoming US-Pak talks on South Asian security, including nuclear/missile proliferation. However, it ignored Bhutto's suggestion that the US propose multilateral talks involving the five permanent Security Council members, Japan and Germany and the two neighbours on issues like proliferation and Kashmir.

The statement also reverted to an extra-cautious formulation where Pressler Law is concerned, recording that "President Clinton expresses his intention to work with Congress to revise Pressler amendment to facilitate both a stronger relationship with Pakistan and nuclear non-proliferation aims in South Asia." Noticeably, it contains no reference to terrorism, despite effusive talk about Pakistan being a "frontline state against terrorism." Instead, there is more than one reference to narcotics, an area where the US has been unhappy with Pakistani efforts.

F-16s Blocked

Nearly two squadrons of F-16s—contracted and paid for by Islamabad, manufactured for and painted over with its Air Force insignia—will stay at the Monthon Davis Airbase in the Arizona desert for some more months, entangled in the Pressler imbroglio, it transpired after the talks. There was little Clinton could do immediately to release the 28 fighter planes.

Evidently, the F-16s did not even top the agenda. "The first consultations with Capitol Hill were about flexibility in other areas, such as cooperation in economic areas and counter-terrorism", said Elien Laipson, Director of the near East and South Asian affairs of the National Security Council.

So, despite all the fine sentiments expressed by Clinton, Bhutto would appear to have returned with nothing more than assurances.

US is Prepared to Mediate: Benazir

On her return to Islamabad, the Pakistani Prime Minister, Bhutto stated at the airport in Islamabad that the US President, Bill Clinton recognised Kashmir as a core issue and also observed that other regional problems would remain frozen till the Kashmir dispute was resolved. She claimed that the Clinton Administration was "prepared to respond positively to the Pakistani proposal of mediation", she termed the US stand as "a moral victory" for her country. Bhutto who was accorded a warm welcome by thousands of people at the airport said that now "it is upto India to accept the US mediation to resolve the Kashmir Issue."

Bhutto said that according to the US President, only a free referendum in Kashmir could gauge the true will of the people. Replying to another question, she said that if India rejects the US President's offer for mediation on Kashmir, the entire international community would be justified in believing that the responsibility for not exploring possibilities to resolve the Kashmir problem lay on New Delhi.

Tall Promises but no Gains

During her visit to Washington, Benazir Bhutto could not persuade the President to jointly fight the threat of religious extremism. She went back home laden with promises of 6 billion in investments. Clinton promised that he would try to convince the Congress to permit at least the F-16s being delivered, Benazir claimed. Benazir said that she had been 'encouraged' by Clinton's remarks. Could it be that she was merely encouraged by the prospect of getting those 658 million minus the considerable storage charges for the planes? Some saw disappointment in her entourage. In any case, the Clinton-Banazir talks lasted two hours and they could not have talked only about "F-16s or money back." Apart from the de rigeur anti-narcotic campaign, the real promise was in Benazir's own commitment of a relentless war against religious extremism.

Now that the cold war is over, the US priorities in the region were different. The spectre of Soviet communism had been exercised, but a new spectre of Islamic fundamentalism has risen. New Islamic States had emerged from the wreckage of the Soviet Union... This is at a time when Islamic mili tancy is on the upsurge from Algeria in the West to Philippines in the east. The Central Asian Islamic States may also be carried away by Islamic revival. In the context, Pakistan is of some use for the US policy-makers, especially to resist Islamic upsurge. This is what the US Defence Secretary meant recently when he declared Pakistan as a "Modern Islamic State." This phrase has obviously caught the imagination of the Pakistani Prime Minister. "Ever since then she has been projecting the importance of her country as a bulwark against the raging Islamic militancy in this part of the world. She has also repeatedly asked the US to help Pakistan to fight terrorism. But her own record is blemished by her open arming and encouraging of terrorism in neighbouring Kashmir. It appear's her appeal to the US to help Pakistan in fighting terrorism is meant more as a public relation exercise aimed at the American public. Her own aims are different. Her one-point programme in foreign affairs has been Kashmir. Pakistan's entire international effort is directed at rousing the world opinion on Pakistan's side in the Kashmir dispute...

"The most important item on Benazir's political agenda would be to persuade Washington to exert more pressure on India to accept external arbitration—to be more specific, US arbitration on Kashmir, and to reduce Indian forces in the state in the name of human rights."

"As far as the present US policy is concerned, it appears to be now tilting towards an independent Kashmir rather than for its accession to Pakistan. This option has been ruled out by Pakistan. Thus eventually Pakistan and the US may not be able to find common language on this issue, apart from expressing their concern for violations of human rights in the state."*

Poll without Hurriyat in Kashmir, a Farce: Bhutto

Soon after her return from the USA, Prime Minister of Pakistan, Benazir Bhutto held a Press Conference in Islamabad saying that the planned elections in Kashmir in July without the All-Party Hurriyat Conference would prove a "farce". She said Pakistan was gratified by the fact that the United States recognized the disputed status of Jammu and Kashmir and "agrees with us that a durable solution to this dispute will have to take into account the wishes of the Kashmiri people."

The Clinton administration, she stated, was prepared to "respond positively to our proposal that the US mediate a solution of the Kashmir issue. It is now upto India to accept such mediation."

Pakistan Insincere to Dialogue Offer: Rao

Just four days later, on April 20, the Indian Prime Minister addressed the bi-annual combined Commanders

---

* "Prime Minister Banazir Bhutto's visit to Washington" By Kalim Bahadur, *Pioneer*, August 4, 1995.

Conference of all three Defence services in New Delhi, he accused Pakistan of not making any 'meaningful response' to India's standing offer of a bilateral dialogue to resolve all outstanding issues. P.V. Narasimha Rao said India would remain on guard and at the same time continue with its quest for normalisation of relations with Pakistan. He said that there has been total peace along the line of actual control on the Sino-Indian border since the Agreement on Maintenance of Peace and Tranquality, signed during his visit to China in 1993 and the joint working group was working with a view to find mutually acceptable solution.

"Most recently we have had extensive enteraction with countries like the United States, United Kingdom, Russia, Singapore, Nepal, Iran and Maldives. These contacts at the highest level were designed to project India's views on international peace and security. But Pakistan had continued its anti-Indian activities supporting terrorism in Jammu and Kashmir and promoting India-baiting on the international scenario, the Prime Minister noted with regret.

Somewhat later, on June 12, in an interview given to Le Figaro, during his visit to Paris, Rao stated his Government was willing to settle the Kashmir issue within the framework of the Indian Constitution, but admitted that the issue was "complicated, because it is not only the Kashmiris who are involved in it." "We are ready to talk with anybody as long as the Kalashnikovs are left outside", he stated. Accusing Pakistan of dreaming to seize Kashmir by force if necessary, he added that it had been dreaming of it since 1947. India had been "very moderate" in responding to Pakistan's nuclear provocations and that it had irrefutable proof that foreign mercenaries and agent provocateurs were responsible for burning down the 15th century shrine at Chrar-e-Sharief. India was worried about Pakistan's nuclear programme. "We tried to attract the world's attention to this danger, but in vain", he said.

U.S. Report Exposes Pak Support for J & K Ultras

In a major development, the Clinton Administration exposed the Pakistan Government's clandestine support for Kashmiri militants, thus giving the lie to Islamabad's oft-repeated claims to the contrary.

The State Department's annual report, 'Patterns of Global Terrorism, which was released in Washington (on April 28), said "There were credible reports in 1994 of official Pakistani support to Kashmiri militants." It also said "some support came from private organisations, such as the Jamat-i-Islami, Pakistan's largest Islamic party." The State Department document noted that "Pakistan condemned the kidnapping in June and October 1994 of foreign tourists by Kashmiri militants in India." It also made a reference to the Pakistani claim that "India provides support for separatists in Sindh province."

According to informed sources, the revelation may make it difficult for the Clinton administration to persuade Congress to agree to its proposal for a modification in the Pressler Amendment to provide some kind of assistance to Pakistan. Under the Pressler Amendment, the then Bush Administration in 1990 had cut off the US military and economic aid to Pakistan in protest against its nuclear weapons programme.

The State Department report said India continues to face significant security problems owing to insurgencies in Kashmir and the North-east. "Targetting of foreigners by Kashmiri militants resulted in several high-profile kidnappings in 1994, including abduction of British and Americans in October and the abduction of British hikers near Srinagar in June", it added.*

Discuss Bilateral Issues at SAARC: Leghari

Pakistani President, Farooq Leghari struck a sour note at the inauguration of the eighth SAARC summit in New Delhi when he referred to his country's problems with India and suggested that bilateral issues should be discussed at the South Asian Summit. India has always protested against Pakistan bringing up bilateral problems at such conferences, but Pakistan has always violated such wishes.

---

* "US Report exposes Pak support for J&K ultras by C.K. Arora in Washington, *Pioneer,* April 30, 1995.

This time, particularly because the SAARC Summit was taking place in India, the Indian Prime Minister, P.V. Narasimha Rao, reacted to Leghari's remarks rather mildy. Answering Leghari's forthright statement Rao offered to resume the stalled dialogue between New Delhi and Islamabad. "We are open to reviving the dialogue. There are no insurmountable barriers to resuming it", Rao told the Press after a 45-minute meeting with Leghari.

Leghari was, however, trenchant in his criticism of India in his speech at the SAARC Conference. In a hard-hitting speech, he implied that Indo-Pak problems were standing in the way of any forward movement by the SAARC. He made no direct reference to Kashmir, but asserted that movements for self-determination, freedom, democracy and respect for human rights across the globe could not be denied. Lasting peace was possible only if the principles of the UN charter are followed and commitments undertaken bilaterally and internationally are fulfilled." He called for an exercise in stock-taking on the progress made by SAARC in its first decade.

Also during his talks with the Indian Prime Minister, Leghari opposed the Indian move to hold elections in Jammu and Kashmir. By holding talks with Hurriyat leaders in New Delhi, Leghari aroused further controversy and the Bharatiya Janata Party leaders in the Rajya Sabha strongly protested against the meeting that he had with the Hurriyat leaders, as they felt that this violated all diplomatic norms. The issue was raised by Sikander Bakht, leader of the opposition in the Rajya Sabha, who said the meeting in which Kashmir elections were discussed was "most objectionable, since no foreign power should be allowed to interfere in the country's internal affairs." "I am shocked how the government could permit the Hurriyat leaders to meet the Pakistani President on Indian soil, since Islamabad has all along been aiding separatist forces in Kashmir", said Bakht.

Hank Brown's Amendment in Senate

Despite all argument against supply of arms to Pakistan, however, Republican Senator Hank Brown in third week of

September re-introduced an Amendment in the US Senate to provide embargoed military equipment worth $ 370 million to Pakistan and to restore economic relations between Washington and Islamabad, which were snapped five years ago under the Pressler Law. The amendment, introduced in the Foreign Operations Act, also sought to modify the ten-year old Pressler Law, under which the United States in 1990 had banned American economic and military assistance to Pakistan because of the latter's nuclear weapons programme. A similar attempt by Senator Hank Brown during the discussion on the Defence Appropriation Bill on the Senate floor last month had failed for want of adequate support.

Besides provision of arms to Pakistan, other than 28 F-16 fighter bombers, the Amendment called for the restoration of bilateral cooperation between Pakistan and the United States in the economic and other fields. These included trade and investment, multi-lateral peace-keeping operations, suppression of terrorism and drug-trafficking, military training and release of repaired parts of mainly F-16 fighter bombers.

In an emotional speech during the debate on the Foreign Appropriations Bill, Brown said the integrity of the word of the US and the credibility of the US President were at stake in the issue of delivery of the military equipment and return of the money to be realised on sale of the F-16s. When Pressler Law came into force, it prevented the delivery of 1.4 billion dollars worth of equipment Pakistan had paid for. The US could not say now that it would not deliver the equipment and also not repay the money. Brown argued that the Pressler Amendment was country-specific as it applied to Pakistan, but did not limit India which developed its own nuclear weapon domestically.

Meanwhile, Senator Larry Pressler sought an intelligence briefing on the security situation in South Asia for senators before they voted on Senator Hank Brown's amendment seeking to provide embargoed military equipment worth $370 million to Pakistan. Brown did not object, but went ahead with his plea.

He made a forceful plea to his fellow Senators to exercise

a conscience vote on his Amendment to facilitate the supply of the arms package to Pakistan. Two Democrat Senators, Tom Harkin and Carolyn Mosley-Braun were drafted as co-sponsors to back up the amendment of the Colorado law-maker, Brown, whose latest Amendment was similar in every way to his earlier proposal except in one aspect: it did not preclude sanctions against Pakistan for transfer of missile equipment or technology under the Missile Control Technology Regime (MTCR).

Democratic Senator Dianne Fainstein, joining Senators John Glenn, Larry Pressler, Cari Levin and others in opposition to the Amendment, predicted that India would now feel obliged to deploy the Prithvi missile and obtain more military equipment to counteract what the USA was now giving Pakistan.

Senators Glenn and Pressler said giving Islamabad the equipment after all the 'lies' of its leaders, including former President Zia, and Prime Minister, Benazir Bhutto, had told about Pakistan's nuclear capability would make a mockery of the US nuclear non-proliferation policy. Brown replied that US Presidents have lied too on national security issues. Eisenhower lied about the base in Pakistan for the U-2 shot down over Pakistan, Kennedy lied about the US arming of the Cuban exiles in the Bay of Pigs invasion, and Truman would have lied had been asked about America's possession of the nuclear bomb when it was still a secret. Brown and others argued that Pakistan has been a loyal ally and that it is not right to take Pakistan's money and give neither the equipment nor return back the money.

US Military aid to Pakistan will Trigger Arms Race

India promptly gave the warning that the US Senate's vote for transferring weapons to Pakistan would be seen as legitimisation of Islamabad's clandestine nuclear programme. A spokesman of the Ministry of External Affairs expressed the hope that the US administration would reconsider the issue and reflect on the issue and reflect on the consequences of its policy before taking any further steps. Asserting that the transfer of arms to Pakistan would endanger the peace and stability in South Asia and trigger an arms race, the spokesman declared that "all necessary measure would be taken to offset its effect on India's security. The proposed sale of American arms must be seen in the light of Pakistan's acquisition of missiles from third countries and its involvement in international terrorism.*

The former Union Home Minister, S.B. Chavan said that the US decision was bond to create tension in the region. "India hoped the authorities in Washington would take note of the strong public reaction in this country over American moves."

Pakistan Jubilant

While a Jubilant Pakistan greeted the scrapping of the Pressler Amendment and the passage of the Brown Amendment was described as the "first significant step in dealing with the discriminatory Pressler Law" by Pakistan's ambassador, Maleeha Lodhi, the step caused widespread feelings in India, and led to some bitter comments, as in an article by the former Foreign Secretary, S.K. Singh, who looked at the event as "back to cosy cold war days for US and Pakistan." He said by passing the Amendment, and giving a new arms package to Pakistan, the US Government had put India in a fix. There were angry reactions in New Delhi, and it looked as if the decision of the Clinton Administration "to ram an arms package to Pakistan through the US legislature has introduced an uncertain element in Indo-US ties, particularly in the burgeoning area of business" which began flourishing with the Indian Prime Minister, Rao having launched the free market economy in India.

India gave the warning of an arms race in South Asia, particularly because the USA overlooked Pakistan's advancing nuclear programme. India felt that the US was legitimising Pakistan's clandestine acquisition of nuclear weapons, even while receiving massive US military and economic aid. The proposed transfer of US military equipment—which was actually valued at far more than $ 370 million as the package would eventually be composed of, it was suspected in India—was

* "*Indian Express*" Diplomatic Editor, September 23, 1995.

also viewed in the light of Pakistan's widely acknowledged acquisition of ballistic missiles from third countries and its major and direct involvement in international terrorism.

The USA took steps promptly to convey to India through diplomatic channels that President Clinton has reassured India that there was no intention to re-estabilish a defence supply relationship with Islamabad, and that President Clinton was keen to visit India in the near future, to demonstrate continued US support for India's economic programme and security interests and a partnership based on convergence of interests and ideals.

India, Pakistan battle it out at UN on Kashmir

Soon after, India and Pakistan engaged in a wordy duel over Kashmir—for the first time in the 1995 session in the UN, Pakistan having decided against moving any resolution on Kashmir in UN General Assembly or its committees this year (1995) after having badly burnt its fingers while making such an attempt last year-in the UN General Assembly, after the Pakistani Foreign Minister, Aseef Ahmad Ali, accused New Delhi of repressing Muslims in Kashmir and launching a feverish arms race. Ali's speech contained veiled criticism of the Indian political leadership when he spoke of threats of war coming from New Delhi. In a well-reasoned response, the Indian deputy permanent representative to UN, Nalin Surie, said the despite Pakistani provocations, India did not have any interest in hostilities and talk of threat by the Pakistani Minister was only a figment of his imagination. "Nevertheless, though we are disappointed that Pakistan does not wish to normalise relations or have bilateral talks, we have noted that their military leaders who continue to be the most influential section of their leadership, have repeatedly said they anticipate no conflict" Surie charged Pakistan with sponsoring terrorism in Kashmir and Afghanistan, and Islamabad had now unleashed terror on its own people. "Karachi is in flames because the government of Pakistan is practising a brutality on its own people with which victims of terror in Kashmir are all to familiar... In 1971 (at the time of East Pakistan operations), state terror unleashed by Pakistani forces in what was then part of their own country, led to three million deaths, a scale of extermination and genocide that compares easily with anything unleashed under fascism", Surie charged.

The US House-Senate Conference Committee approves of Military Package

After nearly a month that the US Senate had approved of the $370 million military package for Pakistan, the US on October 25, House-Senate Conference Committee also adopted the Brown Amendment by passing the Foreign Operations Appropriation Bill by a decisive 10-4 vote, thus paving the way for the transfer of the controversial arms package.

Having been stalled for months at the US Senate, the measure was seen through in September. It was then submitted to the Conference Committee, where representatives from the House as well as Senators were subject to intense lobbying by both Pakistan and India through their caucuses, professional lobbyists and even ex-Congressmen. However, what swung the vote in Pakistan's favour was the lobbying of the Clinton Administration on behalf of a nation characterised as a "realistic and longstanding ally."

Although Representative Joe Knottenburg of Michigan attempted to introduce an Amendment seeking to sell the arms to a third country and reimburse Pakistan, it was easily defeated. Others who voted against the Brown Amendment were Nancy Pelosi, Democrat from California, Sydney Yates, Democrat from Illionis and David Obey, Democrat from Wisconsin.

In a statement released soon after the decision was finally announced, the Indian Embassy in Washington said that it viewed with "serious concern and much regret" the adoption of the amendment. The statement maintained although the Indian Government was "happy that the F-16s will not form part of the military package", it hoped that the arms would only be "a one-time waiver to the Pressler Amendment." The Embassy statement added that it was deeply disappointed that "these concerns have apparently not been taken into account." It also suggested that the "remarkable progress" in Indo-US relations could be "adversely affected" to some extent.

The package to be transferred to Pakistan included three P-3C Orion reconnaissance aircraft, Harpoon missiles, MI-198 howitzers, C-Nite night-vision kits, TPQ-36 radars and TOW anti-tank missile launchers, besides spares for F-16 fighters. From the outset, Pakistan spared neither effort nor expense to hire a formidable army of professional lobbyists. It employed eight lobbying firms, many of which concentrated tenaciously on wavering senators or representatives. Pakistan spent upwards of $2 million, whereas India only $600,000 on one firm. In the final analysis, what made the tussle unequal was the fact that the Clinton administration, working through the White House as well as the State Department, was keen on seeing the package delivered to Islamabad.*

Ironically, the US Congress adopted the bill just hours before former Prime Minister, P.V. Narasimha Rao delivered his speech at the United Nations.

India expressed strong resentment at the adoption of Hank Brown Amendment, allowing fresh arms supply to Pakistan by the United States Senate saying it would lead to an arms race in South Asia and force India to spend more money on defence, former External Affairs Minister, Pranab Mukherjee, said expressing his desappointment and concern at the development, overriding the Pressler Amendment.

Mukherjee said that this would lead to an unintended arms race in the sub-continent as India would have to meet the threat from Pakistan's enhanced military capabilities through the impending acquisition of latest aircraft and weapons systems including Orion aircraft and Harpoon missiles.

Deal to Make Up for F-16s loss—France to Sell 40 Mirage Jets to Pakistan

The French Government two days later cleared the way

* "US law-makers clear arms for Pakistan" By Ramesh Chandran (Washington), *Times of India*, October 26, 1995.

for the sale of 40 Mirage fighter jets to Pakistan, according to senior government officials in Islamabad. The sale of the jets, if finalized, would fill what Pakistan calls its defence gap created when the US Congress blocked the shipment of F-16 fighter planes bought by Pakistan.

Earlier in the day (on October 26), Foreign Minister, Sadar Aseff Ali said in Islamabad that Ms. Bhutto had discussed the sale with M. Chirac during the Pakistani Prime Minister's brief stopover in Paris on her way home from the United States.

"Pakistan has already purchased submarines and we are now looking at the possibility of buying French planes", Bhutto told reporters in Paris. "We are happy to say President Chirac has given the go-ahead", she added.

With this, the Indo-US relations received a temporary setback. Pakistan was jubilant over its success in persuading the US Congress to agree to the supply of military equipment after five years of intense lobbying. (Pakistan had contracted for a $1.4 billion worth of arms and F-16 aircraft with the US which was freezed since 1990 by invoking the Pressler Law which banned arms supply to Pakistan on account of its nuclear ambitions. President Bush could not certify in 1990 that Pakistan did not possess nuclear capability.)

Rao Snubs Pak for Raising J&K Issue

The same day that the US Senate Congress Conference approved of the Brown Amendment, extending fresh arms supply to Pakistan, the former Indian Prime Minister, Rao was in New York. Delivering his address at the golden jubilee commemorative session of the United Nations, Rao said Ms. Bhutto had repeatedly, during her address at the session made references to Kashmir in her five-minute speech at the session. But he did not want to bring bilateral issues to the UN, thereby snubbing Pakistan for doing so. "I am deliberately keeping bilateral matters out of this short intervention", he said. Bhutto in her speech had already said: "The Secretary General has described the Kashmir dispute as the oldest item on the UN agenda. Forty eight years of occupation has not crushed the spirit of noble people committed to the right of self-determination and the ideals of the UN..

Brown Amendment may force Review of Defence Policy

In India, the reaction was immediate to make the Government review its defence policy in view of the US House Senate Committee's decision to transfer arms worth $368 million to Pakistan. A number of influential leaders expressed the view that the Government should adopt a more realistic attitude to US policies with regard to South Asia. They felt the end of the cold war has not changed US policies in the region. The Congress Working Committee member, Jitendra Prasad stated "The US package of arms for Pakistan is totally unjustifiable. The Indian Government should review its defence policy. There is also need to build world public opinion on the deteriorating security environment in the region." Another CWC member and All India Congress Committee General Secretary, Buddha Priya Maurya said "I am sure the Indian government is aware of the consequences of the US decision and would now think in terms of deploying Prithvi missiles." Congress Party spokesman, V.N. Gadgil was also wary of US Committee's decision, saying it raised doubts whether the US was serious at all about fighting terrorism.

The academic community concerned with national security matters speculated on the concessions that Pakistan might have made, like on its nuclear programme, in order to get the toe-hold on the US defence supply platform. Dr. Satish Kumar of the Jawaharlal Nehru University said "what causes concern is not the quantum of arms released to Pakistan, but the motive behind the move. India can absorb the impact of this arms induction, but it cannot accept the justification given by the US that it is trying to help a moderate Islamic state which is working to curb drug trafficking and terrorism."*

---

* "Widespread anger over US arms supply to Pakistan" By Mahendra Ved, *Times of India*, October 26, 1995.

US asks India to Behave Responsibly

The US asked India to 'react responsibly' on the Brown Amendment. Nicholas Burns, the State Department spokesman, said the US Administration strongly favoured the Brown Amendment which "we believe supports the position that President Clinton took in April during Pakistani Prime Minister, Benazir Bhutto's visit to the US. We believe the Amendment will help us forge a stronger and more flexible relationship with Islamabad, which is needed... The Brown Amendment is a one-time release of equipment that Pakistan has already paid for and does not establish an arms supply relationship with Pakistan. So, we continue to expect that India will react responsibly to the developments and recognise that US relations with India and Pakistan are not a zero sum game."

Chavan Accuse US of Training Pakistan's ISI

S.B. Chavan, former Union Home Minister, on October 24, while addressing officers and jawans (forces) of the Indo-Tibetan Border Police, accused US military officers of training, guiding and providing assistance to the Pakistani Inter-Services Intelligence (ISI), "which has been carrying out subversive activities in some neighbouring countries, including India." In an apparent reference to the United States in this connection, Chavan said: "This country says that it stands for world stability and a global move to fight terrorism", making a reference to the US President, Bill Clinton's call on Sunday, October 21, before the UN General Assembly.

"They talk of international conventions and about the need to uphold the unity, integrity and sovereignty of nations. And yet on the other hand, they have been instigating our neighbour, Pakistan's ISI to carry out subversive activities in the neighbourhood" Chavan said. Interestingly, US Deputy Chief of Mission, Mathew P. Daley, sat through the entire function held at Tigri camp, near Delhi. He declined to comment on Chavan's accusations.

While referring to the recent US move to supply arms to

Pakistan, Chavan said: "We destroyed the US supplied Patton tanks (which were use in the 1965 and 1971 Indo-Pak wars. Now they have given (Pakistan) F-16 fighters. But our armed forces are always ready to counter such weapons. These countries think that by supplying weapons, they will scare us into submission."

Rao asks Pakistan to Quit Occupied Kashmir

About this time, India's former Prime Minister, Rao, went to Cartegena (Colombia) to attend the NAM's 11th summit conference. This was just before Rao was visiting the US on the occasion of the 50th anniversary of the United Nations. Pakistan's bid to raise Kashmir issue at the NAM was thwarted at the three-day summit held at Cartegana, the picturesque Carribean coastal town. The draft declaration put up before the 50-odd NAM countries fell far short of Pakistani expectations on Kashmir dispute with India. The Pakistanis had raised the issue at the Jakarta summit three years ago, but the draft declaration put up before the summit only said that the chairman of NAM may play a role in the settlement of bilateral disputes if both parties to the dispute consent to NAM's mediation.

However, coming to speak after Pakistan's Benazir Bhutto had yet again transgressed norms to air her falsehoods on Kashmir, the Indian Prime Minister had perforce to reply and refer to Kashmir. It was a matter of fact, no-nosense restatement of India's stand. "The accession of Jammu and Kashmir is an established fact in international law", he declared. The 'illegal occupation' over a part of the State, i.e., Pakistan-occupied Kashmir, the Indian Prime Minister declared. Rao emphasised that the agonies of the Kashmiri people were caused by "outside support for terrorist depredations in the State." While the Pak Prime Minister was direct and accusing—describing Kashmir as the "oldest dispute" and accused (India) of killings, kidnapping and rape etc.—Rao was indirect and circumlocutory. He talked of "the spread of small arms" which sustained the terrorist movements and ethnic conflicts...and for countries such as India, "to prevent proxy wars across borders and exacerbation of ethnic conflicts that have become the bane of most pluralistic States."*

India tells Pak to stop Interference

Almost simultaneously, there was the fiercest clash of the session over Kashmir, in a UN Committee, where Pakistan's ambassador Kamal Hasan repeated allegations of violations of human rights by Indian Security Forces in Kashmir and called for implementation of the UN resolutions (of 1948 and 1949). However, Nalin Surie, Indian Representative, came out forcefully calling upon Pakistan to put its own house in order and stop promoting terrorism and interfering with neighbouring countries like India and Afghanistan. "Let Pakistan address the fires within is own country rather than attempting to sow discord and fuel terrorism in its neighbouring countries." He charged Pakistan with coveting Indian territory of Jammu and Kashmir and urging Pakistanis to support 'jihad' (holy war) in Kashmir, thereby seeking to instigate terrorism in the Kashmir. He referred to a recent letter sent by Pakistan's opposition party, Mohajir Qaumi Movement (MQM) to secretary-general, Boutros-Boutros Ghali, pointing out massive violations of human rights by Pakistani authorities of its own citizens, including mass arrests of innocents and political victimisation of the MQM. Surie said: "How can those who are being accused of crimes against humanity by a section of their own people, have the temerity to make baseless allegations against another sovereign state? India had banned discrimination on any ground whatsoever. But the Pakistani constitutional system was based on religious discrimination and its electoral system prescribed apartheid-like separate electorates for religious minorities."

Surie's reference was to the 22 million Mohajirs—Muslims from India who voted with their hearts at the time of the partition of the sub-continent and moved over to Pakistan in 1947 to Pakistan—and were still suffering from discrimination mainly in Karachi and also in other parts of Pakistan and were looked upon as second-class

*"Rao asks Pakistan to quit occupied Kashmir" By V. N. Narayan, *Hindustan Times*, October 20,1950.

citizens. They left their ancestral homes and settled in their dream country. Pakistan only to be persecuted there, almost as a class of people inferior to Pakistani Muslims. Hundreds of them are killed in police atrocities every year. The MQM, demanding 'equal rights' has evoked such violent state suppression that Karachi has become an inferno,threatening both Pakistan's economy and political stability. The Pakistan premier has blamed the conflagration on the Indian Consulate in Karachi and closed it. Leaders of the business and industry have protested against the Government, and the Opposition has warned that the former East Pakistan scenario was being re-enacted. The Movement has now given warning of a "civil war."

Sindh Muslims were treated as colonial subjects by the Punjabi-dominated government. Hence the 'Jiye Sindh' movement founded by the late G.M. Syed. In 1944, he had made the Sindhi Provincial Assembly pass a resolution favouring the creation of Pakistan. Later, he called this "the gravest political blunder of my life" and said the religion-based concept of Pakistan was anti-thetic to a modern state. Seeking self-determination for Sindh, Syed stayed 'incarcerated' for the greater part of the life of Pakistan.

The situation brought together ethnic Sindhis and Mohajirs. At the recent World Sindhi Congress in London, Syed Mohammad Shah, a former member of the Sindh Assembly, recalled the separation of Bangladesh and said: "I foresee a situation building up towards that again...millions of Sindhis have been deprived of their livelihood...We have become third grade citizens. We now demand implementation of the 1940 resolution providing for self-determination for the constituent peoples of Pakistan.

(With East Pakistan becoming Bangladesh, Pakistan rulers blasted the 'two nation theory', forfeited half their country and reduced Muslim population to less than India's. Bihari Muslims became permanent refugees just for remaining loyal in Pakistan during the programme).*

---

* "Sinister Pak hand "By Rukmini Menon *Hindustan Times*, November 16, 1995.

(Surie also reminded the delegates of the remarks made by the Afghanistan representative in the General Assembly after Pakistan's statement in the general debate. The Afghan representative had described Pakistan's reference to his country as "antagonistic, indicative of interventionist intentions and an incitement to ethnic hatred which should be condemned as an international crime." In the light of these facts, Surie said, Pakistan should focus on 'healing the ills of its own country and living in peace, goodwill and amity with all its neighbours).'

CHOGM no Forum for Bilateral Talks

Pakistan never missed an opportunity, at any international forum, to raise the Kashmir question. It did so again at the CHOGM (Commonwealth summit) held at Auckland on November 9. Pranab Mukherjee, India's former External Affairs Minister, while heading the Indian team issued a stern warning to Pakistan calling upon it to desist from raising the Kashmir issue at the Commonwealth Summit, saying it would tantamount to violating the CHOGM Charter. He accused Islamabad of repeatedly attempting to internationalise the issue.

In a world apart, at Accra, capital of Ghana, former Prime Minister, Rao, speaking at Ghanian Parliament, rebuked Pakistan for internationalising the Kashmir issue instead of resolving it through bilateral negotiations and vowed to completely stamp out cross-border terrorism from the Indian soil. Citing the example of Punjab, where the Government had been able to control military, Rao said "The People of India have nothing to do with terrorism. Their earnest desire is to return to a life of peace in which they can work to improve their condition of existence. But Pakistan instead of initiating dialogues to resolve Kashmir and other outstanding problems with India through bilateral negotiations was raising the issues at various international fora... I have written to the Pakistan Premier Benazir Bhutto soon after she assumed office offering to have talks. But so far, there had been no response from her"

US Arms given to Pakistan worth well over $1 billion

Sophisticated arms that Pakistan is now getting from the US are worth more than a billion dollars and not merely $368 million sanctioned to it in the wake of the passage of the Hank Brown Amendment this amount was calculated by defence experts after considering the published prices of the US equipment meant for sale to Pakistan. Under the deal, Pakistan is to get three P3C Orion maritime surveillance and strike aircraft. Each P3C Orion aircraft costs $100 million. three Orion aircraft including $90 million worth of support package (spares and components) would alone cost $370 million .

Pakistan is also to get 27 Harpoon missiles. Each missile cost $10 million. The cost of 27 Harpoon missiles including $81 million worth of support package would cost $351 million. In addition, Pakistan is getting weapon-locating radar costing $15 million, ground Electronic Warfare (EW) package costing $10 million and airborne EW package for $1 million. These prices are exclusive of the 30 per cent support package for each equipment. Pakistan will also get F-16 overhaul facilities, aircraft spares and spares for ground equipment.

The defence experts say that the deal is worth more than $1 billion as the US government has undervalued the millitary hardware for Pakistan and was charging one-third of the actual prices.

India has disagreed with the US administration that the military sales under the Hank Brown Amendment and cleard by the US senate, would not tilt the military balance in favour of Pakistan in the sub-continent. They say the supply of arms to Pakistan should be seen by the US government in the light of the deals Islamabad is striking with France and Ukraine.

Pakistan is negotiating the purchase of 40 Mirage 2000-5 fighter aircraft and not 20 as reported earlier. Pakistan is also considering purchasing another 40 Mirage 2000-5 aircraft. It is also negotiating with France the purchase of AEW helicopters and Augusta class submarines with M-39 missiles. Pakistan is seeking the latest T-72C tanks from Ukraine which are far superior to Indian T-72 M1 tanks. The Pakistani tanks will have an updated engine, a new fire control radar and have nuclear, biological and chemical warfare protection. More then 500 tanks are involved in the deal.

Pakistan is also buying from Ukraine 120 BMP-3 armoured personnel carriers, 240 self-propelled 152 MM guns and 24 air defence system.

While Pakistan is going ahead with a rapid arms buildup, no project has been cleared for several months by the Indian defence ministry for modernisation of the forces. Inordinate delays have been made in the production of the Light Combat Aircraft (LCA) and the Advanced Light Helicopter (ALH). For the last 10 years no decision has been taken for the advanced jet trainer for the Indian Air Force. The case upgradation of MI 35 helicopters, conversion of the 130 MM gun into 155 MM gun and the purchase of T-72 tanks are pending with the ministry of defence.*

US has Evil Designs on Kashmir: Chavan

The former Union Home Minister, Shankerrao B. Chavan, on December 5, shortly after the US sanctioned fresh arms to Pakistan, sharply hit out against the United Sates of having "evil designs" on Jammu and Kashmir and blamed it for instigating and continuing violence in the State. Launching a sharp attack in the Rajya Sabha (the Upper House of Parliament) on the Clinton Administration, Chavan asserted that the US wanted "a foothold" in Jammu and Kashmir and like Pakistan, did not want an atmosphere conducive for Assembly elections.

Chavan made the observations, replying to a short-duration discussion in Indian Parliament on Jammu and Kashmir. He said it was not only Pakistan which was creating problems in the Valley, but "some Big Powers" also. Pressed by Opposition members to specify which nations (were creating problems in the Valley), Chavan replied: “I have not hesitation in naming America.” Chavan asserted that the US wanted a

---

* "United News of India *Times of India*, December 4, 1995.

"foothold" in J&K and like Pakistan, did not want an atmosphere conducive for Assembly elections.

Chavan was also critical of one-time waiver of Pressler Amendment which had cleared the way for export of US weaponery worth $1 billion to Pakistan. He said this would lead to an escalation of the arms race on the sub-continent.

In an obvious swipe at the recent Indian visit of US Assistant and Secretary of State, Robin Raphel, the Home Minister declared: "Every time we see a change in the attitude of the Kashmir people, some US official comes here and makes a statement that Kashmir is a disputed territory." In a reference to the US, the Home Minister said: "These people are only interested in themselves. These people are neither interested in India nor Pakistan but want a foothold in Jammu and Kashmir."

US dismisses Chavan's Charges as Baseless

A "distinctly offhand" US official promptly dismissed as "complete nonsense" the allegation made by Chavan in Parliament that the US was fomenting trouble in Kashmir. "Mr. Chavan has a pretty consistent record of making such off-the-cuff remarks. It is complete nonsense", a state department official said in an almost light-heated reaction.*

The same day, December 5, the US embassy in New Delhi, dismissed as "without any basis" the charges by Home Minister Chavan that Washington was fomenting trouble in Jammu and Kashmir. The reaction by an Embassy spokesman came when he was asked to comment to the Home Minister's Rajya Sabha remarks that the US was responsible for the trouble in Jammu and Kashmir and that it had "evil designs"on the border State.

On the other hand, sources in the Government said that Chavan's remarks on the US designs on Kashmir were not off-the-cuff utterances, but based on information that had been checked out well. Intelligence agencies under the Home

---

* "US dismisses Chavan's charge as baseless" By Chidanand Rajghatta, *Indian Express*, December 6, 1995.

Ministry had, of late, been worried about one fallout of the Government's policy of transparency in Jammu and Kahsmir—the increasing activity of US officials in the Valley. The continuing Al-Faran hostage drama in South Kashmir, and its unexpected spin-off in the form of frequent trips of US officials to the Valley, had been worrying India's national security planners. Many in the Indian Government had long been concerned about the extraordinary amount of interest in Kashmir shown by the Americans. Many felt the US would like to see the Valley Independent, as it is strategically located in the midst of South Asia, Central Aisa and China.

When queried on the subject, Government sources expressed great dismay. "Although Ambassador, Frank Wisner is a down-to-earth person, it is the INR (the US State Department's intelligence wing) people who are causing all the problems", a source claimed. The source said that the INR team of two women officers had recently completed their tenure in India (one of whom was posted as an Ambassador in a neighbouring country), and had been replaced by two male INR officials, one of whom was 'highly aggressive'. The other an African-American, is often seen both in Kashmir and in Kashmiri circles in the capital. The Assistant Secretary of State, Robin Raphel before her current posting, was at one time very active in Kashmir. Nowadays, her views and statements on the issue drive the Indian establishment up the wall. The American activity goes to show that the Indian establishment will have to live with such views from American officialdom for sometime to come.*

A day later, the US Charge d'Affaires, Mathew Daly, was summoned to the External Affairs Ministry, by Vinod Grover, Secretary (West), to convey India's displeasure over the statement made by the US official. (The American Ambassador, Frank Wisner, was then in Washington for scheduled consultations). Daly was told that India took strong exception to certain derogatory remarks made by a US State department official against Chavan, saying the use of such 'undiplomatic

* "A baseless charge, says American Embassy" by a Special Correspondent, *Pioneer*, December 6, 1995.

language is regrettable and unacceptable'. While there may be differences of opinion on issues between countries, "we do not expect such observations, which are not in keeping with diplomatic practice", he was told. (The US official, while responding to Chavan's charge in the Rajya Sabha, that Washington was harbouring 'evil designs' on Kashmir was quoted as having said that "Mr. Chavan pops off like that once a month or so on his own. He is an embarrassment to his colleagues in the Indian government)."

US Policy on Kashmir—Evidence backs Chavan's Statement

Ample evidence was available to suggest that Washington's policy on Jammu and Kashmir was not entirely innocent of pernicious designs, according to official sources in New Delhi. These sources did not attach significance to outburst of the United States' State Department describing as "complete nonsense" the remark by S.B. Chavan, that the US has evil designs on Kashmir.

The United States has a long record in promoting the theory of a 'third option' for the state that has been troubled by Pakistans's overt and covert activities since the last more than four and a half decades. This position is couched in the off-repeated concern for the wishes of the Kashmiri people which is widely regarded as a euphemism for delinking the Valley from the rest of the State. And that delinking is believed by many to be the forerunner for a greater US role in the affairs of the Valley. The US interest, say the sources, revolves around getting for itself a foothold in the Valley which can then be used as a launching pad against China in the future. The land route from the Valley into China goes through the Sinkiang region of the Communist State, an area that the US believes to be the 'soft underbelley' of Beijing. Having identified China as a long term threat to its global politico-economic role, Washington needs a firm foothold in the Valley in order to be able to hurt Beijing.

That can only be realised if Delhi's role over the Valley is loosened. The National Conference President, Dr. Farooq Abdullah, has let the cat out of the bag with his disclosure that the US Assistant Secretary of State for South Asia,

Robin Raphel, had conveyed to him that Washington supported the demand for greater autonomy as also the conversion of the Line of Control into a 'soft border'. According to defence experts, the 'soft border' would make the Valley vulnerable on account of the fact that the natural trade routes from the region cross the Pir Panjal ranges into the Mirpuri areas. The increase in Washington's engagement in this part of the world can be seen from the dramatic successes scored by the Taliban militia in Afghanistan. Washington's statements on Afghanistan, when it is normally quick to comment on another country's internal affairs, have been most reticent. Taliban is regarded as the best US option in checking Iran, on the one hand, and the Central Asian States, on the other. While Iran is regarded as a rogue State, the CAS are considered to be the 'soft underbelly' of Russia.*

Informal US Arms Embargo against India

The United States has in effect imposed informal sanctions on India on major bilateral arms sales in order to maintain a balance of power in South Asia between India and Pakistan. Deputy Assistant Secretary of Defence for Near Eastern and South Asian Affairs, Bruce Reidel, indicated on December 7, 1995 before the House Sub-committee on Asia and Pacific that the US has abstained from major arms sales to India fearing that it might alter the existing military balance of forces. He also made it clear, "this will not be an area for immediate, bold steps." He said "one traditional aspect of military co-operation which the Department of Defence is not pursuing in South Asia is arms sales. Arms sales to Pakistan, of course, continue to be prohibited under the Pressler Amendment." However, he claimed that despite this, "The bottomline is that US-Indian defence ties are better now than at any time in past 30 years."

Robin Raphel Reacts to Chavan's Criticism

Assistant Secretary of State, Robin Raphel said Pakistan,

* "US Policy on Kashmir—Evidence backs Chavan's statement," Express News Service, *Indian Express*, December 9, 1995.

India and all countries in the region were very much aware of the US policy of isolating Iran. "As for Pakistan, they share a border with Iran. They are more recently concerned about India developing a relationship with Tehran. That bothers them."

Before the hearing, Raphel received from the Indian Embassy in New Delhi the then Home Minister, Chavan's sharp criticism of US policy on Kashmir. Raphel said generally that "there is residual suspicion in India of US geopolitical aims left over from the Cold War when India was generally aligned with the Soviet Union. We take these concerns seriously as they can undermine our efforts to develop the kind of bilateral relationship that both countries want and need... We have been working to allay this suspicion through robust dialogue with Indian decision-makers and increasing co-operation in a broad spectrum of fields.

Plebiscite not Possible in Kashmir: Raphel

At a hearing before the House of Representatives Sub-Committee on Asia and Pacific on December 6, 1995, Raphel said the United States no longer felt that a plebiscite was possible to settle the Kashmir issue. She announced that the plight of the Kashmiri Pandits would figure in the next human rights report for the first time ever.

Though Raphel had never in her previous Statements called for a plebiscite, she introduced other ideas which angered India, but were welcomed by Pakistan. She indirectly acknowledged that Pakistan was giving material support to the terrorists in Kashmir, saying: "Specifically, with Pakistan, we have urged them to do everything they can to stop military support for Kashmiri militants going across their borders. This only enhances rather than reduces tensions...We have urged the Government of India to engage politically with the Kashmiri leadership."

Pak Islamic University hub of Terrorist Activities

Kathy Ganon, writing for the Associated Press, stated from Islamabad that Pakistan's Islamic University, where the alleged mastermind of the World Trade Center bombing once hung out, is "a hub of terrorist activities." According to a confidential government report acquired by the Associated Press, "The University has now become a direct security threat to the country." The report was prepared nearly seven months ago by Pakistan's domestic intelligence agency, the Federal Investigation Agency. The report which has never been made public, was prepared following the February arrest in Pakistan of Ramzi Yusuf, who was believed to have masterminded the 1993 New York Trade Center bombing that killed six people. (Yusuf, who was handed over to police by a South African that he had befriended at the Islamic Unviersity, was quickly extradited to the United States where he is awaiting trial).

The Report says: "According to various investigations and the statements of accused persons, this University has become a hub of terrorist activities. Eighty per cent of the staff and most board members of the Saudi-funded university are not from Pakistan and therefore the Government of Pakistan has hardly any control on the University." Nearly 1,000 foreign students, many from Arab countries, attend the sprawling two-storey Islamic University built adjacent to one of the world's largest mosques. Like the University, the imposing white marble mosque whose four towering minarets are a national landmark was financed by the Saudi Arabian govenment. However, according to the report, most of the University teachers and board members are Egyptians. The University's bank accounts are located in Jiddah in Saudi Arabia and Cairo in Egypt. The University flourished under Pakistan's military dictator, Gen. Mohammed Zia-ul-Haq, who recruited Islamic mercenaries during the 1980s to fight Soviet invasion troops in neighbouring Afghanistan. Thousands of Arabs from the Middle-East and Northern Africa came to Pakistan, welcomed by Gen. Zia as well as the United States and Europe, who sought to use their Islamic fervour to defeat Russia in Afghanistan, according to analysts. According to the report: Unfortunately there has been no severe action against such illegal students and foreigners (many from middle East and Northern Africa) who stayed on after Muslim rebels threw out the communists from Afghanistan in 1992) and thus they have found Pakistan a safe haven for their activities.

Islamic Schools give Arms Training, Admits Benazir

Prime Minister, Benazir Bhutto, has admitted that some Madrasas (Islamic schools) in Pakistan are giving military training to their students in the cause of Islam. She made this statement during a meeting with a group of Ulema (Islamic scholars) who called on her in the State Guest House in Lahore a few days ago. She asked them to help the government curb the menace of terrorism in the society.

The meeting took place in the wake of escalating tension between the government and religious groups ever since the arrest of 40 army officers on charges of plotting an Islamic coup in September. Religious parties have described this action as an attack on pro-Islamic elements within the army. But dauntless Bhutto has responded by making large-scale arrests of members of militant Islamic groups after the bomb blast in the Egyptian Embassy last month. Bhutto has gone so far as to allege that the Islamic militants in Pakistan are getting support of the American Central Investigation Agency (CIA).*

---

*Islamic Schools give arms training admits Benazir, *Pioneer*, December, 6, 1995.

Chapter 6

The Beleaguered State: International Power Ploy

There was a daring act of terrorism in Jammu and Kashmir even as the year 1992 opened. On January 24, the office of the Director General of Police in Srinagar was bombed in which many senior officers were hurt. That was in Srinagar, in the Valley, and there had been stray incidents of terrorism in Jammu town and other places like Doda, but there had been no corodinated act of terror, as erupted in Jammu city on the occasion of the Republic Day celebrations on January 26. The J&K Governor General, K.V. Krishna Rao (retired) had a close encounter with death when three remote-controlled bombs went off even while he was addressing the Republic Day rally at Maulana Azad Stadium in Jammu, which was more than just a grim reminder that the battle against terrorism in the State was yet to be taken to its logical conclusion. The incident left at least eight people dead and scores of others injured. It would not have occurred but for an obvious security lapse which was a shocking indictment of the administration such as it existed in the troubled State.

Siege of Chrar-e-Sharief

The next major attack by terrorists to destabilize Jammu and Kashmir and prevent elections (which were then due before July 17), was something more disastrous than the capture of the Hazratbal Shrine in the Valley more than a year before. News came in the beginning of February that terrorists led by a notorious Pakistani mercenary, 'Major' Mast Gul, had established complete control on the South Kashmir township of Chrar, about 30 km. away from Srinagar, threatening to use the ancient Shrine there as the shield. Both the Border Security Force and the Army were forbidden from venturing into the thickly populated township at the centre of which was located the ancient Shrine of "Chrar-e-Sharief." Militants were allowing passage only to ration-laden trucks bound for a nearby Security Forces camp at Pakharpora via the township.

A survey by the sucurity agencies established the number of militants holding on inside the town as between 150 and 200. Of them, a large number were foreign mercenaries. The militants belonged to three dominant pro-Pakistan outlawed groups viz., Hizbul Mujahideen, Harkat-ul-Ansar and the recently surfaced mercenaries-dominated group, Lashkar-e-Toiba.*

The militants stepped up their surveillance of the township and they were questioning all wanting to enter the town. 'Major' Mast Gul, leading the militants in Chrar, had reportedly sent a wireless communication message to the troops stationed at the Radar station, five kms. from the town, challenging them to enter (the town), authoritative sources disclosed. Later, Mast Gul established his control over the shrine and the adjoining areas, and the Indian Army pickets kept a watch over the situation from a distance of about 3 km., perhaps apprehending what Mast Gul's intentions could be. The fear was: lest the militants should just light a few match sticks and set the beautiful centuries-old shrine and destroy it.

---

* *Indian Expres*, New Delh, February 7, 1995.

Meanwhile, the statutory resolution approving the extension of the President's rule till July 17 in Jammu and Kashmir was approved by the Indian Parliament, with the confidence that a further extension would not be necessary after that date. The Government expressed its determination to hold elections in the State. Certain preliminary moves such as the revision of electoral rolls had already been put into motion.

OIC asks UNHRC to Investigate Human Rights Violations in Kashmir

Towards the end of February, the Organisation of Islamic Countries (OIC) submitted before the United Nations Human Rights Commission (UNHRC) a memorandum on Kashmir at Geneva, alleging that India had deprived the people of Jammu and Kashmir their basic right of self-determination and it called upon the United Nations to investigate human rights violations in the State. It called on India "to halt its repression in Kashmir and withdraw its forces, in accordance with UN Security Council resolution and called for full and unrestricted access to international organizations including Amnesty International and the International Committee of the Red Cross." Later, Pakistan made a move on similar line before UNHRC.

Finally, India turned the tables on Pakistan. In the final analysis, Pakistan filed to go on the offensive and India did not have to fight it with its back to the wall. Delegates from various countries to the UNHRC attributed this change of position to the position taken by the leader of the Indian delegation, Ghulam Nabi Azad, an Indian Minister, who hails from Kashmir. Azad exposed Pakistan's claim of being an Islamic state. He pointed out that even in the holy month of Ramzan, sectarion strife fuelled by the Government (of Pakistan) had taken over 160 lives in Karachi where even the sanctity of mosques had not been spared from gun and grenade attacks. Pakistan was demanding self-determination in Jammu and Kashmir, but denied this right to the people of Pakistan-occupied Kashmir (PoK) by virtue of Article 7(ii) of its Constitution. In another part of Kashmir, illegally held by Pakistan, Northern Territories, even the basic rights of representation were denied and no elections had been held there todate.*

Farooq demands Autonomy—before Elections

With elections approaching—the date for which would be before July 17—Dr. Farooq Abdullah, former Chief Minister, took a U-turn from his previous softening stance and declared that there was no question of his party, the National Conference, participating in State elections unless the Centre conceded some political autonomy. "As the President of the National Conference, let me tell you that the Party will not participate in these elections unless you give us autonomy. They can push through any kind of elections they want, but we won't take part in it", he stated.

Although the NC leader had initially ruled out participation in polls subsequently he softened his stand, indicating he was willing to contest polls. His changed attitude was pronounced following several statements by Chavan, to the effect that if the NC were to stick to its stand, it would 'miss the bus', as had happened to the Akalis after their boycott of the 1992 Punjab Assembly polls.

The NC leader, who recently returned from Geneva (where he was a member of India's delegation at the UNHRC), said "We, in the delegation at Geneva, watched the Russians sign away on Chechnya without so much as a peep. A time will come when international pressure will build up and put us in the same position unless an initiative is taken in Kashmir...The Central leaders should give us regional autonomy, if this did not come, my party would stay away from the polls."†

In a month, on April 19, Governor Krishna Rao came out with a statement pointing out that although the Government would like to hold elections by July 18, it found difficult to motivate the traditional parties to participate in a meaningful political process. These parties had been exhibiting a luke-

* "India Turns Tables on Pakistan" by Subhash Kirpakar, *Times of India*, March 8,1995.

† "Farooq insists on autonomy before election" by Aditya Sinha, *Pioneer*, New Delhi, March 20,1995.

warm response in reactivating their cadre in the present circumstances. A powerful deterrent in the political process was the ongoing strike by the Valley-based Government employees, who were protesting against the dismissal of 22 employees for their alleged links with militants. The Chrar-e-Sharief crisis was also haunting the poll process in the Valley. Many militant outfits and other organisations had been demanding to lift the seize (by the Army) around the holy town. At a function sometime later, Dr. Abdullah dared T.N. Seshan, Chief Commissioner, to hold free and fair polls in the strife-torn State of Jammu-and Kashmir. "Your job is not easy, particularly in my State, where activities are governed by guns which have come from Pakistan." "Even if there is half a chance, we will have full elections in the State", Seshan announced in reply.

Rao discusses with Political Parties on Autonomy Demand

After arriving from London for a visit to the Valley, on April 3, Dr. Farooq Abdullah, President of the National Conference, in a talk over the Doordarshan (Indian TV set) said his party would participate in the elections provided "internal autonomy" was given to Jammu and Kashmir. About the grant of an economic package to be given to the State before the elections, Dr. Abdullah said it was very necessary for the State as all bridges, school buildings, hospitals and other public property had been damaged in the past five years (of terrorist activity) and a lot of money was needed to reconstruct these again.

The Prime Minister, P.V. Narasimha Rao, too made a move in a few days thereafter, saying the Government would hold discussions with political parties on the issue of autonomy for Jammu and Kashmir. The offer brought two different reactions from the political parties. Whereas the Bharatiya Janata Party pointed out that any move to grant more autonomy to the State was fraught with great danger as it would 'open Pandora's box', the Communist Party of India welcomed the Prime Minister's offer, saying it was a positive response to the demand of secular political parties.

Shabir Shah, the popular 'Azadi' Leader

One significant development of late was the frequency with which Kashmiri leaders committed to 'azadi' (freedom), began speaking out Shabir Shah, undoubtedly the most popular leader in the Valley, spent more than a fortnight in Delhi. Soft-spoken and undemonstrative, he could not have attracted much larger crowds in Srinagar except as a symbol of 'azadi'. He certainly did not represent fundamentalism in any form. Unlike other politicians he tried to establish links with Jammu and Ladakh and project himself as a secular leader. Shah flatly rejected the proposal for early election designed to set up a Government in the State. But he was not entirely negative. While in Delhi, he suggested that election was feasible to determine who would represent the people in talks with New Delhi on the future of the State. He made the point that if election was not aimed at forming a Government, there would be no need for candidates to pledge allegiance to the Indian Constitution, which he and his colleagues were opposed to.*

Mast Gul escapes after Burning Down Shrine

On the night of May 10-11, led by 'Major Mast Gul' a large number of Pakistani and Afghan terrorists, set fire to the historic shrine of Chrar-e-Sharief, to devastate it and lay it in ruins. The arson continued for two days. Many militants, nine of them foreigners and two men of the Indian Army were killed in the continuing encounter between the security forces and the militants hiding around the burnt-down Chrar-e-Sharief shrine for two days thereafter. The encounter left more than 60 militants dead, while violence in other parts of Kashmir continued despite curfew restrictions.

After he accomplished his 'mission' of burning down the shrine, Mast Gul, leader of the holed-up militants, escaped a day later from the town, leaving behind his men to face the security forces. Local residents captured and handed over to the security forces a top mercenary, Abu Jindal, a close

* "A tiny Window of oportunity in Kashmir"by Ajit Bhattacharjee, *Pioneer*, April 21, 1995.

associate of 'Major' Mast Gul. Jindal, who had fought earlier in Afghanistan for seven years, was caught by the locals while he was trying to flee Chrar-e-Sharief to save his life. He was bleeding profusely when he was caught. During investigation by the Army authorities, who gave him first aid, he said that more than 10 foreign mercenaries were still hiding in the town and were willing to surrender. But they were afraid of the Army men. He also confessed that the 15th-century shrine, which housed the relics of Sheikh Noor-ud-Din Noorani, the Sufi saint, his daughter and eleven Caliphs, was torched by Mast Gul himself. He disclosed that Mast Gul escaped the town after torching the shrine. The militants opened fire at the security forces afterwards with a view to escape from the town.

Announcing the capture of Abu Jindaal, or General Afghani, leader of Harkat group, who is the first of the 40 mercenaries and hardcore militants holed up at the historic shrine for more than four months and who, along with Mast Gul, had master-minded the burning down of Chrar-e-Sharief, Brigadier Mohinder Singh, Commander of the Indian Army operations, said "We have accounted for about 25 mercenaries and militants of the band that had taken positions inside the shrine. We are on the lookout for Mast Gul, who is perhaps injured. Among those killed in the encounter since May 11, was Zafar Kawa, a top activist of the outlawed Hizbul Mujahideen." Lieutenant General, J.S. Dhillon, told reporters "it was a false propaganda of Pakistan that Indian Army was having 600,000 troops in Kashmir. In fact, the Pakistan Army had deployed three divisions of its troops to assist the infiltrators." People not satisfied with the Government's and the Army's version about the burning down of the shrine, took o streets. The summer capital city of Srinagar alone witnessed some 20 demonstrations, including at places like Rajouri Kadal, Nawa Kadal, Jehangir Chowk, Khanyar, Sonwar where Police opened fire and lobbed tear gas shells.

Almost simultaneously with the burning of Chrar-e-Sharief, Pakistan backed militant organisation, Harkatul Ansar, threatened to attack Indian cities. A statement issued by Maulana Mohammad Farooq, leader of Harkatul Ansar group, said "India should remember that the fire of Chrar-e-Sharief will not be confined to Kashmir alone. Now this fire will burn Delhi and Bombay... Our movement will spread to other Indian cities. Our jehad will continue until India ends its illegal and unconstitutional occupation and vacates the land of Kashmir." The statement issued in Muzaffarbad, capital of the Pakistan-occupied Kashmir added that "The burning of the holy shrine of Chrar-e-Sharief will become the cause of India's defeat."

All-Party Meeting Summoned

Promptly, an all-party meeting was summoned in the Indian Parliament by the then Prime Minister, P.V. Narasimha Rao, to take stock of the situation arising out of the destruction of the historic shrine. Even as Rao declared his Government's resolve to foil Pakistan's designs and press ahead with the normalisation process in Jammu and Kashmir, the Opposition parties launched a blistering attack on the Government for its 'total failure' to protect the Chrar-e-Sharief shrine despite repeated warnings. Seething with anger, the Opposition parties threatened to come up in the House with adjournment motions, and even a no-confidence motion against the Government. The only issue on which they offered to support the Government was on a sound initiative to foil Pakistan's 'nefarious' designs to destabilise the country. The Opposition party leaders also asked for the racall of Governor, K.V. Krishna Rao and a revamp of the State Administration. The parties also expressed themselves against embarking on elections without restoring total normalcy in the State. Some of the Opposition leaders held the Prime Minister to blame, by highlighting the fact that it was he who had assumed charge of Kashmir affairs. The Opposition leaders including the leader of the Opposition, Atal Bihari Vajpayee, squarely held the Prime Minister responsible for the Chrar-e-Sherief debacle.

In the course of his observations, Rao said the burning down of the shrine by mercenaries and militants with support of a "neighbouring country" was only going to "steel our determination" to go ahead with the process of normalisation in Jammu and Kashmir. On the specific issue of Chrar-e-Sharief, Rao said the State Government had adopted a certain approach which "perhaps did not succeed." But this should not be viewed as a total failure of the Government's policy to deal with the overall situation in Jammu and Kashmir.

Leader of the Opposition, Vajpayee, briefing newspapermen said virtually the entire Opposition castigated the Government for its "total failure." Vajpayee, who had set the ball rolling at the meeting said: "The Government wanted to provide safe passage to the mercenaries. But most of them have been killed or wounded. In the end, the most regrettable aspect was that the plot of the terrorists had succeeded. They not only destroyed the shrine, but did so on the auspicious day of the Id, the most important religious festival. By their action, they have made Kashmir once again the subject of international media attention",Vajpayee declared.

Leaders of the Janata Dal, the Communist Party of India, the Communist Party of India (Marxist), Samata Party, Janata Party, Samajwadi Party and Revolutionary Socialist Party, who attended the meeting, were equally critical of the failure of the whole Government mechinery, including the Central Government, State Government and the Intelligence network.

Representatives of most parties opposed the idea of going ahead with election at this juncture. The Prime Minister was, however, keen on holding them. "We said that the Government first ought to put down the militant activity with a heavy hand and then think in terms of elections", Vajpayee pointed out.

Prime Minister announced a Central assistance of Rs.150 million for rebuilding houses and shops in and around Chrar-e-Sharief shrine which were destroyed due to the activities of the militants. The Jammu and Kashmir State government simultaneously announced sanction of relief to fire victims of Chrar-e-Sharief, whose immovable property, including houses were torched by militants.

Pak Plan to Step up Proxy War

Almost simultaneously with the burning of the Chrar-e-Sharief, news came in from Poonch that Pakistan's Inter-Services Intelligence Organisation (ISI) has streamlined its "command structure" to intensify its proxy war in Jammu and Kashmir. According to highly-placed intelligence sources in Poonch, as part of the revamping process, the ISI also shifted its headquarters for originating Kashmir operations from Muzaffarabad to Kotli, situated south of erstwhile Poonch district.*

Also almost simultaneously, Benazir Bhutto, Pakistan Prime Minister, in an interview to the *New York Times* expressed the fear that Pakistan might lose plebiscite on Kashmir. She said in the interview that "if the option of independence is given to the people (beyond the option of whether they would like to join Pakistan or India), Islamabad could lose such a plebiscite." She told the *New York Times* that Pakistan could not agree on an independent Kashmir and that "the question of an independent Kashmir is a ploy to divide the Kashmiri vote.The Hindus are going to vote for accession to India because they are the minority."

Bhutto analysed: "If you are talking about the Muslim majority deciding between accession to Pakistan or an independent Kashmir, the Muslim vote could get fractured and we could find ourselves with the *status quo*, where the Hindu minority accepts Indian rule and the Muslim majority does not accept it."†

Prime Minister ready for Something 'Short of Azadi'

Rao's announcement on May 16 in the Rajya Sabha that he was willing to consider giving something short of 'azadi' and hold talks with Kashmir leaders in the framework of the Indian Constitution was found to be intriguing in some

* " Pak Plan to step up Proxy War" by R.S. Charka, *The Tribune*, Chandigarh, May 10, 1994.

† "Pak may lose plebiscite on Kashmir—Benazir" By T.V. Parasuram (Washingaton), *Pioneer*, May 17,1994.

quarters and welcomed in other circles. Rao's offer came at a time when following his talks with the Chief Election Commissioner, T.N. Seshan, Home Secretary, Padmanabhiah called on Seshan and told him that the situation was conducive for holding elections in Jammu and Kashmir.

Dissidents in the Congress pounced on Rao's statement saying it implied 'creating a Republic within a Republic' and that it meant turning the clock back to the 1949 situation. "What is the value of saying we will keep defence, foreign policy and currency with us when in Kashmir only the almighty Dollar and not the poor Indian rupee will have respect?' asked a Congress dissident requesting anonymity. He went on to say that the readiness to give something short of 'azadi' meant conceding that Kashmir was under India's illegal occupation, an area not under Indian domain and almost saying that it is not an integral part of India.

Dr. Karan Singh, former Sadr-e-Riyasat of Jammu and Kashmir, welcomed Rao's statement and pointed out that he had consistently been advocating a negotiated solution. "The Governor has to be political or someone political has to be assigned the task of holding these talks. I would like to see a structure being set up to enable a dialogue to begin. I welcome a dialogue with Kashmiri leaders", said Dr. Karan Singh, who was also once Cabinet Minister and India's Ambassador to the US.

The Government's decision to extend President's rule in Jammu and Kashmir beyond July 17 was the result of a realistic appraisal of the situation in the troubled State. While the burning down of Charar-e-Sharief by the militants was one of the immediate causes for the Government's rethinking about the holding of elections, it could not have overlooked the opinion of the Opposition parties which were, by and large, not enthusiastic about opting for the polls at this point of time.

The Chrar-e-Sharief episode highlighted the futility of talking of elections in Kashmir at this stage, pointed out Lieutenant General (retired), S.K. Sinha, in an article "Elections in Kashmir—An Unwise Move" published in the *Hindustan*

Times on May 22. "If we are not in a position to ensure the security of such an important holy shrine despite previous warning, how can one expect adequate security being provided to thousands of polling booths and hundreds of contesting candidates. Even if elections are held under the shadow of the gun, what message will get conveyed if there is a total boycott of elections by voters or if the vote tornout is ridiculously low?...There is also the question of the 300,000 Kashmiri Pandits languishing in refugee camps, outside the Valley. These victims of ethnic cleansing have for all these years suffered neglect and may now get defranchised.

Extension of President's Rule in J&K

The Union Cabinet on May 29 decided to extend President's rule in Jammu and Kashmir, beyond its expiry on July 17. The Cabinet which met under the Chairmanship of Prime Minister, Narasimha Rao, resolved to continue efforts to hold Assembly elections at the earliest. The meeting decided on the extension of President's rule in view of the Chief Election Commissioner, T.N. Seshan's assessment of the ground situation in the Valley after his visit to Srinagar over the weekend. The CEC who met the Prime Minister on his return from the State, expressed apprehensions of violence if elections were held in the immediate future and was in favour of staggering the polls, when they are held. He had however, not committed to holding elections by any specific data but would make known his decision later. The state had already been under President's rule for five years during which it has witnessed unprecedented violence unleashed by the militant groups aided from across the border. An official source said that the Govenment was keen on holding the elections before July 17, but the burning down of the Chrar-e-Sharief had come as a setback to its moves for revival of the democratic process.

Destruction of Chrar, A Severe Blow

Previous to the burning of the Chrar-e-Sharief, serious moves were afoot for holding Assembly elections in Jammu and Kashmir—and before the expiry of the spell of President's rule on July 17. Almost the entire election material was ready. Revised lists of voters were expected to be put up any time for verification by the electorate. Notification had been issued for the delimitation of 87 constituencies, 11 more than in the previous elections, and indications were that four more might be added to ake their total number to 91. Buses and trucks were being hired for two months. However, despite all this preparedness, the National Conference Chief, Dr. Farooq Abdullah, had left for the Haj pilgrimage, causing consternation in his party which would like him to be around at the critical time. The word going round in well-informed circles was that a new name might emerge on the political scenario. This was of a dancer-turned-militant, Kuka Parrey, who was said to be ruthlessly opposed to the pro-Pakistan Hizbul Mujahideen.

But the entire idea of having elections in Jammu and Kashmir by July 17 had to be abandoned because of the Charar-e-Sharief incident. It was such a severe blow.

Rao called an all-party meeting to say that India was well-aware of the continuing attempts by mercenaries and militants supported by Pakistan to upset the normalisation procees. "It is a clash of will. And if we carry on in a resolute manner our will prevail over their evil designs. While we are engaged in this process, there will be temporary setbacks, but this should not deflect us and success will follow", he observed. He said that he was having consultations with various political parties on a policy framework to deal with the situation. He agreed with the Opposition that there were several lessons to be learnt from the incident at Chrar-e-Sharief. The Government had noted these lessons and had taken up follow-up measures. He wanted a master plan for the entire Chrar-e-Sharief area to be taken up.

Among the Kashmir group of ministers who attended the meeting were S.B. Chavan, Dr. Manmohan Singh, Pranab Mukherjee, Rajesh Pilot and Bhubanesh Chaturvedi. Pilot observed that mercenaries had no respect for mosques and shrine in Jammu and Kashmir and were using them as hideouts. CPI (M) leader, Harikishen Singh Surjit,; BJP leader, Sikander Bakht; and R.N. Mirdha of the Congress underlined the need for a political consciousness on evolving a policy to prevent the misuse of religious places as sancturies for anti-national elements. Samata Party leader, Rabi Ray, said the government owned an explanation to the nation why it has been on the defensive on the whole issue. The nation's prestige had suffered because of this. Pakistan would now gain mileage out of this. In fact, it had already launched a propaganda offensive against India. He demanded that the government should come out with its Kashmir policy. Janata Dal leaders, Shrikant Jena and Inder Kumar Gujral asked the government if it had intercepted information that the mercenaries were planning to destroy the shrine, why did it not take the Opposition leaders into confidence right then. Neither the Prime Minister nor the Home Minister had an answer to this.

Chrar Incident Greatest Setback to Political Process

The postponement of elections in Kashmir was a definite setback to the Government's efforts to convince the international community of its capability to normalise the situation in the State despite interference from Pakistan. Even though Prime Minister Rao's commitment to hold Assembly elections in the State had been widely endorsed abroad, leaders of many countries had stressed the point that a political process must be credible to the internationally acceptable. The envoys of some of the European Union countries, who were invited by the Central Government to visit the Kashmir Valley of late, also held the view that the administration needed a through overhaul, starting from the Governor, who was regarded by some as unpopular. The British High Commissioner, Sir Nicholas Fenn, had just visited the State. In the assessment of the envoys of the Western countries, the State adminstration had failed to provide the healing touch and to minister to the needs of the people. They felt that the people by and large were fed up with militancy and were anxious to resume normal lives, but complained that the administration had failed to weed out terrorism and to provide them security. The envoys were told that the militants had ruined their lives and the State's economy and that the administration must put it back on the rails as soon as possible.*

American ambassador in India, Frank Wisner, also visited the State and met the Governor, Krishna Rao, who said the Government was committed to restore democratic set-up in the State and to normalise the situation despite Pakistan's efforts to thwart the process. He apprised the visiting envoy of Pakistan's involvement in militancy in the State and pointed out that Pakistan did not want normalisation of situation, nor did it want revival of the political process in the State. The ambassador also held separate talks with the separatist leader, Shabir Ahmed Shah, Yasin Malik and leaders of All Parties Hurriyat Conference, and businessmen and industrialists of Kashmir, who wanted a solution to the crisis through tripartite talks between India, Pakistan and Kashmiri leaders.

Elections were put off, but according to the purveyors of the scene, insurgency fatigue was also setting in. More people were co-operating with the security forces. The pressure on insurgens had increased and there was more dissension in the militants' ranks. This was the view of officials who had been in the thick of counter-insurgency operations eversince its inception in 1989-end. Even some Kashmiris favoured a poll if the All Parties Hurriyat Conference and leaders like Shabir Shah, Yasin Malik and others agreed to contest or at least agreed to participate. But Yasin Malik had gone to the extent of threatening self-immolation if the election process was initiated. Maulana Abbas Ansari, Shia leader, Prof. Abdul Gani of the Muslim Conference, Mirwaiz Omar Farooq, Chairman of the Hurriyat Conference and Abdul Gani Lone of the People's Conference ruled out any election, but demanded that the only solution to the Kashmir tangle was tripartite talks between India, Pakistan and representatives of the Kashmiris from both sides of the line of control.†

The "much flaunted initiation of political process" in the troubled State thus went into reverse gear following the

* "Setback for Government on Kashmir" by M.K. Dhar, *Hindustan Times*, May 31, 1995.

† "An election needs the veil of peace, but guns are out" By V.K. Dethe, *Times of India,* June 10, 1995.

Chrar-e-Sharief incident and the subsequent postponement of the proposed Assembly elections. Many leaders and workers of the two main political parties in Kashmir, namely the National Conference and the Congress started fleeing the Valley to the safe environs of Jammu and Delhi. The trend increased since the attempt made on the life of Mian Altaf, a prominent Congress leader, who is the son of Mian Bashir, spiritual and political leader of the Gujjar Muslims in the State. The jeep of Mian Altaf, who was a former legislator and a Minister from Kangan constituency in Kashmir, was blown up by a landmine. He along with his two bodyguards, were seriously injured and shifted to All India Institute of Medical Science in New Delhi, for treatment. In the past two months, militants killed six leaders and workers of the National Conference. One political leader of the NC said that fear psychosis amongst political workers had increased manifold following the Chrar-e-Shrief incident. "It was the greatest setback to the normalisation process and all the gains of the past two years have gone down the drain and we are back to square one", was his view.*

'Al-Faran' Decamps with Foreign Tourists

No sooner than Mast Gul and his band set fire to the Chrar-e-Sharief and escaped to Pakistan (where he appeared later to talk to the Press about his great achievement), a new group of terrorists, styling themselves as 'Al-Faran' appeared on the scene, and decamped with half, a dozen foreign tourists camping near Sheshnag in Kashmir Valley in the begining of July. One of the hostages, John Childs, an American, succeeded in escaping from 'Al-Faran', the militant outfit that had come out with the threat of "serious consequences" if the 22 detenus whose release it had demanded were not set free by July 15. A handwritten note in Urdu copies of which had been circulated to the local newspapers in Srinagar said that if the demands were not accepted, the Government would be responsible for the "consequences." The handout said that "all the western powers were anti-Islamic, rather enemies of Islam." The US

* "Poll protagonists fleeing the Valley" *Indian Express*, June 10, 1995.

is the head of all such anti-Islamic, forces and the Kashmiri separatist organisations were told not to beg for freedom from America, but "fight for it."

John Childs was rescued by helicopter borne by State officials almost 15 hours after the escaped from the captivity of his kidnappers from the mountains close to Sheshnag in South Kashmir on July 7. Lieutenant-General, D.D. Saklani, Adviser (Home) and the Director General of Police, M.N. Sabharwal, who were scanning the mountainous ridges and dense forests in the afternoon on July 8, spotted and picked up John Childs wandering in the area in their chopper and brought him to Srinagar. "It was a breakthrough", Gen. Saklani said, still hoping that, "the other hostages would be back safe and sound."

Childs had been abducted along with his campatriot, Donald Fred Huchins, and two Britons, Paul Wells and Keith Monigam and Dirk—Hasert from Germany from Liddervat, 20 kms. west of Pahalgam, a tourist resort in South Kashmir on July 4. According to Saklani, the five hostages, one of them being Childs, were being taken from one place to another and made to stay and eat with the shepherds in the mountains and jungles in Sheshnag area. On the intervening night of July 7-8 at 2 a.m., when the militant guards were asleep and 'not alert', Childs moved out of the mud thached hut and started moving aimlessly towards isolated areas and away from the habitat of the shepherds. Childs had blisters on his body when he was soptted and picked by Gen. Saklani and the State Police Chief. "He took lots of cups of tea and brand-toasts on reaching Srinagar at my residence as he was awfully hungry", Gen. Saklani told reporters.*

The fifth foreigner held captive by Al-Faran, a Norwegian national, Christian Ostro, who came to India for a course of study, and was paying a visit to Kashmir at the end of it, was killed by the abductors in a gruesome manner, in order probably to tell others that they should make no attempt to escape. The four others held by Al-Faran since July 4, were

* "American hostage escapes", *Hindustan Times*, July 10, 1995.

Paul Wells and Keith Monigam from the U.K., Donald Fred from the USA and Dirk Hasert from Germany. In the middle of September, the abductors demanded $50 million or its equivalent for releasing them. The Al-Faran militants had earlier sought the release of 15 hardcore terrorist in exchange for the hostages, were no longer insisting that their colleagues held in Kashmir jails be set free. The Government on its part, maintained that it would neither acquiesce to the demand of releasing the terrorists in exchange for the hostages nor pay any ransom. The foreign countries, from which the tourists came, could however pay the money if they wanted to, it maintained. In essence, this would mean that the Government would not like to be in the forefront if the money deal or the quantum of it became a feasible alternative.

This was the Government's move, it was stated, in order to pre-empt future efforts by the militants to take people as hostages and release them after striking a bargain over the quantum of money to be paid for their release... This, however, raises the question that if the foreign countries concerned were willing to pay up the sum on their own without bringing the Indian Government to the fore, it would perhaps have been done quietly by now and the release of the hostages worked out. The main drawback here, of course, would be that it can become a precedent for such attempts in the future with the foreign nationals becoming ready targets of terrorist and militants who whould want to hold them hostages for extracting money out of these and other countries. What was of primary concern with the Central Government, however, is the survival of the hostages, for the weather in the area they were being moved about, was becoming increasingly bad with the onset of winter in the mountains. The other point of worry was there was no knowing whether and when the militants might decide to eliminate the hostages.

A week later, Al-Faran snapped contact with the Jammu and Kashmir administration. It said it would resume negotiations for the release of the four foreign hostages only after the Government freed at least 10 jailed militants. Al-Faran told the negotiators that they were breaking off contact because the Government had betrayed them by leaking to the media the fresh offer of Rupees 20 million ransom deal that had been agreed upon for the release of the four foreign hostages. The J&K Police had been negotiating with an Al-Faran intermediary over wireless and telephone, and during their last contact a few days ago, the militant outfit angrily told the Government that the money deal was off. Union Home Ministry sources said that Al-Faran had demanded the release of 21 jailed terrorists. The apparent intransigence of the Government forced them to consider a money deal, but that fell through, leading dismayed officials to say that negotiations had been pushed back to "Square one". During the negotiations, the Al-Faran intermediary reportedly accused the negotiators of betrayal saying that the fact that the terrorists had agreed to a Rs. 20 million ransom to be paid in US dollars in accounts abroad, had been deliberately leaked to the Press. They said they would not now accept any ransom for the release of four foreigners. Al-Faran told the negotiators that in view of the 'betrayal', they would not contact the authorities again. The administration, they said, would have to take the initiative by releasing the jailed militants, following which it would again get in touch with the Government.

Pakistan behind Hostage Crisis

John Childs, one of the western hostages held by Al-Faran in Kashmir, who made a daring escape in July said in West Hartford, Connecticut, USA, on October 13, that he believed his captors were controlled by their superiors in Pakistan. "This was a well-disciplined unit. I feel certain they were getting their orders from Pakistan. I saw radios" said Childs, who escaped on July 8. (Pakistan had been denying allegations of direct involvement with Kashmiri rebels).

In course of a lecture at the University of Hartford's World Affairs Council. Childs recounted his ordeal. He appeard on the 100th day of capivity of the four surviving hostages of the Al-Faran guerillas. "I am sure the four still held by Al-Faran are suffering. The winters are very harsh in the Himalayas. I hated our captors. We were constantly bullied by gun-wielding militants... We were not physically tortured but there was a form of psychological torture. For example they slaughtered a sheep in front of us, cutting its throat and beheading it in much the same manner they later killed Hans Christian Ostro." (Ostro, a Norwegian was taken prisoner on July 8, the day that Childs escaped. Ostro was beheaded by his captors in mid-August).

Childs, who was rescued by members of the Indian Army after his escape, discounted the guerillas' allegations that the Indian Government was behind the abductions. He said he was rescued by an Indian Army helicopter that was searching for a German hostage who had been abducted a short time earlier. "I was debriefed for three days by members of the Indian Army and the US Consulate... I am certain my captors were Al-Faran militants. Indian officials say that Al-Faran is the front group for the pro-Pakistan Harkat-ul-Ansar, which has been involved in past kindnappings. During my four days of captivity, we the hostages were kept constantly on the move, spending the nights at shepherd's camps... I don't think they had any particular goal, other than not geting caught by the Indian Army. I found out later that the Indian Army was not far behind us... I was able to escape after a lone sentry fell asleep early in the morning of July 8. I tip-toed out of the encampment, boots in hand, and later hid in a snow cave before making my way down the mountain, toward the down of Pahalgam. I was making my way down the mountain when I was spotted by the helicopter."

According to an Associated Press message, Childs 41, an engineer was in India on business. "After concluding my business, I was on a brief hiking trip in the mountains when I was captured by the guerillas. Several of the guerillas spoke a little English. We were able to establish some rapport with them but we (the captives) all hated them because of the intimidation", Childs said.*

The Director-General of Police, M.N. Sabharwal, disclosed on October 29, that an 'indirect' contact with Al-Faran, the militant outfit holding four Western tourists captive for the

* "American who escaped from Al-Faran Clutches", *Pioneer* and "Pak behind hostage crisis", *Hindustan Times*, October 14, 1995.

past nearly four months was on. Talking to newsmen in Jammu, the DGP said "efforts are on for the safe and early release of the hostages." He maintained that the hostages were safe and "in good condition." The Police were also aware of the whereabouts and the movement of the captives and their captors. To a qestion whether the diplomats (of the countries the hostage belonged to) were having their own channels of communication with the abductors, Sabharwal replied "this does not appear to be true because we share information and combined efforts are on to secure safe and early release of the hostage.

The recent visits of the abductors to the villages in south Kashmir were aimed at getting medical help for their captives."Donald Hutchings, the American, who is unable to walk because of acute frost bite and is not having the normal diet owing to a stomach upset, needs specialised treatment. As his condition refuses to improve, the captors are making desperate efforts to reach the doctors. The *Hindustan Times* newspaper representative had recently disclosed that the abductors and the hostages were spotted in south Kashmir villages. The abductors had earlier taken two medical assistants from Marwah for the treatment of the hostage when they were in Wadhwan valley in Doda district about a month ago."

The partners of the four foreign tourists held hostage left for home on October 26, saying "it has been 114 days since Drik Hasert, Don Hutchings, Keith Mangan and Paul Wells were taken hostage in Kashmir. For all that time we have waited anxiously for news of their well-being praying for their safe return to us and struggling to remain optimistic that they will be returned to us soon." In a statement, before leaving for home, they appealed to the Al-Faran militants to release the men unharmed without delay. The statement was signed by Anne-Katrin Henning, Jane Schelley, Julie Mangan and Catherine Moseley. It said the four hostages were innocent tourists who had never done any harm to the people of Kashmir.*

---

* "Indirect Contact with Al-Faran", *Hindustan Times*, October 26 and 29, 1995.

Government's efforts to Negotiate with 'Al-Faran'

While the Government has repeatedly ruled out any exchange of captive militants for the hostages, it is also not ready to risk a commando-type military operation to rescue as it might have endangered the lives of the foreigners—particularly as there could not be an element of surprise in the hills.

Dr. Farooq Abdullah returned to Srinagar in the beginning of October after a long stay abroad. The euphoria over elections in the State notwithstanding, the National Conference decided to play it cool and instead pursue its demand for a fresh autonomy package from the Centre. These decisions were taken at a meeting of NC heavy-weights. Dr. Abdullah was advised by the Working Committee members to display an utter indifference to the Centre's proposed plan for elections.

NC in no hurry for Elections

The NC was in no hurry for the elections. Its leadership favoured elections only after the next general elections in the country in 1996. A senior party leader said in course of an informal chat: "The pressure from within the country and abroad is building on to the extent that even if the Bharatiya Janata Party comes to power, we are sure to get internal autonomy." The Party is expecting a major support from the Left Front which was likely to submit a memorandum to the President. Besides, the NC leaders were aware that the Western nations favoured internal autonomy for Kashmir to settle the dispute.*

Just a week later, former Prime Minister, Narasimha Rao met Dr. Abdullah breaking the ice over Kashmir, to work out a formula that might enable the NC's participation in the Assembly elections in the State. Dr. Abdullah flew in from Srinagar along with his trusted associates, Mohiuddin Shah and Bashir Ahmed Kichloo, and they were joined in New Delhi by other senior Party leaders. Mohammad Shafi (Uri) and A.K. Rather, who came from Jammu. Dr. Abdullah

---

* "National Conference to pursue demand for J&K autonomy", by Aasha Khosa, *Indian Express*, October 8, 1995.

led them to the meeting which lasted till midnight. The groundwork for this meeting had been made by the State Governor General, Krishna Rao, who believed that the elections would be meaningful if the National Conference and even the Hurriyat Conference took part in them. The National Conference leaders stuck to their demand for the restoration of the pre-1953 dispensation in the state as a pre-condition for its participation in the elections which the Government was keen to hold in December, 1995. The meeting was significant for it marked the resumption of a political dialogue had been abandoned in the past fuelling NC's suspicion that New Delhi was propping up its rivals in the Valley.

Later in an interview to the *Indian Express*, Dr. Abdullah said: "We are once bitten, twice shy." He feared 'betrayal' by the Centre if the NC participated in the polls merely on the basis of assurances of fulfilling pre-conditions. "We want something concrete, or otherwise we will wait and watch. Anyway this Government is in power for only the next six months", he added (speaking of Rao's Government in the Centre). The centre was yet to respond to the NC 's demand in any concrete manner, barring the statement the prime Minister had made in Parliament to the effect that the Centre was ready to concede anything to Kashmir, except 'azadi' (freedom). On the issue of restoration of the pre-1953 dispensation, that is, all subject excepting defence, foreign affairs and communication, he said, "You have eroded Article 370 of the Constitution completely which is the bridge between Kashmir, this State, and the rest of India... We are not beggars asking for something from them. We say this is our right and we are fighting for our rights."

The National Conference leader indicated in an interview to *United News* of India earlier in Jammu that the basic thrust in his talks with the Prime Minister would be on the NC demand of autonomy within the limits of the Indian Constitution. "I do feel that Mr. Rao wants to win the hearts and minds of the people of the State, but at the same time he has certain compulsions and he also has to satisfy the hawks within the party", Dr. Abdullah said. He acknowledged that there were some problems in the Home Minister and "some people" were averse to the idea of granting autonomy. "I am sure however, that the Home Minister will have to toe the line Mr. Rao whenever the issue is finalised and decided", Dr. Abdullah stated.

Dr. Abdullah also expressed the hope that a majority of the pro-Independence elements, including Shabir Shah, would react positively to the grant of autonomy and would participate in the polls in that event. The pro-Pakistan elements are in a tiny majority. Lashing out at the Hurriyat Conference, Dr. Abdullah said it was a divided house and was full of inherent contradictions. "While Syed Ali Shah Geelani and Abdul Gani Lone were for merger with Pakistan, Hurriyat Chairman Omar Farooq is undecided", Dr. Abdullah remarked.*

No Consensus on Election Timing

A Day after Rao conferred with Dr. Abdullah and his associates, the former Union Home Minister, S.B. Chavan, invited the Opposition leaders of Parliament for talks, but the special all-party meeting failed to arrive at a consensus on the timing of the Assembly elections in Jammu and Kashmir. (The National Conference and the Hurriyat Conference were unrepresented at the Home Minister's meeting but Yasin Malik, who was present in New Delhi told the Press that his organisation wanted the people's will to prevail).

At the special all-party meeting convened by Chavan, the major political parties did not favour the government's move to held elections before the end of the current spell of President's rule on January 17, 1996,—except the Congress Party. At the same time, they clarified that they would participate in the election whenever it was conducted. Among those who attended the meeting were Chaturanan Mishra and M. Farooqi (CPI), Madhavsinh Solanki and Ved Prakash (Congress), S.P. Malaviya (SJP), Jaswant Singh (BJP), George Fernandes (Samta Party), Chitta Basu (Forward Bloc), E.

* "P.M. favours J & K autonomy", *Hindustan Times* and "Farooq sure of autonomy before poll" by S.M.A. Kazme, *Indian Express*, October 21, 1995.

Ahmed (All India Muslim United League), P. Tirky (RSP), Jaipal Reddy (Janata Dal) and Ram Gopal Yadav (Samajwadi Party).

The opposition parties told the Government before going in for an election, it must ensure the participation of regional parties like the National Conference since it enjoyed greater clout in the State and was capable of playing a more concrete role in the poll. "We suggested that the Centre announce a political package so as to ensure the participation of the National Conference", said S. Jaipal Reddy, the Janata Dal leader, whose view was shared by most participants.Chavan re-iterated that the government was not against granting greater autonomy to the State but would discuss these matters with the elected representatives.

By raising the issue of restoration of the pre-1953 dispensation of the State, as a pre-condition for participating in the elections. Dr. Abdullah was known to have raised a very basic question, and wanted to be a step ahead of other contenders, such as Shabir Ahmed Shah or Yasin Malik, who were wanting independence for Kashmir. He perhaps wanted to tell the Kashmir there was another way still available to them that was equally good and to which he was ready to lead them to. This was his term of autonomy which he wanted the Prime Minister Rao to agree to, by accepting the pre-1953 dispensation of the State.

His demand for restoration of the pre-1953 dispensation meant the implementation of the Delhi Agreement, as reached between Jawaharlal Nehru and Sheikh Abdullah, and announced by the former in Parliament on July 24, 1952. The provisions of the Agreement included, among other things, continuance of special citizenship rights for 'State subjects', flying of a separate flag for the State with the national flag also finding a supremely distinct place, abolition of the hereditary rulership and vesting of the residuary powers in the State.

Farooq wants Pre-1953 Position

To go back to the past, the bonhomie after the Delhi Agreement had vanished in about a year. The relations between the Centre and the Sheikh developed strain as the latter chose to refer some of the provisions of the Delhi Agreement to sub-committees of the State Constitutent Assembly. He fuelled New Delhi's suspicion with hostile comments. To cite just one, he organised a rally in Srinagar on July 13, 1953, saying "It is not necessary that our State should become an appendage of either India or Pakistan. Twenty eight days later, the accord was given a formal burial with the arrest of the Sheikh, after being awakened from sleep in the hill resort of Gulmarg. Another accord was reached between the Sheikh and India Gandhi on November 13, 1974. The agreed conclusions envisaged, *inter alia*, that the State Government could review certain laws made by Parliament and extended to the State after 1953. The Accord paved the way for the Sheiks's return to power on February 25, 1975, with the help of the Congress which commanded a majority in the State Assembly.

The third Accord was unwritten even though its two architects, Rajiv Gandhi and Dr. Abdullah glowingly referred to it. Its seeds were sown in 1985 and it flowered into Dr. Abdullah again becoming the Chief Minister on November 7, 1986, and then leading the Congress-National Conference coalition to a victory in the much-maligned March, 1987 elections. The pact never percolated to the rank and file of the two parties as it was demonstrated by their total capitulation to terrorist forces 1988 onwards.

The return to the past was easier said than achieved. Any understanding with the towering Sheikh Abdullah could work because he and his local population had a rare rapport and mutual respect. Pakistan and China were both shaken by his accord with Indra Gandhi. Pakistan went to the extent of expressing its 'disquiet and concern ' at the UN and China called it "India's annexation of Kashmir." Dr. Abdullah knows full weel that he does not have that stature.

Next Elections before January 17: Chavan

A few days later, on October 22, Chavan in an interview to the Delhi Doordarshan (TV), ruled out further postponement of the Assembly elections in Jammu and Kashmir and indicated that polls could be held in the State before January 17, when President's rule was due to end. Chavan said the law and order situation had considerably improved in the State and elections could be held with usual precautionary measures. If polls were postponed any further, it would only encourage militants to go on creating further trouble, he held. Speaking about his meeting with various party leaders, the Home Minister said, nobody was opposed to istallation of a popular government in the State through elections, through there were dfifferent views on the timing of the polls.

Pak lied to US about its Nuclear Programme

In the beginning of November, the Government decided to ignore the U.S. disapproval of India's handling of the ongoing disturbances in Jammu and Kashmir. The Clinton Administration had recently again attempted to keep open the question of the State's accession to India. Even though evidence provided repeatedly by India as well as international agencies had confirmed Islamabad's role in fanning terrorism in the Kashmir Valley and in Afghanistan, the US Government had been choosing to bankroll Pakistan's arms purchases. While Pakistani Prime Minister, Benazir Bhutto spared no attempt to internationalise the Kashmir issue, the US assistant Secretary of State, Robin Raphel, who was on a tour of Pakistan, Afghanistan and India, made little effort to conceal her unconcern for Indian interests in Jammu and Kashmir. India appeared set to ignore Raphel's visit, slated for between November 4 to 14.

The Government was seeking to persuade the Natonal Conference leader, Dr.Farooq Abdullah, of participating in the Assembly elections. Meanwhile, news also came in on November 1 of the US House of Representatives adopting the Hank Brown Amendment and clearing $368 million worth of sophisticated arms for Islamabad—brushing aside criticism that military aid to Pakistan would begin an arms race in the sub-continent. The adoption cleared the way for providing Pakistan anti-submarine planes that could fly all the way to the tip of India without refuelling, engine upgrades for Pakistan's nuclear-capable F-16s, anti-ship Harpoon missiles, air-to-air sidewinder missiles, anti-tank tow missiles and night-fighting equipment for helicopter gunships, among other arms. In addition to the weapons, Pakistan was excused from paying storage charges for the F-16s it had bought but which the US could not deliver. The Amendment enabled the Administration to sell the planes to a third party or parties and give the money to Pakistan, which Pakistan hopes to use for buying modern French Mirage warplanes.

The Brown Amendment was a negation of the US House's earlier Pressler Amendment, which Democratic Congressman from New Jersy, Frank Pallone, recalled was imposed because "Pakistan had deliberately lied to the United States about its nuclear programme." He said the United States had earlier agreed to release the equipment to Pakistan if it could agree to cap its nuclear programme, but Pakistan would not agree to do any such thing. "Now we will giving Pakistan $368 million worth of military equipment without any commitment to stop the proliferation of nuclear weapons and this will heighten regional instability in South Asia."

Rao's New Proposal

Just two days later, on November 4, the former Primer Minister of India, P.V. Narasimha Rao, while on a state-visit to Burkina Faso (capital of a West African country, Ouagadougou) proposed a comprehensive autonomy package for Jammu and Kahmir. He announced the government's decision to hold elections in the troubled state which has been under the President's rule for five and a half years. In a broadcast to the nation, Rao reaffirmed that Article 370 of the Indian Constitution under which Jammu and Kashmir enjoys a special status, shall not be abrogated.

Mr. Rao proposed that the Governor and the Chief Minister could be renamed "Sadar-e-riyasat" and "Wazir-e-Azam" respectively "if the legislature so desired." He also proposed that the 6-point Indira Gandhi-Sheikh Abdullah pact of 1975 (which was signed by G. Parthasarathy, on behalf of Indira Gandhi, and Mohammad Afzal Begum on behalf of Sheikh Abdullah respectively) could be adopted to meet the needs for holding an election in the state. The highlights of the 'agreed conclusion' were :

6-point Indira-Sheikh Pact of 1975

Jammu and Kashmir, which is a constituent unit of the Union of India, shell in its relations with the Union continue to be governed by Article 370 of the Indian Constitution.

The residuary powers of ligislation shall remain with the state; however, Parliament will continue to have power to make laws relating to the prevention of activities against the soverignty and territorial integrity of India.

Any provision of the Indian Constitution which had been applied to the state with modifications will be altered or repealed by presidential order; but provisions already applied without modification are unalterable.

The state will be free to have its own legislation on matters like welfare measures, cultural matters, personal law and procedural laws. The state government can review the laws made by Parliament or extended to the state after 1953 on any matter relatable to the Concurrent List and may decide which of them needs amendment or repeal. In future the state government shall be consulted regarding the application of any such law to the state.

Any law made by the state legislature seeking to change any provision of the state constitution relating to (*a*) the appointment, powers and immunities of the governor; and (*b*) the control of elections by Indian Election Commission, eligibility for inclusion in the electoral rolls without discrimination, adult suffrage and composition of the Legislative Council will need the President's assent.

No agreement was possible on the question of nomenclature of the governor and the Chief Minister. (Sheikh Abdullah wanted the titles to be *Sadar-e Riyasat* (head of State) and *Wazir-e Azam* (Prime Minister)

Rao s' new proposal to resolve the Kashmir issue was obviously the outcome of his 90 minute talk with the J&K leader, Dr. Abdullah, he had just before emplaning for Burkina Faso.

Rao said in a broadcast recorded at Burkina Faso: "This article is the product of our very aiduous and devoted labours in the Constituent Assembly." Recalling that "historically the rest of India shares a special kind of relationship with the state of Jammu and Kashmir as delineated in Article 370 of the Indian Constitution", Rao said "It shall be our endeavour to strengthen within the Constitution, the authority of the state of Jammu and Kashmir, keeping in view the aspirations of the people."

Political observers noted that Rao was proposing terms that go well beyond the 1975 Indira Gandhi-Sheikh Abdullah Accord, as aspects of the 1952 Delhi Agreement between Jawaharlal Nehru and Sheikh Abdullah were incorporated. The change in nomenclature of the highest constitutional offices could not be agreed upon in 1975.

Rao's offer, combined with the expression "if the legislature so desired" indicatad that the autonomy package would be debated and legislated by the Assembly that would come into being after the elections. There was no across-the-board give-away by the Central Government in its open-ended offer.

The Government also formally wrote to the Election Commission conveying its decision that polls be held in December. The Commission was requested to decide the poll dates. The Prime Minister's announcement were later adopted as a decision of the Union Cabinet at a Cabinet meeting held under the presidentship of the Union Home Minister, S.B. Chavan.

Rao's announcement was generally welcomed as it broke a long-standing deadlock in Kashmir. Most observers felt that elections would pave the way for restoration of democratic rule and put an end to violence. The elections were not likely to be a smooth affair, especially in the Valley since many militant outfits sponsored by Pakistan were resolved to frustrate the democratic process. A large-scale violence was not ruled out. The elections were also expected to be a highly publicised affair with the world media and human rights organisations focussing their attention on them. The voters' turnout in the Jammu and Ladakh regions was expected to be high. In the

Valley, the interior might not pose much problems, but the problem areas would be along the Line of Control (LoC) and the Doda region in Jammu which have been the hotbed of militancy. Besides, special arrangements were contemplated for postal ballot to facilitate voting by a large number of Kashmiri immigrants, both Hindus and Muslims, who have fled the State. The State Chief Secretary, Ashok Kumar, expressed full preparedness for the polls, saying the ground situation was conducive to hold elections.

They Promise everything but after Elections

Just before leaving for the West African country, Rao had a crucial 90-minute meeting with Dr. Farooq Abdullah, the key politician in the State it was one of his many such meetings—for Rao was in a hurry to meet the deadline of January 17, 1996, when six years of President's rule over Jammu and Kashmir were to be over. He was keen to see that a Government was ushered in, ending the violence and terrorism in the State. But in his meeting with Dr. Abdullah he reportedly failed to secure a categorical commitment from the National Conference leader regarding his participation in the proposed poll in Jammu and Kashmir. He however decided to go ahead with his plans to complete the exercise in the troubled state by mid-December, to hold elections in the State. Rao had explained to Dr. Farooq Abdullah that the question of the restoration of the 'pre-1953' status should be left to be decided by the elected representatives

Returning to Srinagar, Dr. Farooq Abdullah advanced the dates for the meeting of the Working Committee of the National Conference to November 7. Dr. Abdullah was accompanied by his party heavy weights like Mohammad Shafi, Bashir Ahmed Kitchloo and Ghulam Mohiuddin. Dr. Abdullah told the BBC in an interview that he would recommend to the working committee of his party to boycott the proposed elections. "The level of violence in the State is too high to be conducive to free and meaningful poll. The average daily toll is around 40 to 50. Fifty thousand Kashmiris have been killed so far. How can one think of elections in such an atmosphere", he had asked the BBC interviewer. "I am not going to befool and mislead Kashmiris", he added. Asked about the response of the Prime Minister to his party's demand for restoration of the pre-1953 position to the State, Dr. Abdullah said.

"I am not going to befool and mislead Kashmiris...They promise everything but after the elections." "This is what they (Central leaders) did to my father, Sheikh Mohammad Abdullah, and never fulfilled it", he said.

There was already an anti-poll mood when the NC Working Committee met. Even as the Chief Election Commissioner, T.N. Seshan and two Election Commissioners., M.S. Gill and G.V.G. Krishnamurthy, went to Srinagar to meet the National Conference leaders to ascertain their views about a coming poll (to be held sometime in mid-December), the National Conference categorically conveyed to them its inability to participate in the December polls. The National Conference leader, P.L. Handoo, who is a former Minister and one of the senior-most party leaders, met the three member Election Commission and conveyed to them that "bad law and order situation, wintry weather and inadequate notice period" dictated a postponement of the polls. The postponement be therefore ordered by at least six months, Handoo demanded.

The National Conference leadership explained that the Party wanted to have more time to reconsolidate its position before facing the electorate and it would continue to reiterate its demand for the restoration of the 1952 position to Jammu and Kashmir. In the National Conference Working Committee no clear line seemed to have emerged yet as to how the Party should react to the appeals for participation in the polls when "it has got much less than the expected share of autonomy for the State." The party working committee was still continuing its deliberations on issues of autonomy and participation in the elections, a general view had emerged that the National Conference would want the polls to be postponed.

Congress (I) favours Early Elections, but not NC

The Congress (I) was the only important political party which favoured early elections while representing its view before the Election Commission. The Congress (I) leader, Ghulam Rasool Kar was the only leader who strongly favoured holding of elections as he said. Sheshan stated that during his meetings with political parties, barring the Congress Party and the Panthers' Party, other parties such as the National Conference, Janata Dal, the Communist Parties and the National Front were opposed to holding of elections.

During the visit, the Election Commission Members also had "a good discussion with the people and political parties of the three regions, Ladakh, Jammu and the Valley." This has provided us valuable inputs for taking the decisions. Political parties in Ladakh have supported the holding of elections in December, Gill stated. Seshan said the Commission would take all points of view, including those of the National Conference into consideration before making a final decision.

A day later, Dr. Farooq Abdullah, National Conference leader, announced that his party would not participate in the State Assembly elections proposed to be held in December because the conditions were not conducive enough for holding free and fair polls. He told a Press conference in Srinagar that his Party would not participate in any elections until the basic principles on which Kashmir acceeded to India were accepted."While the gun is still ruling supreme in the Kashmir Valley, Doda, upper reaches of Rajouri and Poonch are still disturbed and the National Conference demands that the 1952 position has not been conceded. We would want that to be fulfilled. Kashmir acceeded to India on the basis of certain conditions—that the Central Government can retain Defence, Foreign Affairs and Communications while the State would hold all the other subjects. We want to return to that position. Other matters can be discussed. There are certain laws which we can retain and a few others we cannot." Dr. Abdullah termed the Prime Minister's package as a welcome step in that direction, though it was not sufficient, for it did not fulfil the aspirations of the people of Jammu and Kashmir.

Dr. Abdullah was categorical in stating that the National Conference would not oppose the holding of polls. "However, we are not going to participate in the polls, neither are we going to boycott it", he said, while drawing a comparison with the All Parties Hurriyat Conference (APHC). "That is the difference. We are not participating, they are boycotting it... We are part of India and we will remain part of India."*

The Union Home Minister who a day earlier had told the J&K Congress Chief Ghulam Rasool Kar that the Centre would go ahead with its plans for holding elections in the State now said that the Government had considered all aspects of the matter in great detail and was convinced that the situation in the Valley was conducive for the restoration of the democratic process. "Perhaps the Election Commissioner was looking for 'ideal conditions' for the conduct of a poll in the State, but everybody is aware that the conditions in J&K are not being allowed to be normal and the main factor in this regard is the cross-border terrorism and the supply of arms, men and material from across the border to fuel terrorism and violence in the State.

J&K Congress Committee President, Ghulam Rasool Kar in his sharp reaction, described the Election Commission decision as 'regrettable', since he believed that the conditions in the State could not be more conducive than what they were at present for holding elections. He thought elections could have helped in ending the miseries of the people suffering from militancy. The Bharatiya Janata Party President, Lal Krishna Advani, welcomed the Election Commission's decision and said his party had all along been asserting that the situation in the State was not conducive to holding elections. The BJP had been consistently opposing elections in the State at this stage. The BJP leader, Dr. Murli Manohar Joshi had earlier assailed the Government for striking a 'dubious deal' with the National Conference leader, Dr. Farooq Abdullah and demanded that Rao's Kashmir package be withdrawn, for "there are no soft options in Kashmir." While clarifying that his party was not opposed to elections in the State, the CPI(M) general secretary, Harkishen Singh Surjeet, stated that it wanted a proper atmosphere to be created before elections were held. In veteran CPI leader, M. Farooqi's view, it made little sense to hold elections in

* "*Hindustan Times*," November 10, 1995.

J&K without the participation of the National Conference, which is the largest party in the State and had ruled over it almost all the time. His Party wanted more autonomy for the State before holding any elections there. The Janata Dal also recorded its concurrence with the Election Commission's decision. Senior JD leader, Jaipal Reddy said "We welcome the decision as we share the Commission's assessment of the situation in J&K." As expected, Hurriyat Parties would not also participate in the poll.

Election Commission rejects Union Cabinet's recommendation to hold Election in December

It was an anti-climax to the Government's massive preparations to hold elections in Jammu and Kashmir. Two days after its return from the troubled State, the Election Commission composed of Seshan, Gill and Krishnamurthy, held a prolonged deliberation and unanimously rejected the Union Cabinet's recommendation for holding Assembly elections in the State in December. The Commission pronounced that the prevailing law and order situation in the State was "not conducive for the conduct of a fair and free election." The Commission decided that it cannot recommend elections to the State and it would wait for the creation of conditions appropriate to the holding of a fair and free election. The terrorism-affected State thus headed for another spell of President's rule after the expiry of its present term on January 17,1996. It means that the State would be deprived of popular rule for six-and-a-half years, the longest in any State in the country. The Governor's rule was first imposed in the State for six months in January, 1990 under the State Constitution. It has since been followed by a continuous spell of President's rule. It was clear that the term for President's rule in the State would have to be extended by another six months.

The Prime Minister, on his return from abroad, held separate meetings with Madhavsinh Solanki, All India Congress Committee General Secretary in-charge of Jammu and Kashmir affairs, Ghulam Rasool Kar, Jammu and Kashmir Congress President and top dissident leader of J&K Congress, Mian Bashir. The impression that Congress leaders got was that the relationship between Narasimha Rao and the National Conference President, Dr. Farooq Abdullah, had come under strain following the latter's decision to boycott the polls. The Election Commission's decision was apparently influenced by the National Conference's boycott decision which left the Congress as the only major party willing to enter the fray. The National Conference's participation was being taken for granted after a meeting between Rao and Dr. Abdullah, following which the Government promised the restoration of the nomenclatures of 'Sadar-e-Riyasat' and 'Wazir-e-Azam' in place of Governor and Chief Minister respectively. According to highly reliable sources, what led subsequently to the hardening of National Conference's posture was Dr. Abdullah's insistence that the Government gives a prior commitment about restoring the nomenclatures. He wanted a formal notification to be issued in this regard. The Government, on the other hand, referred to difficulties involved in the process. It pointed out that the change of nomenclatures could be done only by amending the State Constitution and the competent body to do so was the elected Assembly.*

In a two-page press not issued after the meeting of the three member Election Commission, it was said: "The Commission has come to the conclusion (while rejecting the Centre's recommendation about holding elections in Jammu and Kashmir in December) that the sum total of factors available at present in the State of Jammu and Kashmir are not consistent with the conduct of a fair and free election. The Commission has therefore decided with total unanimity that it cannot recommend at present to the Governor of Jammu and Kashmir the initiation of elections to the J&K Assembly by the issue of a notification and that it would wait for the creation of conditions appropriate to the holding of a fair and free election."

Union Government regrests Election Commission's decision

The Union Government soon after issued a statement regretting the Election Commission's decision not to hold

---

* "*Indian Express,*" New Delhi, November 11, 1995.

polls in Jammu and Kashmir. The Government contended that the mood of the people in the troubled State had distinctly changed, clearly bringing out their disenchantment with the militants and of Pakistan. The then Union Home Minister, S.B. Chavan reacted bitterly and sarcastically to the Election Commission's decision against holding elections in Jammu and Kashmir at this juncture. In a statement, Chavan remarked "It is a matter of regret that the Commission took such a view. Perhaps, the Commission was looking for 'ideal conditions' for the conduct of a poll in the State. Everybody is aware that the conditions in Jammu and Kashmir are not being allowed to be normal and the main factor in this regard is the cross-border terrorism and the supply of arms, men and material from across the border to fuel terrorism and violence in the State. The entire population of the State had been in the grip of the fear of the terrorists' gun since 1989.

The government had considered all aspects and was convinced that the situation in the Valley was conducive for restoration of democratic process in the State. In fact, it was hoped that this process itself would contribute further to the restoration of full normalcy and peace apart from giving the people a representative Government. The Government had been trying to restore the democratic process."

Also, the Election Commission's decision was said to be "bereft of any mature nuancing." For instance, it was stated that the Commission had failed to recognise that Jammu and Ladakh, between them accounting for more than half of the J&K population, have been denied popular rule for five and a half years for no fault of theirs. A newspaper editorial said "And now the Commission's no-poll diktat has meant the throttling of the democratic aspirations of the people of the two regions, if not also that of a section in the Valley.*

Abdullah's Popularity Rating Goes Up

For one of these politicians often described by the militants' supporters as 'discredited', Dr. Abdullah's popularity rating

* "*The Economic Times*, New Delhi, November 13, 1995.

in Kashmir had gone up following his demand for autonomy and decision to boycott elections. "Today, all roads lead to his Gupkar Road residence with politicians, family friends and the public congratulating him on his stand. The security around his residence is visibly less today and even Dr. Abdullah appears more confident and relaxed. Even the visitors, surprisingly, are not hiding their faces under burqas or over-sized caps for the fear of militants..."Ultimately, though, the National Conference will have to fight the fundamentalists who are behind the insurgency to wrest public support back from them", said a National Conference leader who was unhappy with the postponement decision."*

As soon as he came to New Delhi, the National Conference President, had a 90-minute long breakfast meeting with the US. Assistant Secretary of State for South Asia, Robin Raphel, who was visiting the Indian capital coincidentally. During the talks, Dr. Abdullah reportedly told Raphel that his Party believed that the accession of Jammu and Kashmir to India was final and all that it wanted was autonomy within the framework of the Indian Constitution. Dr. Abdullah later told a newspaper representative that the US Assistant Secretary of State was sympathetic and she felt that his suggestion was "one positive way for the solution of the Kashmir problem." The Hurriyat Conference "waited in vain for a positive response to its request for an appointment with the American visitor, who was winding up her tour of the country."

The fact remained that Rao's announcement on Kashmir did not introduce anything new. "The Prime Minister, mindful of his political compulsions, chose the half-way mark (both politically and chronologically) by opting for the 1975 accord. The main provisions of the accord were that Article 370 of the Constitution would not be abrogated and that any post 1953 laws could be repealed by the legislature (that was to be formed after the elections). That the Legislature would have to take the initiative for obtaining autonomy was in line with the Government's stand that it would only deal with

* *Indian Express*, New Delhi, November 12, 1995.

elected representatives. The BJP's likely attack during the coming general elections—that Mr. Rao was following a policy of appeasement—could be countered by saying that he was only implementing what already existed." The Prime Minister would not have to take an initiative, even though he would be seen to be taking one. Nothing new has been introduced into either the Constitution or the political equation between New Delhi and Kashmir, except for a promise, and Kashmiris know what to make of New Delhi's promises.*

Major beneficiary is Farooq

The major beneficiary of the Election Commission's decision to postpone election in Jammu and Kashmir was Dr. Farooq Abdullah, as it was helped the National conference leader re-establish himself firmly in the State's politics, writes Aditya Sinha, known political commentator on Kashmir in the *Pioneer* on November 11, 1995. "What remains to be seen is whether Dr. Abdullah will seize the opportunity and generate enough political activity in the Valley so that elections can be held in February. At a Press Conference in Srinagar, he claimed it would take him a couple of months to convince his people to accept what was offering them and return to the political mainstream... The National Conference may have had the compulsion of having to show Kashmiris that it was not enthusiastically rushing to accept the "Ouagadougou offer" Now however, Dr. Abdullah must realise that this is all his party is going to get, and somehow find a way to participate in elections, even if it means doings so reluctantly."

It was now clear that elections could not take place before mid-March, because of heavy snowfall in the Valley and also in many other places in the State. Since the Lok Sabha polls were also due and must be held about the same time, the Government is not in favour of holding the elections simultaneously because of logistical problems. Some, like former Jammu and Kashmir Governor, Girish Saxena, were of the view that the polls in Jammu and Kashmir could be held four to five weeks after the Lok Sabha elections, but the

---

* *Pioneer*, New Delhi, November 7, 1995

Government appeared to be of the view that the Jammu and Kashmir elections should precede, and should be held a month before, probably in the end of March, in order for the ruling Congress Party to get the best results in the general elections. The ruling party, the Congress, also felt that the National Conference and a section of the Hurriyat Conference may participate in the polls, apart from the national parties, lending the execise a semblance of legitimacy. The Election Commission's order that conditions were not appropriate for the holding of a fair and free poll in the troubled state now, left Parliament with no other option but to extend President's rule in Jammu and Kashmir, which would end on January 17, 1996.

It was clear, amidst all the controversial happenings, that elections were the first step towards breaking the impasse in the troubled state. It was also clear that a pre-poll package being demanded by Dr. Farooq Abdullah is neither possible politically nor legally and constitutionally. The issue of Kashmir could not be tackled in isolation but within the context of India. Apart from anything else, Dr. Abdullah surely knew that reverting to 1952 meant an amendment in the Jammu and Kashmir Constitution and this could be undertaken only by the State Assembly after it was elected and began functioning.

Towards the end of November, the then Home Minister, Chavan clearly stated in the Lok Sabha that the Government was not thinking of any change in Jammu and Kashmir policy in restoring democratic process in the State at the earliest, although the opposition which had threatened to table an adjournment motion, was angry with the government for its 'failure' on the Kashmir front. The BJP, whose members walked out of the House and chanted "no dialogue with terrorists", sharply differed with the other opposition parties. The BJP was opposed to any move to "put the clock back to 1953", more specifically to the proposal of reverting to the 'Sadr-e-Riyasat' and 'Wazir-e-Azam' nomenclatures. As for the elections, Lal Krishna Advani asked: "What is a greater failure than the fact that a constitutional authority had to vote the government's decision." The non-BJP opposition parties, however, made it clear that they were not opposed to the autonomy package. Their was against the Government for not consulting other parties and the Election Commission before taking the initiative unilaterally. Their plea was to adopt a policy of "national consensus."

Making a statement before the House, Chavan reiterated the Government's 'disappointment' at the Election Commission's view that the state was not yet ready for polls. He spoke of the Government's efforts to achieve normalcy, and claiming all-round progress in containing "so-called militancy", he was defensive only on one count. Efforts to strengthen the civil administration and its normal functioning were yielding positive results, though perhaps not to the desired extend. "The security forces had clearly gained an upper hand. Ther was a perceptible change in the attitude of the people. The pro-peace forces had been reactivated and people in general had moved away from the psyche imposed by militants and terrorists, towards the mainstream of their normal live and activities."

Chavan's Criticism of US

In a week thereafter, on December 4, Chavan speaking in the Rajya Sabha (the Upper House of Parliament) made a trenchant criticism of the US role in Jammu and Kashmir. He accused the US of having "evil designs" on the State and said "it is not only Pakistan which is creating problems in the Valley, but 'some big world power' also which are responsible for the trouble in Kashmir." Pressed by Opposition members to specify which nations, Chavan said "I have no hesitation in naming America. I have no hesitation in saying this. Recent history shows that America has evil designs as far as Jammu and Kashmir is concerned." His remarks were received with loud cheers and thumping of desks by the entire House.

Replying to a short-duration discussion, Chavan was also critical of the one-time waiver of Pressler Amendment which had cleared the way for export of US weaponry worth $1 billion to Pakistan. (The real value of $368 million worth of arms and ammunition the US supplied to Pakistan had meanwhile been computed, at the present price, at $1 billion). He said this decision of the Clinton Administration to go ahead with arms supplies to Pakistan was in reality calculated to gain "a foothold" in Jammu and Kashmir." He said this would lead to an escalation of the arms race in the sub-continent. "Ultimately, both will have to spend huge amounts on defence", rather than on developmental activity or poverty alleviation.

In a reference to the US, the former Home Minister remarked: "These people are only interested in themselves. These people are neither interested in India nor Pakistan, but want a foothold in Jammu and Kashmir. Every time there is a change in attitude in the Valley, with the situation improving some US Government official will come here and make a statement that Kashmir is a disputed territory." (The obvious reference was to the comments made by the Assistant Secretary of State for South Asia, Robin Raphel's remarks on these lines, calling Jammu and Kashmir a 'disputed territory'). This resulted in further complicating matters. Chavan said he was more than convinced about America's role in Kashmir after the Brown Amendment was passed, providing for a $370-million arms package for Pakistan. Nobady was convinced with the US explanation that this was a one-time waiver and wondered how President Clinton would certify that Pakistan has no nuclear capability.

He warned the Benazir Bhutto Government in Pakistan against creating a situation which could result in a confrontation with India.

Chavan also said the Government was ready to help Kashmiri migrants return to the Valley. He said a massive developmental programme had been launched for the State. More than 1,000 unemployed youth have been recruited in paramilitary and other forces. Several self-employment schemes have been launched. He also said a Rupees 10,050 million plan had been approved for Jammu and Kashmir this year.*

US Embassy Dismisses Chavan's Charges

The US Embassy in New Delhi dismissed as "without any

* "US dismises Chavan Charge as baseless" by Chidanand Rajghatta, *Indian Express*, December 6, 1995.

basis" the charges by Chavan that Washington was fomenting trouble in Jammu and Kashmir. The reaction by an embassy spokesman came when he was asked to comment on Chavan's remarks in the Rajya Sabha that the US was responsible for the trouble in Jammu and Kashmir and that it had 'evil designs' on the border State. The spokesman said the US had been for a long time encouraging India and Pakistan to negotiate a settlement to the 'Kashmir dispute', taking into account the wishes of the people in Kashmir. The US also wanted the violence in Kashmir to end to lessen the sufferings of the people in the State, the spokesman added.

Without doubt, Chavan's criticism of the US for its "evil designs" on Kashmir was one of the sharpest made by an Indian leader in recent years, particularly because it was made in Parliament. A few days ago, the then Prime Minister, P.V. Narasimha Rao, although in less direct language said that the Clinton Administration's recent decisions and statements seemed geared to keep Kashmir on the boil. He had also pointed out that the US policy was seemingly aimed at blocking a peaceful settlement on the Kashmir issue. Chavan went to the extent of alleging that every time the situation seemed to be on the mend in the Valley, some US official came here and made a statement describing Kashmir as a disputed territory.

US not using Diplomatic Language: India

India on December 6 conveyed to the United States its 'displeasure' over the language used by the US State Department, while reacting to Chavan's observation in Parliament about the American objectives in Jammu and Kashmir. The US Charge d'Affaires in India, Mathew Dailey (the US Ambassador in India, Frank Wisner, being away to the US), was summoned to the Foreign Office by Vinod Grover, Secretary (Wast) in the Ministry of External Affairs. The Indian official told Dailey that Chavan had made the statement in the Rajya Sabha and members of Parliament were exercised over the use of expressions like 'nonsense' in the State Department's reaction. Grover told the American diplomat that New Delhi expected use of 'diplomatic language' in the conduct of bilateral relations...Later, Dailey told the Indian official that Washington was 'upset' over Chavan's statement in which he had accused the US, among other things, of instigating violence in Kashmir.

Meanwhile, Chavan met a South Asian delegation of the European Parliament, composed of Ms. Anita Pollack, Thomas Mann, Ms. Patricia Mekenna and Robert Evans. He told them that after six years of turmoil created by Pakistan sponsored terrorisms, the local militants had realised their folly and therefore Pakistan had taken recourse to deploying foreign mercenaries. Chavan said the situation in Punjab had been similar to that of Jammu and Kashmir, but after holding elections there, it had become quite normal.*

US Policy on Kashmir: Evidence Backs Chavan's Statement

Washington's policy on Jammu and Kashmir was not entirely innocent of pernicious designs, official sources stated in New Delhi, soon after. These sources did not attach much significance to the outburst of the United States State Department describing as "complete nonsense" the remark by the Chavan, that the US had evil designs on Kashmir. The sources contended the US has a long record in promoting the theory of a "third option" for the State that has been troubled by Pakistan's overt and covert activities since the last more than four and a half decades. The position is couched in the oft-repeated concern for the wishes of the Kashmiri people which is widely regarded as an euphemism for delinking the Valley from the rest of the State. And that delinking is believed by many to be the forerunner for a greater US role in the affairs of the Valley. The US interest, said the sources, revolved around getting for itself a foothold in the Valley which could then be used as a launching pad against China in the future. The land route from the Valley into China went through the Sinking region of the Communist State, an area that the US believed to be the 'soft underbelly' of Beijing. Having identified China as a long-term threat to its global politico-economic role, Washington needed a firm

---

* "US not using diplomatic language " *Hindustan Times*, December 7, 1995.

foothold in the Valley in order to be able to hurt Beijing. That could only be realised if Delhi's rule over the Valley was loosened. The National Conference President, Dr. Farooq Abdullah, had let the cat out of the bag with his disclosure that the US Assistant Secretary of State for South Asia, Robin Raphel, had conveyed to him that Washington supported the demand for greater autonomy as also the conversion of the Line of Control into a 'soft border'.

According to defence experts, the 'soft border' would make the Valley vulnerable on account of the fact that the natural trade routes from the region cross the Pir Panjal ranges into the Mirpur areas. The increase in Washington's engagement in this part of the world could be seen from the dramatic success scored by the Taliban militia in Afghanistan.

Washington's statements on Afghanistan, when it was normaly quick to comment on another country's internal affairs, have been most reticent. Taliban is regarded as the best US option in checking Iran, on one hand, and the Central Asian States, on the other. While Iran is regarded as a rogue state, the Central Asian States are considered to be 'soft underbelley' of Russia.

Meanwhile, there was further support for Chavan with the former External Affairs Minister, I.K. Gujral and Natwar Singh issuing a statement that said, "The language used by the spokesman of the US State Department is unfortunate and unacceptable." They went to add that "It is extraordinary that an official of the US Embassy in New Delhi should phone the Secretary of the Ministry of External Affairs and discuss the Home Minister's parliamentary statement with him in such an off-hand manager dismissing Chavan's well considered statement which has been well received by all parties."

(The same day India had taken strong exception to certain derogatory remarks made by a US State Department official against the Home Minister, saying the use of such "undiplomatic language" was regrettable and unacceptable. The US Charge d'Affaires, Mathew Dailey, was summoned by Vinod Grover to convey New Delhi's displeasure over the statement made by the US official. (The American Ambassador in India, Frank Wisner was away in Washington for scheduled consultations). An official spokesman said Dailey had been told that while there may be differences of opinion on issues between countries, "we do not expect such observations, which are not in keeping with diplomatic practice." The US official, while responding to Chavan's charge in the Rajya Sabha, that Washington was harbouring evil designs on Kashmir, was quoted as having said that "Mr. Chavan pops off like that once a month or so on his own. He is an embarrassment to his colleagues in the Indian government.")

US Meddling in Kashmir

Senior leaders of the Congress Party, and all other parties, were enthused by the stand the Government was taking on USA *vis-a-vis* Kashmir issue. They were happy that the Prime Minister, Rao, too had only a few days ago, on November 29, at a meeting of Congress Parliamentary Party criticized the US policy on Kashmir, for the first time. According to a Cabinet Minister, the Union Home Minister had the support of the entire party for his stand against "US meddling in Kashmir." Chavan could not have made the statement without clearance from the Prime Minister, "who after the Brown amendment has realised the danger in giving a mild response when faced with threats to Indian interests." Moreover, one factor behind the current expression of official anger at US policy was the two recent visits of US Assistant Secretary of State, Robin Raphel, to the sub-continent, in September and November. In her visits to Afghanistan, Sri Lanka, Pakistan and Bangladesh, Raphel had aimed at putting pressure on these countries to the US-way of going about their problems. This had not been to the liking of the Indian leadership, who felt that the countries in the region should settle their differences between themselves, without any outside mediation. According to a senior Congress Party leader, "the cold reception given to Raphel indicates the region's uneasiness at US efforts to create a surrogate power so as to further its interventionist agenda. According to a senior policy analyst in Delhi, "the Bhutto gameplan of accepting the role of US surrogate will backfire and lead to the growth of anti-American feeling in Pakistan". In case of Kashmir, the security analysts say that "should the state get azadi, it would not be a moderate state, but a fundamentalist one that would be a haven for terrorists to operate from and within which would rage a civil war between the extremists and the Shias, Hindus and Buddhists ." However, they add, "it may take a few more years for Washington to understand this."*

At the end of his nearly two-week long tour of the Jammu region, Dr. Abdullah, talking to newsmen, said his Party was not against elections. The National Conference wanted a people's Government in the State. He was also in favour of 'panchayat' elections to check corruption and lack of accountability (of government expenses). But the National Conference would participate in the elections only after a political package was announced. There was a provision in the Constitution to restore autonomy before polls, he reminded a questioner. In this context, he also made it clear that he was not satisfied with the 1975 Sheikh-Indira Accord which promised to review all Central laws extended to the State after August, 1953. He demanded restoration of pre-1953 status by way of which the State has its own Prime Minister as head of Government and Sadr-e-Riyasat as head of State, and full control over all matters, barring defence, communications and external affairs. He would return to the State only as 'Prime Minister' and not as Chief Minister. He made it specific that the National Conference would participate in the elections after a political package was announced.

Dr. Abdullah stated there was widespread corruption in the State. During his tour of the border districts of Rajauri and Poonch, he found that "money was being taken for appointments even in the police." Dr. Abdullah again took upon himself to defend the US. In reply to a question, he said that he did not come across any evidence during his tenure as Chief Minister which suggested American hand in the turmoil in Kashmir. Referring to the visit of the US

* "Congreesmen support Chavan's criticism of US", by M.D. Nalapat, *Times of India*, December 7, 1995.

Ambassador, Frank Wisner to Kashmir in summer this year, Dr. Abdullah said he was the only ambassador to have told the Hurriyat Conference to participate in the elections.

No Dissidence in J&K Congress Now

At the two-day State-level training camp of the Congress Party, differences between the major groups were resolved. "All the differences have sorted out", claimed Major Ved Prakash, All India Congress Committee Joint Secretary, who went to Jammu to coordinate the arrangements for the two groups in his party to come together. In this context, he pointed out that Mian Bashir Ahmad had been appointed Chairman of the State-level campaign committee. However, the party differences were resolved after the announcement of the campaign committee, and both camps refrained from making comments about official camp or dissident camp. In spite of this however, no voice of friendship was heard immediately from either group we did by PCC President, Gulam Rasool Kar or Mian Bashir Ahmad.

However, the Congress Party's decision to hold the elections in Fabruary or March did not have the support of other political parties in the State. The National Conference, and even the BJP, the two major parties, had yet to make their intentions clear about the election. Dr. Abdullah had been saying that his party would participate in the poll only if the pre-1953 status was restored and the State was given a decent economic package. The BJP was also for holding elections in the State in the near future, but its first priority was containing the militancy. So if these and other parties did not go in for elections, it would be a futile attempt by the Congress to come out with an election plea—and it would be something like what happened in Punjab in 1993.

As a matter of fact, the Union Government was still licking its wounds after its plan to hold elections in December was sabotaged both by Dr. Abdhullah and the Election Commission when the elections were postponed.

A controversy was going on whether the Government should once again succumb to pressure tactics of the National

Conferences on the 1952 status issue. For all these years, the Central Government had pampered the National Conference, going out of the way to keep it in good humour and had allowed it to do whatever it wanted to in the Valley. But it was now being realised that a large amount of funds which the Centre had been doling out in Kashmir from time to time had not made any difference is so far as the people's ecomomic well-being was concerned as these funds were wrongly used. The people were fed on religious propaganda and were deliberately kept backward and poor which had generated a tremendous resentment in the minds of young generation who wanted to end the dynastic rule in the Valley. The moment they got the opportunity they revolted and took to arms.

Twice during the year, the much-awaited Assembly elections which were looked upon as saviour of utter helplessness had to be put off; once because of the burning of Chrar-e-Sharief and the second time beacuse the election Commission held elections could not take place in a fair and free manner. The second time elections were put off, the people had been deprived of their right to go for elections for five-and-a-half years, which was because complete anarchy ruled in the State on account of terrorism. When, in the last stage, talks began on holding polls in December, 1995, the National Conference, on which the Central Government had high hopes, declined to participate. The NC President, Dr. Abdullah, wanted autonomy for the State. "Till the Centre grants us the pre-1953 position, we will not participate in any election, even if we have to wait for 100 years", Dr. Farooq Abdullah had declared on November 9, a day after the Election Commission concluded its visit to Leh, Srinagar and Jammu. The next day the Commission announced its decision of not holding the polls in the State as "free and fair" elections were not possible in Jammu and Kashmir in the prevalent conditions."

'Political Package' Demand by Abdullah

This was a rude shok to the Governor General, K.V. Krishna Rao, who had been wanting to vacate his office for a long time. He had promised to the people that he would get them an elected Government installed by the year-end. Equally shaken was the PCC Chief Ghulam Rasool Kar, who described the situation as 'unfortunate'.

Now when the elections had still not become a reality in the State, a debate was going on whether these can be held or not. Now another condition had been laid to the holding of elections, that is a political package, which was being demanded by Dr. Abdullah. The All Party Hurriyat Conference leadership also failed to work out a formula to resolve the Chrar-e-Sharief crisis. The Hurriyat also found itself the object of mysterious attacks on its leaders. There were attempts on the lives of Syed Ali Shah Geelani, Abdul Ghani Lone and Mohammad Yasin Malik, whose leadership of JKLF was questioned. Then Shabir Siddiqi declared himself as the Chief of what he called the "real JKLF." The Hurriyat leaders blamed the Government for these attacks and the Government denied the charges, while offering security to them.

In his reaction to the developments in Jammu and Kashmir, the BJP President, Lal Krishna Advani, expressed the view that the history of the State be summed up as an "unending tale of blunders by the Congress." Speaking at a 'Save Kashmir' public meeting organized by the Delhi unit of the BJP, Advabi said "we object to the J&K assembly—after elections—being given the option to return to the pre-1953 position or of having a Sadar-e-riyasat and a Wazir-e-Azam, instead of a Government and a Chief Minsiter." This would be another blunder in a series that has comprised the Kashmir policy of successive Congress governments.

He cited several such "blunders" and recalled scenes and instances from Ketan Mehta's film on Sardar Vallabbhai Patel's life called 'Sardar'. He said the first 'blunder' was 'the unfortunate' decision of the then Prime Minister, Jawaharlal Nehru to retain the charge of accession of Jammu and Kashmir, entrusting the rest to the then Home Minister, Vallabhbhai Patel. The second one was the decision to go to the United Nations complaining about the 1948 invasion and loss of territory to Pakistan. Patel had opposed it, he reminded his audience. He related how the then Home Minister tried desperately, and failed, to stop Nehru from announcing on the All India Radio the Indian Government's decision to seek UN intervention. Advani proceeded to attack Article 370 which gives special status to Kashmir. He said this Article and other such decisions are threatening to put the clock back "to the time when the Bharatiya Janasangh (BJP's previous incarnation) gave the call opposing two Constitutions in the country—one of India and the other of Kashmir", he said and added: "But we will not allow the clock to be put back. In fact we will push the needle forward and will remove Article 370 from the Constitution the day we are voted to power at the Centre."

EC Order on J&K Polls Challenged

The Election Commission's decision not to hold elections in Jammu and Kashmir was challenged in the Supreme Court on November 18. President of the Panther's Party Bhim Singh filed a petition pleading that the Election Commission's unanimous decision, after a day-long tour of the Valley, be quashed so that citizens of the State could have a democratically elected government.

The petition traced the background of militancy in the State, the Pakistani aggressions and the unending Central rule. It also rasied the vital issue whether the EC has the jurisdiction to interfere with the government's mandate to hold elections in a particular State.

The petition stated that the State Governor Gen., K.V. Krishna Rao had already recommended to the Union of India and the Election Commission that the time was 'conducive' to holding elections in the State where the term of President's rule would expire on January 17 (next year). It had suggested December 20 for holding polls, so that an elected assembly could come in operation.

The petition sought a judicial pronouncement on the Commission's power to direct a Governor or the President of India not to issue a notification for holding elections for an indefinite period, thus throttling the entire democratic process.

A few days later, in the beginning of December, the Government of India, too, filed a Special Leave Petition before the supreme Court questioning the Election Commission's powers to veto the elections. The Court decided to hear both the petitions together.

Chapter 7

Attempts to Restore Democracy

The 1987 Elections and Proxy War

The failure in the battle of ballots in the 1987 elections in the State was said to have pushed the Muslim United Front (which got only four seats in the 75-member Assembly) towards a battle with bullets, or this is how it was explained even in Pakistan's favour in the beginning. The first of the militants in 1989, both of Jammu and Kashmir Liberation Front (JKLF) and the Hizbul Mujahideen, were recruited from among the MUF candidates and their election agents in the years of 'proxy war'. Later, by about 1992, was militancy taken over by regular foreign mercenaries such as the Harkat-ul-Ansar and its several fronts, which upstaged the whole agenda of Kashmiriyat with Islamic fundamentalism, to lead to a state of insurgency in Kashmir. They played havoc in the State perpetrating inhuman torture on the people in the State, particularly in the Valley, killed and maimed thousands of Kashmiris, ravaged the area mercilessly for years and drove out the nearly 300,000 Kashmiri 'Pandits' and some 50,000 Muslims and 20,000 Sikhs.

The State has, after mid-1989, gone through an unprecedented political turmoil, accompanied by the longest period of terrorism, rather softly called militancy, that started out in the Valley with local Muslim young men being trained in Pakistan and sent over to commit murder and mayhem, in the garb of 'proxy war' against India. From about the beginning of 1992, it turned into a full-fledged terrorism against India, as Pakistan began sending out terrorists of its own and of other countries, such as Afghanistan, Arabia and the Middle East, a collection it was presiding over from the days of the Afghan war. Jammu and Kashmir was being administered by direct rule under Governors, Jagmohan, Girish Chandra Saxena and General (retired.), K.V. Krishna Rao, for years. General (retd) Krishna Rao has been pressing for a return of the popular rule.

Terrorism has ruled over the State for the longest time—even longer than it has in Punjab, where too Pakistan had sought to spread its terroristic network, but failed.

Governor's rule was imposed on Jammu and Kashmir on June 19, 1990 for six moths under the State's Constitution and on the expiry of that period, the State has been under President's rule eversince. Terrorism in the State particularly in the Valley and in parts of Jammu, notably the Doda district, has meanwhile played havoc, killing as Dr. Farooq Abdullah, the former Chief Minister put it, some 50,000 people, injuring and maiming twice that number; terrorists raping thousands of women, in the beginning Hindu women, but when Hindus fled and went out of the Valley, then Muslim women. They wrecked havoc in the State throughout these years.

Dr. Abdullah's is an exaggeration, for he might have used the figure of killings in the State covering all these years from Independence, but certainly some 13,000 People have been killed in the days of 'proxy war' and insurgency in the Valley (839 sq. km.), inhabited by 3.5 million people. The number of custodial deaths is not known, but these could run into hundreds. Others including the

People's League leader, Shabir Shah, have put this figure of killings by terrorists on militants and militants killed by the para military forces and the police at around 40,000.

Efforts to build Consensus for Elections

Since early 1994, Rao had been quietly implementing a policy designed to create conditions of normalcy in Kashmir. Welfare programmes were started, roads, hospitals and schools were rebuilt and electoral rolls completed. At the same time, it was ensured that newly-raised battalions of the Rashtriya Rifles as well as more Army personnel were deployed in the Valley to combat insurgency. M.D. Nalapat, wrote in the *Times of India* that "Rao favours early elections in Kashmir and that in domestic sphere, he is busy building up a consensus for greater autonomy to the state within the Indian Union, and has reportedly secured sympathetic reactions from major political groups, and his intention, in the words of a high-level policy-maker, is to ensure that Kashmir is seen as a national and not as a partisan issue".

Among the probable parties in the poll, Dr. Farooq Abdullah's National Conference had been demanding an 'autonomy package' before polls, the thinking at the highest level is to negotiate the package only after a government gets elected. The February, 1975 Kashmir Accord between Sheikh Abdullah and Indira Gandhi in regarded as a model for resolution of the question of greater autonomy for Kashmir within the Indian Union. The Prime Minister has already made it clear that the accession of the State to India is the 'final and irrevocable' thus rebuffing informal attempts buy some powers to re-open the 'Third Option' (of independence for the Valley). While this option was tacitly pursued by some powers after 1954, it was given up after the 1971 partition of Pakistan.

According to high-level policy-makers, however, after the Soviet Union disintegrated in 1991, some powers restarted efforts to revive the 'Third Option' The Union Home Minister's recent comments in Parliament about the involvement in Kashmir of a country other than Pakistan was an 'implied rebuff' to such efforts.

That the level of Pakistan's involvement in the Valley is still high is evident from the seizure of '12,500 Kalashnikov rifles and 4,700 pistols' from militants this year. Despite this, the perception in Delhi was that even fundamentalist elements in the Valley have got fatigued by militancy. However, fear of death prevented any open expression of this feeling, and even those Kashmiri leaders who were opposed to violence were forced to support the gun in public.*

Change comes—'Azadi' cannot come through Armed Insurgency

For nearly two years, there is a change in the Kashmir situation. The Pakistani insurgency, against the presence of the Indian Security Forces does not really take the form of an uprising for more than a year. That has abated partly because realisation has dawned in the ranks of militants as also their patrons across the border that 'azadi' (or rather freedom from India) cannot be achieved through armed insurgency, and that it is a long haul. But more significantly, what is unmistakable is the disillusionment with Pakistan due to Islamabad's diplomatic setbacks at the UN fora of Geneva and New York in 1994 and 1995.

Also in 1994, more than 1,000 militants, including a number of prominent secessionist leaders were released by Narasimha Rao. This was done to create conditions conducive to the restoration of democratic political processes through reactivisation of the local administration and stepping up of economic development activity. Work on the revision of constituencies under the State Constitution and election law was already under way. All these measures had a definite and positive impact on the situation. It was soon after that well-known leaders like

---

*"Prime Minister favours early elections in Kashmir" by M. D. Nalapat, *Times of India*, March 29, 1995.

Shabir Shah, Mohammad Yasin Malik, Amin Inquilabi, Prof. Abdul Gani, and Syed Ali Shah Jeelani rose from among them to form the All Party Hurriyat Conference. The APHC was composed of some 34 organizations.

Also slowly, Rao was preparing the stage for holding elections in the State, and had set different steps in motion. However, anyone thought to be holding talks or negotiating with the authorities became targets of the militants. The liquidation of the J&K Liberation Front leader, Idris, who was a prominent aide of Yasin Malik, by the activists of Hizbul Mujahideen for his role in the lifting of the siege of the Hazratbal shrine, showed their long reach and contained a warning to both Yasin Malik and Shabir Shah. The prolonged 'siege' and stand-off of the Chrar-e-Sharief, the hallowed Shrine of venerated Sufi saint Sheikh Nooruddin Noorane in Badgam district in South Kashmir, also showed the Security Forces and even the Army as helpless to intervene, an abdication of authority in the face of an extraordinary situation.*

In March, 1996, the Prime Minister's Office sources declared that the preliminary groundwork for holding elections in the State had been completed. The Prime Minister had constituted a seven-member ministerial committee on Kashmir Affairs to accelerate the political process and work out a concrete plan of action for holding elections which were likely to be held in the ensuing summer.

Preliminary Groundwork towards Elections

The committee consist of: S.B. Chavan (Home), Pranab Mukherjee (External Affairs), Dinesh Singh (Minister without Portfolio, who later died), P. Chidambaram (Commerce), Rajesh Pilot (Internal Security—later shifted to another Ministry), H.R. Bhardwaj (Minister of State for Law) and R.L. Bhatia (Minister of State for External Affairs).

The Center reiterated its commitment to install a

---

*"Wishful thinking will not help Kashmir" by M. K. Narayanan, *Asian Age*, May 8, 1995.

popularly elected government to avoid further extension of President's rule which involved to expire on July 18, 1996, a constitutional amendment. The Prime Minister, who is keen on the restoration of normality in the State, met various leaders of Kashmir to get a feedback. The Minister of State in the Prime Minister's Office, Bhubanesh Chaturvedi, along with senior officials, visited the Valley to study the situation. On the directions of the Prime Minister, a team of secretaries headed by K.R. Venugopal, incharge of the PMO, visited Jammu and Kashmir several times and held discussions with the State Government on the measures required to step up developmental activities. The main thrust was on effective implementation of development programmes which could make an impact on the lives of the people in the Valley.

But the Valley's major political players, militant groups, including the moderate, pluralist, secular People's League of Shabir Shah and Yaseen Malik's JKLF set its face against elections. Shah said he would participate in the polls only if these were held under UN supervision to determine the people's will. The Hurriyat said a firm 'no'. Even Dr. Farooq Abdullah was against holding elections before a proper 'autonomy package' was delivered. In Jammu, the Bharatiya Janata Party opposed any talk of autonomy. The Congress (I) was the only party prepared to go to poll.

Intelligence agencies did not expect a polling rate of more than 10 per cent. In 1989, it was under 5 per cent. Such a low turnout, it was said, would not only rob an 'elected' government of legitimacy, but also put it against the Valley's people.*

Prime Minister offers 'Azadi'

Already, however, there were some welcome straws in the wind. Though the militant outfits (on the surface at least) were dead set against participation in elections, leaders like Shabir Shah and Yasin Malik, even while

*"Plan for J & K Poll" by Praful Bedwai, *Tribune*, May 8, 1995.

distancing themselves from Pakistan, had sought to enlarge the ambit of their relationship with parties, forces and groups not only within Jammu and Kashmir, but in the rest of the country as well. Some leaders of the All Party Hurriyat Conference also displayed a willingness to meet and discuss issues with leaders across the national political spectrum.

But the Government of India, by offering to hold talks with militant groups and by trying to involve the militants in its efforts to revive the political process in the State, threatened to derail the carefully laid-out plans of Pakistan. Pakistan feared that India's twin-pronged approach of seeking a political solution even while it continued to exercise the military option would take the steam out of the insurgency. The capacity of a war-weary people to undertake hardship for any length of time is limited, and if they are offered an honourable way out, they might take it. Moreover, Pakistan also feared that India might win over the 'freedom fighter' in Kashmir with all sorts of blandishments. An example of this was Prime Minister Rao's statement offering 'azadi' within the framework of the Indian Constitution.

With the release of the separatist leaders from prison, the Government had already initiated the political process. Allowing these leaders to go to the OIC Summit at Casablanca, letting them attend Pakistan Day celebrations in Delhi and permitting them to meet the Pakistani President in Delhi during the SAARC Summit, were all components of the continuing political process.

Probably, the most potent political weapon which could be used by India to drive a wedge in the militant ranks was the so-called 'third option'. With the Kashmiris being overwhelmingly in favour of independence, something which both India and Pakistan are unwilling to concede, Aness Jilani in an article in *The News* (of Karachi) wrote "the Indians are perhaps striving to get the All-Party Hurriyat Conference leadership to realise that Pakistan has nothing to offer that India cannot give them." In the same article, she argued that the Indian "strategy is simply to wear down the freedom fighters and bring them to the negotiating table. Such negotiations will then exclude Pakistan."*

National Conference wants pre-1953 Status

However, from the way things have gone on so far, it is clear that except Congress (I), none of the other national parties are eager for early elections in the State. The National Conference, the most dominant party until the last elections, has put forth restoration of the State's "pre-1953 status" as the condition on which it would be prepared to go to the polls.

Conceding such a demand, most observers felt is dangerous for two reasons: one, because the NC with its discredited leadership is hardly popular in the State, and two, the Central government would lose its only bargaining chip during future negotiations by agreeing to a reversal to the past. A political package after the elections seems a better bargain.

Even in the Congress (I), opinion was divided. The division was not only between the workers of the Jammu province and the Kashmir province, but within the workers of the Kashmir province itself, which comprises the Valley and the adjoining Ladakh region (Kargil and Ladakh districts). Whereas the party workers in the Jammu province and Ladakh region (8 district), where the situation was almost normal, which wanted elections and have in fact, started working for it—the workers in Kashmir Valley (7 districts) were by and large immobile. Because the fear of the militants has largely benumbed the middle and lower level workers. The position of the National Conference, the main political party in the state—is the same.

The BJP was totally opposed to the holding of elections now because it felt the situation was not conductive for the people to freely vote in the Valley. This indeed is

*"Pakistan and elections in Kashmir", editorial in *Pioneer*, June 16, 1995.

a fact. The party, however, will contest the polls especially in Jammu, whenever these are held.

The two left parties, the CPI(M) and the CPI, want a political package to be announced for Kashmir before the elections, giving 'maximum autonomy' to it within the framework of Indian unity for the protection of 'Kashmiri identity' and socio-economic development of the State. They feel that a pre-election political package would facilitate a large-scale mobilisation of people for the restoration of democratic process in the Valley, and the package should be largely in consonance with the 1976 Agreement between Indira Gandhi and Sheikh Abdullah. The other national parties like the Janata Dal and Congress (T), now called Indira Congress, also do not favour early elections.

The Central leadership of the Congress (I) in New Delhi, however, wants elections at any cost. It is, therefore, working in tandem with the state governor on one hand and its top local leaders on the other, with Dr. Farooq Abdullah and his men and persuading them to participate in the elections. Although Dr. Abdullah has put in a stiff demand for restoration of the 'pre-1953 status' of Jammu and Kashmir, he appeared now likely to settle for an enhanced economic package.*

What appears to be the largest political coalition in the state, especially in the Valley, is the All-Party Hurriyat Conference (APHC) which still insisted on "plebiscite" and seemed adamant on boycotting the polls. While the majority of them wanted 'azadi', some of the constituents still demanded a merger with Pakistan.†

In such a state of 'siege' however, elections could only be held under special conditions. A large deployment of paramilitary forces might ensure limited levels of campaign and at least a trickle of turnout. Staggered elections

*"Playing with fire" by Avatar Krishan, *Business Standard*, November 9, 1995.

†"Preparing for Polls in Jammu & Kashmir" by Ajit Kumar Jha, *Times of India*, October 27, 1993.

were the only possibility with short periods of campaigning. Both the districts in Leh and most areas in Jammu, except Doda, did not pose much of a problem but the Valley, despite all precautions proved dangerous. What most people feared is that under such extraordinary conditions, the Central government might pull off a 'Punjab' in Kashmir, the dangers of which have been proved by the murder of Beant Singh.

Unfair Polls

Such a fear is genuine given that the state has had a tragic tradition of elections, from the first in 1952 to the last in 1987. The National Conference under Sheikh Abdullah virtually bulldozed through, with the help of a totally non-competitive electoral process in 1952. Similarly, it is widely believed in Kashmir that the NC led by Farooq Abdullah, in alliance with the Congress Party, virtually rigged the whole electoral process in 1987 to its advantage and imposed the most unpopular government in the history of the State. The NC-Congress (I) combine cornered 62 out of 66 seats in 1987, contrary to popular expectations. The Muslim United Front (MUF), a broad-based coalition of disparate groups whose election rallies were extremely popular, shocked most observers when it won a mere four seats. Perhaps with the exception of 1977, almost all elections in J&k have been unfairly conducted.*

There is another valid argument. Pakistan is no more able to influence Jammu and Kashmir ultras. India's intelligence has reports that Pakistan's influence on terrorists, particularly from other countries, is on the wane and soon the time may come when militants would not be attracted to Kashmir any more. The way the Al-Faran terrorists are feeling frustrated, with four foreign tourists held hostage by them, is well-known. And as days pass, more and more Kashmiri militants are emerging out of Pakistani influence.

* *Ibid.*

Pakistan ISI Losing Control of Terrorist Outfits

The Diplomatic Editor of the *Hindustan Times* wrote: International terrorism experts believe that Pakistan's Inter-Services Intelligence has lost control of several terrorist outfits operating in Kashmir and is, therefore, unable to persuade them to release the four foreigners held hostage by Al-Faran, a Harkat-ul-Ansar outfit. Many contradictions exist among the various terrorist organisations under the religio-political parties of Pakistan, as well as, between them and the majority of the Muslim. One cannot rule out a war between the guerilla groups operating in Kashmir, in much the same way as it has happened in Afghanistan... Paula R. Newberg, in her report "Double Betrayal", just published by the Carnegie Endowment, says the Endowment providing support does not directly translate into ability to control its beneficiaries. When two British trekkers were kidnapped in the summer of 1994 by the Pakistan-based Harkat-ul-Ansar practical problems quickly became clear.

It is pointed out that Pakistan's strategy in Kashmir resembles its Afghanistan war policy through the provision of weaponry and training, dividing resources, many guerilla groups when choosing favourities, hinging weapon supplies on ideological agreements and, most important, using a local war to pursue a larger, more encompassing, geo-political goal. Anti-Soviet, anti-Communism—Pakistan's global rationalisation for its engagement in Afghanistan has been replaced with an anti-Indian policy to justify its engagement in Kashmir.

According to experts, Pakistan has been making amateurish attempts to deflect its real involvement in the hostage crisis, fearing adverse international opinion. Kidnapping of prominent persons, particularly foreigners has been a recurring feature of Kashmir insurgency, because the external sponsors believe such sensational acts invite the attention of the world community towards Kashmir. This strategy has been adopted by the foreign countries, particularly Afghan and Pakistani mercenaries.

Some of the extremist groups within Pakistan were responsible for the kidnapping of three German Engineers. In November, 1994 three Britons were freed from captivity of their Afghan-Pakistani terrorists in Saharanpur. In the rescue assault, two foreign mercenaries were nabbed and they disclosed their sponsorship by the ISI. These kidnappers had demanded the release of two top Harkat-ul-Ansar activists. The Al-Faran too is demanding the release of these activists, besides others.

Although the Afghan mercenaries are sponsored by Pakistan, given their background, they always do not obey their masters. Having let them loose in Kashmir, Islamabad is now trying to distance itself from them and blaming the Indian authorities for having sponsored the abductions. Pakistan had made a similar allegation at the time of the abduction of Romanian diplomat, Mr. Rado, in 1993, but subsequent arrest of the kidnappers revealed their association with the Council of Khalistan, operating from Pakistan. Despite the Harkat-ul-Ansar having been branded a terrorist organisation by the US State Department, Benazir Bhutto has refused to take action against it.*

Putting off Poll

It was only in the beginning of 1995 that the Government could think of staging elections in the State, not only because the depredations by tyrannical fundamentalists and terrorists had somewhat lessened and it was time to think of elections, but because elections had to be held after the State remained under President's rule for six years—the longest any State has been, and as for Jammu and Kashmir, six years was the limit—and it was time to switch back to normal process, not to violate the Constitution far too much and to see if elections would clear the way for bringing back normality and a process of normal government. The Governor, Gen. (retd.), Krishna Rao, was also understood to be pressing hard for elec-

*"Pak no more able to influence J & K ultras" by 'Our Diplomatic Editor', *Hindustan Times*, September 22, 1995.

tions, for he thought the State had enough of militancy and it was time for him to quit. Five years of President's rule over the State was already over on July 15, 1995, and so the Chief Election Commissioner, T.N. Seshan, and two Election Commissioners, M.S. Gill and G.V.G. Krishnamurthy, visited the state to explore the possibility of holding the poll. But they were frustrated to find that no party, except the Congress (I) was willing to take up the challenge. They ordered putting off the poll.

Dr. Farooq Abdullah, President of the National Conference, came from London for a visit and after a meeting of the Working Committee of his Party, stated that it was not possible for his Party to participate in the poll, unless the Centre announced autonomy for the State and decide in favour of the 'pre-1953' status for Jammu and Kashmir. In other words, he meant that the status given to Jammu and Kashmir under the 1952 Agreement, which could not be implemented, be granted to the State, before his party, the National Conference, could participate in the poll. This meant going back the entire way. It meant that excepting three subjects, External Affairs, Defence and Communications all other subjects be given to the State to administer, scrapping whatever has been done over the years to integrate the State with India. (Meanwhile, over the years, jurisdiction of the Supreme Court of India, the Election Commission of India, the Controller and Auditor General of India, and Census operations and the authority of the Central Labour Laws of the Union of India were extended to the State of Jammu and Kashmir). If that was conceded, the State would become half-independent. The Commission Members paid a second visit to the State after a few months and put off the elections a second time, pronouncing elections as being not possible.

A former Governor and now a Member of Parliament (in the Rajya Sabha) Jagmohan, stated in an interview in the *Times of India*: "Nobody has so far defined what 'azadi' (the slogan often raised by militants in Kashmir) means. Does this mean restoration of the pre-1953 status? if that is the case, it will mean that the benefits extended to the State since then—Census operations, Election Commission and Supreme Court jurisdictions and Central Labour Laws—will have to be withdrawn. Now tell me which way the forsaking of these facilities for 'azadi' would improve the people's conditions? If you are under Supreme Court jurisdiction, you got better justice. Labour laws ensure labour welfare. It is a small self-serving oligarchy which is spearheading the Azadi campaign for their benefit. This small group wants a fieldom, a sort of Sheikhdom, for which the Centre keeps sending money and they continue ruling the State.*

The President's rule was extended twice, as a result, and now due to expire on July 16, 1996. The first time after the burning of the Chrar-e-Sharif and second time because of uncertainties with regard to National Conference's participation in the poll and nearness of the General elections in the country. The Centre has been planning to hold elections in the State as soon as the winter is over, that is by March, 1996, but there seems little possibility of the State elections taking place by then. The Centre has not yet accepted Dr. Abdullah's proposal to grant the 'pre-1953 status' for the State. But the Prime Minister Rao announced from Burkina Faso an election plan and offer which were not acceptable to Dr. Abdullah. No election seems possible by the scheduled time.

Present Situation in which Terrorism has Abated a Great Deal

Terrorism today is much subdued in Jammu and Kashmir. Against the presence of the Indian Security Forces, it no longer takes the form of an uprising. That has abated substantially because realisation has dawned in the ranks of militants, as also their sponsors across the border that 'azadi' (in the sense of 'freedom' from India) cannot be achieved through armed insurgency. It has

*"Polls will only boost secessionism" by Gurmukh Singh, *Times of India*, May 28, 1995.

already been a long haul. Foreign terrorists feel they have come to an end in Kashmir and must look for something new or new pastures. Kashmiri terrorists or militants also feel they have come to the end of their long haul. Significantly, what is unmistakable is the disillusionment with Pakistan due to many setbacks—including its discomfiture at the UN fora at Geneva and New York in 1994 and 1995—and now the knowledge that the present tactics of terrorism has almost come to a dead end and is not making much headway. So, Pakistan is looking for something new to achieve its objective, may be more sophisticated arms which India does not have, and even the final weapon, the atom bomb.

Pakistan is still raging a low-intensity proxy war in the Valley, but the scale is very low and it is almost dying out.

While the Kashmiris still have no love lost for India, from all accounts the common man in the Valley has become completely exhausted by the armed struggle and is thoroughly disenchanted with Pakistan.

Some who had started the movement in the late 1980s, such as Shabir Shah, Azim Inquilabi and Mohammad Yaseen Malik are already talking the language of downplaying the armed aspect of the struggle. Other 'older' militants who are presently in Pakistan-occupied Kashmir (PoK) have sent signals that they, like Inquilabi, wish to return to the Valley.

Furthermore, security officials say that most of the current militant activity is restricted to the groups dominated by foreign mercenaries, such as Harkat-ul-Ansar and Lashkar-e-Tayuba, or the 'hardcore' Hizbul Mujahideen. Then there are efforts by separatist political organisations such as the All-Party Hurriyat Conference to move away from the armed struggle. On January 26, 1995 Hurriyat leader, Prof. Abdul Ghani, emphasised the need for mutual talks between the Kashmiris, the Government of India and the people of India for evolving a national consensus on the Kashmir issue for bringing a permanent and lasting peace in the Valley.*

The basic point is that there is an immediate need to promote a dialogue among the political leaders and parties of the Valley, Doda, Ladakh, Jammu, Poonch and Rajouri. Only such interaction will bring realism to the consideration of the implication of various issues, and help an understanding needed to project a final solution. It is possible to make elections acceptable by reaching out to the politicians, militants and the people. It is also possible to ensure sizeable participation by working towards a ceasefire by other militant groups as indeed the JKLF has indicated.

Parties in the Poll

The Congress (I), the National Conference, the Janata Dal, the BJP, the Communist Party, the People's League, the JKLF and the Hurriyat are all in the political arena. The Congress (I) is non-existent in the Valley and despite economic gains in terms of agencies and petrol pumps, there is little effort to gain strength. The Gujjar leader, Mia Basheer and the Shia leader, Iftikhar Ansari, have a following but with the departure of Mufti Mohammed Sayeed there is no one to keep the factions together. On the Central Front, Rajesh Pilot and Ghulam Nabi Azad lead different groups and the Congress (I) rarely talks in a single voice. The National Conference is in a slightly better shape but seems to be third in the popular ratings. Dr. Farooq Abdullah is used extensively to give speeches to international forums and travels frequently, but amongst the locals the major grudge is that he left in the difficult days to stay abroad. His brother, Mustafa Kamal, who stayed behind is gaining the popular syndrome, but this again is a 'personal' matter for the Abdullah dynasty. Dr. Farooq is supported by Pilot, is close to George Fernandes, and would be willing to go along with most groups if he is the front-runner. He has an excellent public relations posture, is very likeable and excellent company; but all

*"Terror in Jammu" by Aditya Sinha, *Pioneer*, January 31, 1995.

this means little if he lacks the support on the ground. He could well hand over the reins to his younger brother and be a Cabinet Minister at the Centre. He has done well for India at various forums and may be temperamentally suited to this type of role.

Yassen Malik of the Jammu and Kashmir Liberation Front held the spotlight but has over a period of time yielded the top slot to Shabir Shah of the People's League. The latter without doubt has the largest following and both will be the prime targets of the militants who act at the behest of Pakistan. Both are the treading cautiously and will be wooed by different political factions.*

The Hurriyat Leaders Today

The main point about some of the Hurriyat Conference leaders today is that they have mellowed down a great deal from the time they started out. Those who began their movement in the late 1980s, such as Shabir Shah, Azim Inquilabi and Mohammad Yasin Malik, and were taken into custody, have now started speaking the language of downplaying the armed aspect of their struggle. Other 'older' militants who are presently in Pakistan-occupied Kashmir (PoK) have sent signals that they, like Inquilabi, wish to return to the Valley. Furthermore, security officials say that most of the current militant activity is restricted to the groups dominated by foreign mercenaries, such as Harkat-ul-Ansar and Lashkar-e-Tayuba, or the 'hardcore' Hizbul Mujahideen. Then there are efforts by separatist political organizations such as the All Party Hurriyat Conference to move away from the armed struggle. On January 26 of 1995, the Hurriyat leader, Professor Abdul Ghani emphasised the need for mutual talks between the Kashmiris, the Government of India and the people of India for evolving a national consensus on the Kashmir issue for bringing a permanent and lasting peace in the Valley.

*"Kashmir I" by Arun Nehru, *The Hindu*, April 25, 1995.

However, the point remains that the Hurriyat leaders are hopelessly divided. An umbrella organisation of as many as 34 groups never had much of a chance. Shabir Shah, the charismatic People's League leader clearly fancies a larger than life role for himself, while Yaseen Malik insists that what Kashmiris want is to be left alone both by India and Pakistan. It is worth recalling that Malik went on a fast to uphold the rights of Hindu pilgrims to Amarnath last year (in 1995), to travel without let or hindrance, and without damage to his image as a Kashmiri leader. Given below is an account of the Senior Hurriyat leaders and their present arms and aspirations.

Mirwaiz Umar Farooq

The Young son of Maulvi Farooq, who was killed by militants, Mirwaiz 'Umar Farooq Bhairman of All Parties' Hurriyat Conference, has said that the elections which the Central Government plans to hold in Jammu and Kashmir are not acceptable to the people who would want polls to be held under a neutral authority or the United Nations.

He wants both Indian and Pakistani troops to be out of the whole of Kashmir, including the Pakistan-occupied areas, when the Kashmiris vote to decide their future. The elected representatives thus chosen would then talk to India and Pakistan to find a final solution to the Kashmir issue.

The people of Kashmir should be associated with any talks on the future of the State, and a plebiscite should be monitored by the UN troops, as happens elsewhere in the world.

The APHC leader feels bilateral talks between India and Pakistan should continue, but the two countries are not in a position to solve the issue. The discussions have to be tripartite between the representatives of India and Pakistan and the leaders of entire Jammu and Kashmir, including the PoK.

He does not rule out independence as an option, but

this would have to be decided by the representatives of the people of the State from the areas controlled by India and Pakistan. All options would be on the table when talks are held.

He says Kashmir is the oldest unresolved issue on the UN agenda when the world body celebrated its 50th anniversary. "So, we feel that the United Nations has an obligation towards the people of Kashmir. The people in Kashmir have been suffering and the situation has deteriorated because of lack of interest by the UN."

The aim of the APHC, which represents 31 political, social and religious parties, is to strive "politically and peacefully" for a final settlement of the issue. The aim of his visit to the UN, the Hurriyat Chairman said, was to apprise the people, the law-makers, and others in the UN of the realities on the ground and to explain how the international community could play a role in bringing about peace in Kashmir.

The Hurriyat Conference has given a peace plan which includes the immediate stoppage of military and paramilitary activities by the Security Forces and the complete withdrawal of all those arrested in connection with the insurgency. If such steps are taken, the APHC could persuade the militants to stop their activities for a certain period of time so as to enable a political process to take place.

Farooq said "We are not going to the NAM either to lobby against India or Pakistan, but to put our message across that the people of Kashmir are the first and foremost party, and they feel that the international community must listen to what the Kashmiris feel and say." He also alleged repression by the Indian Security Forces, saying that recently they had adopted a new method—threatening the militants' close relations to force them to surrender.

Shabir Shah

Yassen Malik of the Jammu and Kashmir Liberation

Front held the spotlight, but has over a period of time, yielded the top slot to Shabir Shah of the People's League. The latter, without doubt, has the largest following and both are the prime targets of the militants who act at the behest of Pakistan. Both are treading cautiously and will be wooed by different political factions. It is clear that the Governor, the intelligence agencies, the forces and cadres represented by Shabir Shah, Yaseen Malik and the National Conference have to be brought together for final negotiations, and this is what the Government solution does not like in an election when foreign mercenaries and terrorists are still threatening to destroy the gains made in the field. The wide variety of political forces has to be welded together and this is not easy. But then nobody in India is expecting a quick-fix solution. The Prime Minister has to start the process.

Shabir Shah has emerged as the foremost mass leader of Jammu and Kashmir today. What is significant is that he is keen to hold threadbare discussions with the entire political spectrum and especially non-party individuals and scholars. His campaign is for strengthening the unity of the three regions of Jammu and Kashmir and the wide response of his appeal constitute a silver lining in the otherwise depressing scenario. He has emerged as the foremost mass leader of Jammu and Kashmir today.

Both Shabir Shah and Yaseen Malik, popular youthful leaders, have said many a time that their struggle was secular. The OIC did no service to Kashmir when it invited the Hurriyat, having a limited representation in the Valley. There was none from Jammu and Ladakh, the two other regions of Kashmir, Indian opinion has come a long way from the one that prevailed five or six years ago. Most people now recognize the fact that the Kashmir issue is far from resolved and that a final settlement would need Pakistan's association. By communalizing the issue, Islamabad is only strengthening the Bharatiya Janata Party stand, which is parochial and which demands even the abolition of Article 370 that gives Kashmir a special status within India.

Shabir Shah has spent more than 20 years of his life in Indian jails and yet he is not bitter about it. He seems to be quite reasonable and does not take any extremist posture. He said "We have sacrificed more than 40,000 people for our freedom. It is a big sacrifice by any account. What for did we make this sacrifice? Our only demand is that let people of Kashmir decide their future. But we are not laying down any pre-conditions. Also, we do not want the people of the Valley to decide everything. People of Ladakh and Jammu also have the same right. We are fighting for justice and so we do not want injustice to be done to any region. We are all ready to accommodate different points of view. Some people may desire accession with all the people. I went to Delhi and met all sections of people including the leaders of BJP (Atal Behari Vajpayee and Jaswant Singh). I told Vajpayee "you improved India-Pakistan relations, why do you want to do away with Article 370". He replied "We want to be closer with the people of Kashmir." I said "you are ignoring the aspirations of people of Kashmir."

Shabir Shah also said "We stand for all Kashmiris, Hindus, Sikhs and Muslims. We are not at all against Pandits. They are integral part to Kashmir. It is Mr. Jagmohan who created fear psychosis in their minds. We never killed Pandits just because they were Hindus and pro-India. We were fighting establishment and since some Pandits were part of establishment they were killed. So were many pro-establishment Muslims. In fact, the Government of India is not interested in bringing them back because they want to use them as pawns in their power game. When we complain about atrocities against us and violations of human rights, they tell the world "look what the militants have done to these Pandits; most of the Pandits have been given jobs and only poor Pandits are kept in miserable camps."

About Charar-e-Sharief, he said "it was burnt down by the Army. The people of Charar-e-Sharief have defence ordinance shells, which show who burnt it. This ziyarat was of Sheikh Nuruddin, a great representative of tolerant and liberal Islam. It has greatly shocked people of Kashmir. Let there be a dialogue with the people of Kashmir and Pakistan with an open mind. With open mind, we can certainly find a solution.*

Speaking to Sumit Chakravarty, Shabir Shah said Prof. Abdul Ghani's position (of support to Dixon Plan for partitioning the State, as backed by Pakistan) "is totally unacceptable to the People's League." Peoples League chief, Shabir Shah's immediate aim is to 'stitch with needle and thread the minds and hearts of the people of Jammu, Kashmir Valley and Ladakh."

Shabir Shah is, however, cautious and politely declines to directly assail Benazir Bhutto (as does Yaseen Malik, who answering a question, replies: Why should independence of Kashmir lead to balkanization of India and Pakistan). On the Government of India's approach, he charges New Delhi of being rigid and not accepting anything. "Let them accept something. Then we will see what we can do." (According to Yaseen Malik, tripartite negotiations between India, Pakistan and the Kashmiri representatives is a must if the problem is to be resolved amicably).

Shabir Shah campaigns for strengthening the unity of the three regions of Jammu and Kashmir and the wide response of his appeal even in Jammu constitute a silver lining in the otherwise depressing scenario. Indeed, there is an air of expectancy in the Valley despite all the despondency and distress that prevails in the dark and sombre winter setting... especially now when the futility of pinning all hopes on Pakistani support is becoming increasingly transparent to the young militants with every passing day.†

Shabir Shah, perhaps the most popular and sensible Kashmiri leader, who has emerged on the scene today,

*"Evaluation of Kashmir Problem—A Report on Visit to the Valley" by Ashgar Ali Engineer, Human Rights, edited by Balraj Puri, September-October, 1995.

†"New Stirrings in the Valley—Onas on Delhi" by Sumit Chakravarty, *Indian Express*, January 5, 1995.

says: "No elections, no autonomy, only self-determination". He has demanded tripartite talks between India, Pakistan and the people of Kashmir on both sides of the order to find a solution. He would not mind joining the political process and elections provided these are held under UN auspices.

Yaseen Malik

Today, Yaseen Malik, President of the JKLF intends to immolate himself should the elections be held in Kashmir. According to him, elections are no substitute for freedom. The All-Party Hurriyat Conference which is a conglomeration of around 35 political parties and is predominantly pro-Pak has declined to participate in any elections or any other political process.

Malik totally disagrees with Professor Abdul Gani, who speaks the language of Benazir Bhutto that independent Kashmir would set the process of balkanization of both India and Pakistan in motion. That view is not only not shared by the head of the JKLF, but he also conveys his sense of annoyance and indignation at Benazir's statement. Speaking with remarkable candour in his office in the heart of Srinagar, he says: "Why should it (independence of Kashmir) lead to balkanisation of India and Pakistan: Is it part of history that Kashmir was an independent, sovereign state, much before the birth of Pakistan. Who is Benazir Bhutto? Who has given her that kind of authority to speak any damn thing? This is not a Benazir-sponsored movement. The movement was sponsored by the people of Jammu and Kashmir who have suffered, not Benazir."

According to Malik, tripartite negotiations between India, Pakistan and the Kashmiri representatives is a must if the problem is to be resolved amicably. He was keen to see the Government of India accepting the problem as a 'political one and not a single law and order issue."

Yasseen Malik openly said he was not part of the

Hurriyat and the JKLF was not attending Hurriyat meetings.*

Mohammad Azam Inquilabi

Of considerable importance is the reappearance of Mohammad Azam Inquilabi, one of the founders of the Kashmiri movement in Srinagar a few days ago. Inquilabi, founder and chief of Operation Balakote and lecturer in his early days, is articulate and clear about his approach to the outstanding issues facing Kashmir. Though his statements are significant by themselves, his arrival on the Kashmiri political scene and the response from leaders like Yaseen Malik of JKLF and an independent like Shabir Ahmed Shah, have been interesting. Following the release of Malik and Shah, the importance of the 'political struggle' as opposed to the wielding of the gun, has definitely increased. In fact, Shah's public campaigns and his stress of political struggle in the movement for 'azadi' are a reflection of the people's desire for 'freedom' and peace. Further, it is the assessment of the Central Government that a climbdown from a non-violent movement for 'azadi' to participating in a 'credible political process' will be far easier than expecting the hardcore Islamic fundamentalists waging a 'jehad' against the Indian State to join the electoral stream.

It is this thought process along with the pressures from the Western Governments, perceived or otherwise, which has forced the Centre for the first time in five years to make space for the non-violent dissent practised by leaders such as Shah, Malik and now Inquilabi. Though there is no let up to the operations of the Security Forces and the hardships being faced by the people, the fact remains that the Kashmir Valley today has an entire spectrum of leaders from Inquilabi to Abdul Gani Bhatt and Syed Ali Shah Geelani, who speak without the gun. Inquilabi's statement in Srinagar that it was time to 'shed the gun culture and dedicate ourselves to the dem-

*"Terror in Jammu" by Aditya Sinha, *Pioneer*, January 31, 1995.

ocratic struggle' tells its own story.*

Abdul Gani Lone

Abdul Gani Lone of People's League which is also part of the Hurriyat, said that atrocities by the Army and the paramilitary forces have not stopped. He gave many instances of continuing atrocities and torture by Security Forces. In villages, he said, much more atrocites were being committed than in Srinagar. He gave many examples. He admitted that the problem was extremely complicated and it cannot be solved with guns and he showed his readiness to go to negotiating table with an open mind to stop bloodshed and established peace in South-Asia and also for saving defence expenditure of the two countries and for keeping South-Asia free from nuclear armaments. But the Indian Government, too, he felt, should be prepared to negotiate with an open mind.

Syed Ali Shah Gilani

S.A.S. Gilani, leading light of the All-Party Hurriyat Conference, flatly rejects any suggestion of improvements in the ground situation in the troubled state, as indicated by Ghulam Nabi Azad, a former Central Minister (also from Kashmir), who said "the restraint shown by the Security Forces in Chrar-e-Sharief, together with public anger shown against the havoc caused by terrorists and the Government's determination to revive normal political processes, has contributed to an improved situation on the ground."

"The situation has gone from bad to worse", the Jamat-i-Islami leader holds. Asked about the possibility of elections, Gilani said that people might be taken forcibly to the polling booths by the Security Forces but they would resist voting. The Security Forces may organize crackdowns and then take the people to vote. The people are not willing to participate in any election process."

---

*"The gun is not the only voice" by Amit Baruah, *The Hindu*, January 15, 1995.

To a question on the differences within the Hurriyat Conference, he said seven major parties were present in the APHC executive. There was no differences on the major objective of attaining 'freedom from India'. "We are all together on this issue".

Asked about the position taken by Shabir Ahmed Shah, another Hurriyat leader, and Chairman of the Jammu and Kashmir People's League, that the Hurriyat should be made more broadbased and have representation from all areas of the State, Gilani said that most constituents of the APHC were State-level organisations. The Jamaat leader flatly rejected any ideas of 'unconditional talks' between the Government and the Kashmiri leadership, saying that to be effective this must involve the third party—the Government of Pakistan. "There is no point in the Government of India holding talks with the Kashmiris or the Government of India holding talks with the Pakistani counterpart. The talks to be meaningful must involve all three parties. If the Government of India decides to invite only the Kashmiri leadership for talks, it will turn into a futile exercise", he said.

Responding to a question on a recent report prepared by the Geneva-based International Commission of Justice (ICJ) for a plebiscite in different geographical regions of the erstwhile princely State, the Jamaat leader said the basis of the Kashmir case lay in the United Nations resolution, calling for a plebiscite. He, however, provided and escape route on the issue by adding that the 'modalities' for a plebiscite could be worked out in 'tripartite talks'. The Kashmir crisis was a creation of both Pakistan and India, which had made grave mistakes. "I don't say that there are angels in Pakistan", he stated.

Gilani's approach to the Kashmir issue is perhaps the most unrelenting hardline among the 'separatist' Kashmiri leadership. There are others, however , who do not rule out the possibility of unconditional talks with the Government of India on the Kashmir issue. Till, date, not a single leader from the 'new' Kashmiri leadership has spoken a line different from the stated position demanding a 'plebiscite' and 'self determination'. It is more than evident that the fear of the bullet prevents some of them from articulating a position different from the 'norm'.*

In another interview with Asghar Ali Engineer later on, Gilani of Jamaat-i-Islami (which controls Hizh-ul-Mujahideen) group maintained that India should accept that Kashmir is a disputed territory and that Government of India should fulfil its commitment to hold plebiscite in J&K. "We can negotiate with India only on that basis. There is no question of accepting autonomy. We have sacrificed lives of more than 40,000 people and honour of our women for what? for autonomy? Certainly not. We will accept independence, he said. The UN resolution gave only two options—accession to India or Pakistan. There is no third option.

When he was asked how does he expect 66 per cent Hindus of Jammu and the large number of Buddhists from Ladakh to join Pakistan, he pointed out that when Hyderabad and Junagadh were annexed through police action, the Muslim population in these two states had to remain in India. So Hindus and Buddhists from Jammu and Ladakh can join Pakistan. But on being told that Muslims in Hyderabad and Junagadh states were no more than 7 to 8 per cent, he did not reply. All he said was once the Government of India accepts the principle of plebiscite some solution to this problem can also be found. Also, the problem of Pandits came for discussion. He said Pandits were welcome back to Valley without any pre-condition. When it was pointed out that they would return only when they were sure of safety of their life and property, he said 'when our own lives are not safe, how could we guarantee their safety'.†

Professor Abdul Gani

Prof. Abdul Gani of Muslim Conference questions the

*"Poll in the wind" by Amit Baruah, *The Hindu*, New Delhi, March 26, 1994.

†"Evaluation of Kashmir Problem " by Asghar Ali Engineer, Human Rights, Jammu, September–October, 1995.

fact of accession (of Jammu and Kashmir to India) and maintains that Kashmir belongs to Pakistan. "If plebiscite takes place today, I will vote for Pakistan." He accepted the fact that "Jammu and Ladakh are not with us; for us, the main question is of the Valley." He supported a solution on the lines of Dixon Plan that Chanab be accepted as the dividing line. But this suggestion was rejected even by the U. N., "but we are not rigged; we have flexible attitude."

Pakistan had endorsed the Dixon Plan for partitioning of the State, as evident from the opinion of Prof. Abdul Gani, head of the Muslim Conference and a prominent Hurriyat leader, who is at the same time ideologically closest to the Pakistani position. This is totally unacceptable to the People's League Chief, Shabir Shah, whose immediate aim is to 'stitch with needle and thread the minds and hearts of the people of Jammu, Kashmir Valley and Ladakh.' Prof. Gani on the other hand spoke the language of Benazir Bhutto that independent Kashmir would set the process of balkanization of both India and Pakistan in motion. In as exclusive interview, Prof. Gani said: "Benazir Bhutto and myself are persons of small stature. But even China has said that independent Kashmir is repugnant to the People's Republic of China. That view is not only not shared by the head of the JKLF, Yaseen Malik, but he also conveyed his sense of annoyance and indignation at Benazir's statement.

Prof. Gani has emphasized the need for mutual talks between the Kashmiris, the Government of India and the people of India for evolving a national consensus on Kashmir issue for bringing a permanent and lasting peace in the Valley. Speaking to 'Search', a voluntary organisation of eminent jurists, social activists and academicians, Prof. Gani stressed upon the fact that Kashmiris as the affected party should be allowed to play a major role in bringing about peace in the sub-continent. The statement was not only the most positive to date, but he also began to sound very mainstream when he said that the vested interests in the bureaucracy were sustaining militancy land jeopardising all the peace moves by right-thinking people, including the Hurriyat leaders. While Prof. Gani reiterated the need to include Pakistan in the tripartite talks, he stressed that it was Kashmir and not Pakistan that had the major role to play in resolving the issue. All of these things together are interpreted as a petering out of the movement among the majority of the people. Whether they still remain alienated from India will be known in the elections.

Chapter 8

Conclusion

Even as the most momentous century is coming to a close and momentous events are taking place which make for a better world to emerge for its peoples, will there be peace on the Kashmir issue which has troubled the Indian subcontinent over the last nearly fifty years—ever since as India and Pakistan came to be born with the withdrawal of the British, leaving the legacy. The two big countries of South Asia have already seen three wars on the Kashmir issue. Currently, over the last six years or so, Pakistan has imposed a proxy war on India on Kashmir, of which there seems to be no end, though there are indications that the people of Kashmir have no heart any more in this, and the battle is being fought mainly by Afghan and Pakistani militants. Kashmiris, apparently, have become quite disillusioned about what is going on and are unable to make up their mind what they want next.

For, as we approach the end of the 20th century, India and Pakistan are in the running for staging the longest confrontation since it began. This has already erupted into three major conflicts. Judging from current tensions, with no moves in sight to resolve them, the confrontation could well spill in the 21st century. Elsewhere, the French and Germans, who fought the bloodiest battles ever in the first half of the century have become partners in the European community, with no travel and economic restrictions between them. They are members of a common European Parliament. The cold war, which once threatened the world with a nuclear holocoust, has ended without even conventional clash: the previous global rivals are busy evolving closer economic ties.

The Third World, too, has become peaceful, says Ajit Bhattacharjea in his "Only people can hear the political mess in Kashmir", published in the *Pioneer* on February 17, 1955. The war in Vietnam, he says, in which a greater tonnage of bombs was dropped than in the entire Second World War, has ended with both sides attempting to restore some of the damages. In South Africa, the long years of racial confrontation has ended with the Blacks and Whites joining in a Government headed by Dr. Nelson Mandela, a black leader who spent most of his life in a white prison. This was a peaceful denouement that nobody could have anticipated. An agreement between the Palestinians and the Israelis has been reached. This, too, seemed equally unlikely in view of deep-rooted racial and religious discord. Another arena of politico-religious conflict, Northern Ireland, is inching towards a settlement which will give the people there an opportunity to determine their own future. The number of casualties has dropped sharply.

"Only Pakistan and India continue to spew invectives at and injure each other wherever they can, principally in Kashmir. Even after nearly half a century of the first war between them, tensions are high as reflected by the closure of consulates in Bombay and Karachi, and events following thereafter. Both New Delhi and Islamabad engage in the crude tit-for-tat diplomacy of expelling diplomats. This is designed to play up to the political gallery rather than fulfil any diplomatic purpose. The primary objective of their spokesmen abroad is to denigrate each other which reduces the stature of both countries in the world, where they are increasingly viewed as irresponsible delinquents now brandishing nuclear weapons.

"At home, this militant posture has cast intolerable burdens on the common man. India and Pakistan rank among the worst countries in the world in providing the essential amenities of health, education and housing to their citizens, according to UN data. Scarce funds have been diverted from development to defence. The primary target is the neighbouring country... the sustained race for military superiority has recently assumed an even more fearsome dimension. Both India and Pakistan are credited with nuclear weapons. Neither Government has been able to gain the confidence and trust of the other. As a result the border has become a wall deterring the popular reforms of contact, whether in trade, culture, media or professional visits that could modify the climate of hostility. It is this historical background that makes Kashmir the main arena of confrontation. Pakistan claims the State because it has a Muslim majority; India because the National Conference leadership that led it into India in 1947 was an example of Muslim commitment to secularism."

Attempt to Break Deadlock

A major attempt to break the deadlock to reach a settlement on Kashmir was made by the late Indian Prime Minister, Indira Gandhi, during her talks with Pakistani counterpart, Zulfiqar Ali Bhutto, when they signed the Simla Agreement in July, 1972, after the last Indo-Pak war. This was after Pakistan's discomfiture in retaining the then East Pakistan followed by its loss of some territories in Kashmir a war that Pakistan imposed on India in the wake of its defeat in East Pakistan and leading to the creation of Bangladesh. Bhutto signed the agreement with Indira Gandhi, but had apparently no intention of keeping to it, or in any case was soon out of power to adhere to the agreement. Though Pakistan did not wage a formal war thereafter, neither did it allow peace and order to prevail. After a little more than a decade and a half, Pakistan waged a proxy war against India in Kashmir, upsetting the expectations of peace and order flowing from the Simla Agreement. More than 20 years later, D.P. Dhar, who was with Indira Gandhi as her principal Secretary and was behind the architect for the peace treaty known as the Simla Agreement, wrote two articles recently in a newspaper to explain how the Simla Agreement provided a mechanism for the solution of the Kashmir problem, and also envisaged a solution.

But no solution emerged. India is capable of living with the problem till Pakistan which spends about 39 per cent of its budget on defence as compared to about 13 per cent by India, runs out of steam. This is true but statesmanship demands that the Pakistani establishment should be persuaded to realise that the tragedy of partition can be mitigated only by reconciliation. The path of violence will only make Pakistan's problems worse.

After the 1971 war, when India was holding all the cards and could have settled the Kashmir problem for good, our policy-makers negotiating the Simla Agreement were out-smarted by Bhutto to insert in the Kashmir clause the words "without prejudice to the recognised position of either side" at the last minute on a verbal assurance by him that he would convert the Line of Control into the international border. He soon went back on his word and the problem received a fresh lease of life.

India, Pakistan should Settle Differences

It would still be better both for India and Pakistan to try to settle their mutual differences bilaterally, peacefully and without outside intervention, as was accepted by both sides in the Simla Agreement on July 2, 1972, rather than looking for help from abroad. Indians and Pakistanis are ethnically the same people. They speak common languages, share similar music, dance, songs, food and dress habits. It should, therefore, be easier for the two to cooperate with each other in evolving economic, political and social cooperation, as compared to Western Europe which has many more ethnic, linguistic and even religious differences.

"The Malayasian Prime Minister once told me that if India and Pakistan could work together in friendship and cooperation they could help in maintaining peace and promoting progress not only in South Asia but in South-East Asia also", says T.N. Kaul, in his article "The Kashmir Question" in the *Observer,* dated March 4, 1995.

Why is it, then, that Pakistan has turned down all efforts made by India to settle differences bilaterally and peacefully? This may be due to their internal difficulties, rivalries and jealousies. Partly, it may be due to the mistaken belief that by internationalising bilateral problems they are going to get a better bargain. "I should like to remind Madam Benazir, Prime Minister of Pakistan, about the Agreement signed in Simla in 1972 when she was present there with her illustrious father, is there any instance in recent history where territory conquered has been returned to the defeated country within months of cessation of War? Is there any instance in recent history where 93,000 P.O.Ws have been returned to the vanquished nation within months of the cease-fire? Has Madam Benazir forgotten that India's voice was one of the first to be raised against the assassination of her father by the military dictator?... I am mentioning these points to emphasise that internationalisation of bilateral problems, so far as our sub-continent is concerned, has only made them more difficult to resolve. In the post-cold war scenario, it should be even easier for the two countries to sit together. This has been proposed by India several times to Pakistan but we are still waiting for a positive response. This was the essence of the Simla Agreement where a reference was made to a final settlement of the Jammu and Kashmir question. I recall asking President Bhutto across the Conference table in Simla: "Sir, when you were the Foreign Minister of Pakistan at the Tashkent Conference in 1966 , you said that Kashmir was the basic cause of all our differences. Today, you are the President of Pakistan. Are you willing to agree to a peaceful, bilateral and final settlement of the Kashmir question?" He replied, "You are" right, Mr. Kaul, I did say that at Tashkent.

But I did not represent a defeated country then. Today, I do. But as soon as I get back to Pakistan I will prepare the ground for it.. "Unfortunately, President Bhutto was not able to fulfil his promise because of internal pressures particularly from Pakistan's military intelligence."

India made a gesture of friendship to Pakistan at Simla in the larger interest of peace and friendship between the two peoples of India and Pakistan in the hope that the leaders of Pakistan would see the benefit of settling our differences bilaterally rather than buy internationalising them. India still stands by the Simla Agreement. It is Pakistan that is trying to get out of it by creating a situation that could lead to disturbance of international peace and tranquility. Pakistan should realise that she is committing a violation, both of the Simla Agreement as well as international law by training, arming, financing and abetting terrorism in Pak-occupied Kashmir, and even on Pakistani soil, to commit sabotage, subversion, loot, arson and murder in Jammu and Kashmir. This is a dangerous game that can boomerang against Pakistan itself.

The US Thinking

The US thinking seems to be far removed from reality. This in spite of the fact that the US finds much greater trade relations and a vast consumer and capital market in India. Washington foresees Pakistan's stability only with a larger transfer of American arms to that country. Its Assistant Secretary of State, Robin Raphel, is also on record as having said that Pakistan had signed no pact with the US which disqualifies it from receiving military aid irrespective of its nuclear capability! The Americans would also have us believe that the supply of military equipment to Pakistan will not upset the arms balance in South Asia. They are fully aware of Pakistani attempts to obtain Mirage fighter planes from France.

Pakistan's acquisition of French submarines with Exocet missiles should also be no secret to the Americans. Pakistan's defence arrangements with Saudi Arabia and

Turkey for rendering substantial military assistance in the event of a war with India are quite well-known. And what happened to the $3 billion worth of US weapons including missiles supplied to Pakistan during the Afghan unrest? How much of that equipment was siphoned off by the Pakistani military machine for disruptive activities in Kashmir? The US is still keen to supply arms to Pakistan even at the cost of India. What strategic purpose it would serve to the US in the long run is known only to Washington.

General Aslam Beg, the former Pakistani Army Chief, admitted unhesitatingly that his country had assembled a bomb as far back as 1987, but the US had closed its eyes because of Pakistan's active role in promoting resistance to the Soviet forces. The Pakistani leaders have been openly confirming the receipt of Chinese missiles, which in fact are violative of the MTCR guidelines and though the US had imposed some sanctions against Pakistan earlier, these were lifted through a waiver of the Pressler Amendment.

The point that lethal weapons included in the US package for Pakistan give it the capability of reaching up to the tip of India without the need for refuelling is crystal clear. It is also a fact that India at present is not equipped with the necessary means to counter such weapons. The history of the last five decades shows that wherever Pakistan filled its arsenal with US weapons, it started a misadventure against India. Nawaz Sharif's warning about the use of nuclear arms against India on the Kashmir issue is incapable of being dismissed as paranoia. During her last US visit, Prime Minister, Benazir Bhutto's initial denial and later admission of a nuclear centre at Khushab also provided considerable amusement to the media. From the intent of declaring Pakistan as a terrorist state, the US in one stroke provided Pakistan enough encouragement to go ahead with nuclear proliferation. The US lost its moral right to pressurise India into signing the non-proliferation treaty.

The question that naturally arises is what India should

do to safeguard its territorial integrity. The only answer one can find is that it should never give up its nuclear option. It should never succumb to pressure under any guise unless the nuclear haves agree to the total elimination of all weapons of mass destruction. Secondly, India should continue with its missile programme. Agni was fired for the first time in 1989. India became the second outside the nuclear powers to have perfected an intermediate range ballistic missile capability. It is a precursor to an inter-continental ballistic missile, which should come off sooner than later. But it is unfortunate that the Congress Party Government has put the Agni and Prithvi production on hold, not because of any material constraint, but due to its own pusillanimity. The danger of aggression from Pakistan with the help of the American and Chinese arms is real. If the US has failed to apply sanctions against Pakistan and China under the MTCR, how can it inveigh India for developing its own missiles for its own legitimate defence?

US Trying For 'Third Option'

The Americans somehow believe that given their power after the end of the cold war they can solve problems in different parts of the world and create a new world order of their liking. Conflict resolution is the name of the new Clintonian game. Bosnia, Somalia and Chechnya, however, should have by now convinced them about the limits of intended 'Good Samaritanism.'

Washington is certainly making a mistake in believing that India will hand over the Valley to Pakistan as a price for buying peace with it. And for Washington to think that it can push through its famed Third Option—namely an independent Kashmir—is unrealistic. India cannot let any part of the country secede, whether it opts for Pakistan or chooses to be independent. Benazir Bhutto has also—tactically or otherwise—rejected and independent Kashmir. Washington's fascination for an independent Kashmir is not new. The late Adlai Stevenson and many a ranking American fiddled with the idea in the Fifties and the Sixties, but it never took off because it serves nobody's purpose.

The acceptance of an independent Kashmir is bound to lead to a chain reaction and make the disgruntled people in some other parts ask for a separation. Can Pakistan afford to accept independence for the PoK, Gilgit and the Northern Territories: Pakistan's unity is already fragile and it should thank its stars if it can remain one country, but separation of the people of the Pakistan-occupied Kashmir, Gilgit and the Northern Territories is bound to lead to fissiparous movements in Pakistan already caught in ethnic strife. Also, Islamabad cannot relish the prospect of an independent Kashmir within a walking distance from Rawalpindi and its nuclear installations at Kahuta. What kind of broth is being cooked is not exactly known, but it can be that the Americans believe that Jammu and Ladakh should remain with India, the PoK, Gilgit and Northern Territories with Pakistan, and the Valley and the adjoining Muslim-dominated areas of Ladakh and Jammu be made an independent entity. This proposal discussed in the US academic circles in the past envisages the creation of an independent entity consisting of the Kashmir Valley, and the Muslim areas of Kargil in Ladakh and the Doda district in Jammu. This means that the State of Jammu and Kashmir—which has already been divided once—is sought to be partitioned again. This is a prospect which India cannot accept. There could be other proposals in the works, but these are not publicly known.

The Third Option idea is inherent in the American view that there are three parties to the Kashmir dispute: India, Pakistan and the people of Kashmir. The acceptance of this proposition, logically followed, will mean that India has to sit in negotiations on a three-side table with Pakistan and delegate from Jammu and Kashmir—a contingency it cannot accept and would hopefully avoid. To skirt Indian resistance to the three-party negotiations the Americans are apparently encouraging a larger exposure of Hurriyat and other Kashmiri leaders.

Pressure on India

India needs to tell the Americans and all others who wants to see a Conflict-free sub-continent that an already complex situation should not be complicated further. India, Pakistan and leaders from the Valley are being nudged into talks to work out a settlement among themselves. Many in New Delhi see in the effort a sort of pressure on India by the Democratic Administration. That this should have come at a time when India and the United States are engaged in improving their relations, opening up a lot of possibilities, is indeed intriguing.

A resolute Government should have the courage to make it clear to Washington that while it is keen to resolve the Kashmir dispute with Pakistan and its problems—although purely internal—with the people of the State, it cannot accept solutions thought of abroad. Given the history of mediatory attempts made by the West in the wake of the India-China conflict in 1962 and later—these showed a clear tilt towards Pakistan—India cannot take extraneous interest in Kashmir as innocent and accept a solution that will open a Pandora's box of problems in the sub-continent. If India could resist these now and tell all those who want to do good to the sub-continent to be more practical and show greater regard for India's resolve to maintain its territorial integrity. India should also make it clear to Pakistan that the time has come for it to stop meddling in India and sending arms and terrorists into Jammu and Kashmir.

India needs to be blunt with Pakistan in demanding an end to its export of terrorism, and frank with Washington that India's problem with the people of the Valley is of a domestic nature and India has the earnestness and capacity to sort it out politically. Once Pakistan has stopped aiding the secessionists in the Valley, India can discuss such issues with the people as autonomy with the framework of the constitution, devolution and relations among different regions of the State.

US Tilt towards Pakistan

Nearly 20 years after Zulfiqar Ali Bhutto expressed his pious intentions, the situation today is just the reverse, Pakistan having raised its military power almost double, and deploying larger and larger number of militants in Kashmir in its proxy war venture to win over the Kashmir Valley through aggressive ways. Pakistan has been spending double the amount in terms of its gross domestic product on defence than India. Whereas Pakistan's military expenditure has been to the tune of 6.8 per cent (of its budget), India's expenditure has been pegged down to 3.3 per cent. Pakistan has been neglecting many welfare sectors, including health and education of its people to divert the funds for military purposes. Almost three quarters of its population is illiterate. At present India has 1.18 soldiers per thousand citizens as compared to 5.37 of Pakistan and 2.41 of China. Thought Pakistan is one-seventh in population as compared to India, the strength of its armed forces is 803,000, as against 1.1 million of India and 3.2 million of China.

Pakistan's defence expenditure is 26.72 per cent of its total government expenditure, whereas India's expenditure is only 9.46 per cent. With regard to China this figure works out to 8.6 per cent. Pakistan has been trying to acquire most modern and sophisticated arms from any conceivable source in the world. Apart from the latest bonanza from the United States, the clinching evidence of which has been provided by the US satellite pictures. It is also developing Haft-1, 1A and 2 missiles with assistance of China. In contrast, the US bludgeoned Russia into reneging on the deal for supplying cryogenic engines to India in 1992. It also imposed sanctions against ISRO and Glavkosmos. In total disregard for India's feelings, the US administration directed it companies to obtain special permission before exporting any equipment relating to the Indian missile systems. The US has been exerting unrelenting pressure on this country not deploy Agni and Prithvi missiles.

The US tilt towards Pakistan really passes one's comprehension. Its officials consider the "drift" in their Pakistan policy as a mistake. They find it difficult to "write off" 120 million friendly Muslims. Perhaps, the US administration is trying to distinguish good Muslims from bad Muslims. It is also a fallacious argument that the supply of lethal arms would increase the American leverage in Pakistan. Its past record is a mirror to its present performance and future possibilities. From its brazen invasion of Kashmir in 1948 to its proxy war till this day its policies show no promise of reversing its plans of pinpricking and profaning India.

In the present situation that India is *vis-a-vis* the Kashmir problem, many in India have come to feel that probably a tough attitude, rather, than being soft all the time, towards the USA, which is playing the key-role today to help Pakistan, will be of benefit to India today. India's soft-minded leaders have always tried to pander to US wishes and thinking, particularly of late, considering the fact that US, is the only super-power and must be obeyed. But far too much subservience has also not paid off and it is time that India revises its policy in regard to USA, particularly *vis-a-vis* Kashmir and take up a challenging role, as it has in at least the past one year or so. This, many think in India, will bring about a turn in the situation in Kashmir, and the US is more likely to fall in line. India is also in a position to adopt this line, after having opened its doors to the world outside in opening the economy for investments and trade.

A Suggestion on these lines has been made by Lieutenant General, S.K. Sinha (retired), who was recently invited to address the prestigious US security institution RAND at Los Angeles. (RAND is a think-tank serving both the State Department and Pentagon). One return, Sinha wrote for the Hindustan Times in his "US tilt and Kashmir" in which he said that all his arguments were not likely to affect the deliberate decision of tilt towards Pakistan taken at Washington. "India has to be prepared for intensification of the proxy war by Pakistan. The futility of the policy of acquiescing to US pressure on deployment of

Prithvi or Agni missiles and rolling the red-carpet for junior US officials making repeated anti-India pronouncements and allowing them to meet the Prime Minister and other senior officials, should now dawn on the decision-makers at Delhi. India needs to emulate the Chinese approach towards the US. She should endeavour to build more friendly relations with China and some Islamic countries like Iran and Iraq. Simultaneously, she must also continue to maintain a qualitative and quantitative edge over Pakistan's military capability."

Islamic Fundamentalism

Sinha also says if it is true that today the people of Kashmir have become alienated and want to opt out of India, it was the outcome of lavish use of petro-dollars in the past two decades to propagate Islamic fundamentalism and a hate-India campaign through mosques and 'madrasas'. The situation got compounded by the political and administrative lapses of the Indian State. "It has to be appreciated that the question of secession or self-determination in Kashmir is as irrelevant as any such demand for Texas seceding from the USA and rejoining Mexico...As for respecting democracy in terms of the wishes of the people, there are occasions when commitment to an ideal has to take precedence over democracy. Abraham Lincoln rightly held that US people's commitment to the ideal of liberty for all, was more important than the democratic process in the slave-holding Southern States. They had in a perfectly democratic manner chosen to opt out of the Union. To uphold the ideal of Liberty, Lincoln fought the American Civil War, in which the people of the USA suffered more casualties than their total casualties in the First World War, the Second World War, the Korean War, the Vietnam War and the Gulf War put together. Similarly, India is committed to the ideal of secularism and is prepared to make sacrifice for upholding that ideal... Kashmir's secession from India for religious reasons will provide a great fillip to Hindu fundamentalism and jeopardise secularism in India. For the sake of two million Kashmiri Muslims, India cannot be a party to sacrificing the interests of 120 million other Indian Muslims. There are more Muslims in India than the total population of Pakistan. If China can hold on to Tibet, Russia to Chechnya and Sri Lanka to Jaffna, so is India perfectly capable of retaining the Kashmir Valley. However, India does not want to impose a military solution but is keen to resolve the issue politically. She is endeavouring to remove the present alienation of the people of Kashmir and it trying to win their hearts and minds. This process may be slow and long, but there is no other visible solution to the complex Kashmir problem.... It has to be remembered that India had accepted partition but not the two-nation theory. Only Muslim majority areas where the people wanted to be with Pakistan were to comprise that State. Thus a referendum had to be held in NWFP with over 95 per cent Muslim population, to ascertain the wishes of the people regarding remaining in India of opting for Pakistan. The perfectly legal accession of Kashmir was sanctified by moral sanction. Sheikh Abdullah, the popular Kashmiri leader fully supported accession and became the Chief Minister of the State. Plebiscite could not be held because of Pakistan's intransigence. The UN resolution of 13 August 1948 accepted by both India and Pakistan required Pakistan to withdraw her forces from Kashmir, prior to the holding of plebiscite. Pakistan failed to withdraw her forces and to this day, continues to be in illegal possession of a large part of Kashmir.*

Terrorism a Grave Threat to Civilised Living

International terrorism poses a grave threat to civilised living. Graduates from the University of Terrorism, located near Peshawar, were associated with the explosion at the World Trade Centre in New York and the bomb blasts in Bombay. History does not hitherto record a single instance, where the boundaries of a state have been altered as a result of terrorism. God forbid, if this is allowed to happen in Kashmir, it will give a tremendous boost to

---

*"U. S. Tilt and Kashmir" by Lt. Gen. S. K. Sinha (Retired), *Hindustan Times*, October 20, 1995.

international terrorism and Islamic fundamentalism, dangerously affecting the other trouble spots in the world. The world community must guard against this grave danger.

Kashmir has, over time, become a living symbol of India's secularism. Apart from the fact that the Indian Independence Act and the arrangements made thereunder cannot be re-written a half-century after the event, any scheme to separate the Kashmir Valley from India will reopen the wounds of the partition and send millions back on those blood-stained refugee trials. What, then remains for India to do? "First, to defeat Pakistan in the fourth armed conflict it has imposed on India, this time with the help of a small fanatic fringe of the Kashmir Valley's Muslim population. Second, to stand firm against any international meddling, especially a great powers meddling in Kashmir. One of history's great lessons is that great powers act, invariably always, in their own interests. America encourages the idea of an independent Kashmir for its own reasons. China opposes it in its own interests. Third, by reviving the political process in the Valley and last but not least, Pakistan's supporters in the Valley should be clearly told that self-determination is not something to be repeated with every succeeding generation. And certainly in India religion cannot be the basis for it."

It is true though that many Muslim from different parts of India did migrate to Pakistan at the time of Partition, just as virtually the entire non-Muslim population of West Pakistan had sought permanent refuge in India. For economic and other reasons, Muslims from Pakistan and Bangladesh still keep coming into India in their thousands in sarch of freedom and livelihood every year. The small pockets of Islamic fanatics in the Kashmir Valley, if they find life all that unbearable in the multi-religious and secular Indian State, should be given the option of migrating to Pakistan. And if Pakistan is truly solicitious of their well-being, it should not be too difficult for the two countries to amicably negotiate the terms of their orderly transfer to Pakistan. The only viable solution to the Kashmir problem lies in *de jure* recognition of the existing reality. That is what the Simla Agreement is all about.*

Bhutto Regime hopes for Strengthening its Position

According to political sources based in Rawalpindi the Bhutto tactic is to "play upon the pet theories of prominent US officials." For example, according to these sources, "US Vice-President, Al Gore sees visions of a grand civilisational reconciliation between Christianity and Islam, presumably in a future Gore administration." In such a process, the Pakistani side has "shrewdly put itself as an interlocutor." The Pakistani officials add that South Asia "is not at all a matter of concern for President Clinton, who has therefore, allowed the Vice-President and others to set policy there".

The Bhutto regime expects that there will be a period of severe political uncertainty in India after the 1996 polls. As a result, it hopes to get greater concessions from India, especially over Kashmir. According to political sources within Pakistan, the Bhutto regime's game plan in Kashmir is to "firstly wrest near-total autonomy for the Valley, through US pressure on India as well as by militant action." After the militants strengthen their base as a result of the freedom allowed to their activities after autonomy, "they will launch a struggle form unification with Pakistan." Thus, "before the two years when she has to face the electorate again, Ms. Bhutto hopes to annex the Valley, with the total support of the Clinton Administration these sources claim.†

Benazir Bhutto is also thinking in a wrong direction in another way (or is she merely pretending)—thinking that if India vacates Kashmir, it will automatically come to Pakistan. How perverted and wrong the thinking is obvious

---

*"Kashmir—Stick to Simla Accord" by M. Rasgotra, *Hindustan Times*, March 15, 1995.

†"Banazir's Plan for Kashmir Hinges on Indian Polls" by M. D. Nalapat, *Times of India*, October 14, 1995.

from the fact that, as it is, she cannot manage the problem of the MQM, which is like a festering sore on the face of Pakistan. Benazir knows how difficult it is for Pakistani Muslims to adjust themselves with the MQM Muslims. Kashmiri Muslims in their view will be far worse to adjust with. Kashmiri Muslims themselves must have weighed their own future. Will Kashmiri Muslims like to go to Pakistan? And adjust themselves to Islamic fundamentalism that prevails in Pakistan? Certainly, no. What then is Pakistan fighting for? To hand over Kashmir to 'Independent' Kashmir, or in other words, to the US?

Poll Conjectures

In the situation, Pakistan would probably still like to continue with its old thesis—despite the fact that it itself has been divided and torn of from its other part, Bangladesh, and that the MQM still divides Pakistan. Kashmir, where Muslims are not at all like Pakistani Muslims, will also not be like Pakistanis or pro-Pakistan, or want to integrate into Pakistan. What the Kashmiris want is also important.. They do not want to go to Pakistan. They would like to be independent and separate. It means that eventually Pakistan will also support the Independent Kashmir move and would like to hand over the Valley to an informal control by the USA, and thereby have the satisfaction of tearing off Kashmir from India. A well-known writer, Prem Shanker Jha, has also stated in an article that "the Kashmiris may be fed up with India, but they want independence and do not want to merge with Pakistan."

In a controversial article, the new magazine, outlook, has in a recent issue predicted on the basis of a 'poll' of Kashmiri opinion, that 72 per cent of the people there want independence, 19 per cent merger with Pakistan, 7 per cent are for greater autonomy within India and 2 per cent are undecided. The Outlook has also stated that 66 per cent, or two-thirds of the people there disapprove of the increasing Islamic fundamentalism. Among the favoured leaders, Shabir Shah comes first with 37 per cent support and Yaseen Malik second with 13 per cent.

The 'poll' by the magazine has not been known for its impartiality or as reflecting there factual state of affairs. Not enough details are also provided about the profile of the poll. Information about age-levels, professions, sex, locations (where the poll was conducted and whether it was limited to Srinagar) and other sociological factors would have enhanced the authenticity of the report.

Kashmiris to become another Group of Mohajirs?

Questions are already being asked in Pakistan as to what that country can offer to the people of Kashmir that India cannot. Pakistan is under the delusion that people of Kashmir will elect to become another group of mohajirs in the Islamic Republic of Pakistan. A torrent of Propaganda has been pouring into Kashmir in the recent past from across the border, most of it relating to the brave deeds of the 'freedom fighters' of the Kashmir Valley and the sacrifices made by 'Mujahids' who have come from Pakistan to aid their co-religionists across the border who are waging a 'Jehad'. Each report projected on the Pakistan media and with the number of people who have become 'shaheeds' after, of course, inflicting heavy casualties on the Indian security forces. The language is familiar. It could have been drafted by the spokesperson of any security force in any part of the world. The objective is to keep the pot boiling and the conflict continuing—till Kashmir becomes a part of Pakistan. For the sake of record, Pakistan will continue to render 'moral' help to keep the fight going. Whatever other 'help' is needed would continue in a clandestine manner. But that would stop short of anything more than training young boys from Kashmir, arming them, and their induction into the state of mercenaries, who are at a loose end after the conclusion of the Afghan war.

Pakistan is also committed to raise the Kashmir issue in every international forum. Delegations will go to all international gatherings all over the world, whatever be the subject on the agenda of the Conferences—defence, human rights, economy, health care or even environment—

Kashmir issue will be raised. The delegation from Pakistan would consist of diplomats accompanying the entourage of members of non-Governmental organisations and media presence. It is expected that India too would follow suit, including the secessionists from Kashmir. The latest to join the bandwagon have been the representatives of the Kul Jamiat Hurriyet Conference.

In an article published in the *News* (a Pakistani Publication) of May 18, 1995, Anees Jilani wrote: "More important is the question of the future of Kashmir. For some reasons, we in Pakistan have presumed that Kashmiris would opt for Pakistan if given a choice between India and Pakistan. Has it ever occurred to our policy-makers that we could be wrong?" Anees Jilani then referred to the statement of Amanulla Khan, claiming to be the JKLF chief, "Limiting the choice of Kashmiris only to the State's accession to India or Pakistan in tantamount to denying them their very right to determine their own further." Anees Jilani argued: "For argument's sake, if India is forced to vacate Kashmir, what will happen to Azad Kashmir and Northern Areas? First India, even in the face of the fierce uprising against its rules, cannot be expected to vacate the Kashmir Valley without seeking something in return...If India gives up Kashmir, it will ask Pakistan to vacate Azad Kashmir and Northern Areas in return. Is Pakistan prepared to do this?" Eqbal Ahmed in his article in the *Dawn* of May 21, 1995, quotes a former Pakistani army officer: "We ought to do homework, which we do not do. India's position is less frozen than ours. It is readying now for Kashmir's internal autonomy. In time, this could become an attractive alternative to worn-out Kashmiris. India's governing elite should not be under-estimated. It is sophisticated, capable of planning and executing a policy, and its political system is stable." The *Dawn* commentator, Anees Jilani, also dwelt on the decision of the Government of India to permit Kashmiri leaders to participate in Pakistan Day celebrations at the Pakistan High Commission in New Delhi and later to meet the Pakistani President, there, and Said: "The Indians perhaps are striving to get the All Parties Hurriyat Conference leadership to realise that Pakistan has nothing to offer that India cannot give them. Both countries oppose Kashmir's independence."

Have the leaders of the Hurriyat Conference realised this? Perhaps the fact is that the Hurriyat leaders think that Pakistan can offer many more things than India. India can only offer a democratic government, autonomy and peace. But Pakistan can offer continued strife, Kalashnikovs and move important, opportunities to visit world capitals to complain against India, and a future to the people of Kashmir of becoming another group of Mohajirs in the Islamic Republic of Pakistan.

Why the West does not have a Kashmir?

While addressing a group of Indian industrialists recently, the US Assistant Secretary of State, Robin Raphel, emphasised on the need of "a negotiated settlement" on Kashmir. But if faced with a similar problem, would the liberal democrater of the West ever negotiate on what would amount to their countries' unity and integrity. A selective reading of the constitutional history of western countries makes it obvious that the answer to the above question is "No". The western states can constitutionally subvert, if necessary, the democratic rights of one section of its people, if they try to undermine the state. Clearly, the concept of sovereignty in the West is not particularly liberal, since many states are not based on consent.

Prakash Nanda says: Take the case of Switzerland which witnessed a civil war in 1840, following the revolt of the seven cantons (equivalent to provinces) predominantly inhabited by the catholics. These cantons formed a League and attempted to break away from the country but failed. It was made absolutely clear that "Integrity of the territory is not negotiable." This is the case with arguably the world's most representative democracy for more than 700 years...Enforced in 1787, the US constitution was decided by only 13 of its present 50 states. It is a common knowledge that many of the states of the US, particularly in the south and west, were acquired by non-democratic means. The doubts over the viability of the US as a single country were removed only after the 1860 civil war ended. Seven southern states followed South Carolina in adopting an ordinance of "secession from the union" and forming "the Confederate States of America." Southern leaders regarded secession as legally justifiable on the ground of their states' "rights theory of constitution." Sovereignty, they declared, belonged to the states, not to the union. However, President Lincoln, in 1861 asserted that no state had constitutional rights to secede and that he would not "recognise that the union could be divided." The American civil war, like the Swiss case, made it very clear that the authority conferred on the federal government by the various states was "an irrevocable authority."

The constitution of France and Germany also underline the same theme that once formed, the countries cannot be undone. The provinces of the present-day Australia were so distant and isolated from each other that until 1883, all attempts to create some form of union had yielded no results. The constitution now envisages one perpetual federal union and as such no constituent unit can secede there from. "Viewed thus, what India is witnessing in Kashmir is not unique. Kashmir's grievances need to be addressed sympathetically. But to recognise Kashmir's right of self-determination is to challenge the very concept of India. It cannot be acceptable."*

---

*"Imagine West Having a Kashmir" by Prakash Nanda, *Times of India,* November 16, 1995.

Appendices

Appendix I

INDIA'S LEGAL RIGHT OVER JAMMU AND KASHMIR

Instrument of Accession executed by Maharajah Hari Singh on October 26, 1947:

Wherease the Indian Independence Act, 1947, provides that as form the fifteenth day of August, nineteen hundred and forty seven, there shall bet set up an independent Dominion known as India, and that the Government of India Act, 1935, shall with such omissions, additions, adaptations and modifications as the Governor-General may be order specify, be applicable to the Dominion of India.

And whereas the Government of India Act, 1935, as so adapted by the Governor-General, provides that an Indian State may accede to the Dominion of India by an Instrument of Accession actuated by the Ruler thereof.

Now, therefore, I Shriman Inder Mahinder Rajrajeswar Maharajadhiraj Shri Hari Singhji, Jammu and Kashmir Naresh Tibbet adi Deshadhipati, Ruler of Jammu and Kashmir State, in the exercise of my Sovereignty in and over my said State do hereby execute this my instrument of Accession, and

1. I hereby declare that I accede to the Dominion of India with the intent that the Governor-General of India, the Dominion Legislature, the Federal Court and any other Dominion authority established for the purpose of the Dominion shall by virtue of this my instrument of Accession but subject always to the terms thereof, and for the purposes only of the Dominion, exercise in relation to the State of Jammu and Kashmir (hereinafter referred to as "this State)" such functions as may be vested in them by or under the Government of India Act, 1935, as in force in the Dominion of India, on the 15th day of August 1947, (which Act as so in force in hereafter referred to as "the Act)."
2. I hereby assume the obligation of ensuring that due effect is given to provision of the Act within his State so far as hey are applicable therein by virtue of this my Instrument of Accession.
3. I accept the matters specified in the schedule as the matters with respect to which the Dominion Legislature may make law for this State.
4. I hereby declare that I accede to the Dominion of India on the assurance that if an agreement is made between the Governor-General and the Ruler of this State whereby any function in relation to the administration in this State of any law of the Dominion legislature shall be exercised by the Ruler of the State, then any such agreement shall be construed and have effect accordingly.
5. The terms by this my Instrument of Accession shall not be varied by any amendment of the Act or the Indian Independence Act, 1947, unles such amendment is accepted by me by Instrument supplementary to this Instrument.
6. Nothing in his Instrument shall empower the Dominion Legislature to make any law for this State authorizing the compulsory acquisition of land for any purpose, but I hereby undertake that should the

Dominion for the purpose of a Dominion law which applies in this State deem it necessary to acquire any land, I will at their request acquire the land at their expense, or if the land belongs to me transfer it to them on such terms as may be agreed or, in default of agreement, determined by an arbitrator to be appointed by the Chief Justice of India.

7. Nothing in his Instrument shall be deemed to commit in any way to acceptance of any future constitution of India or to fetter my discretion to enter into agreement with the Gòvernment of India under any such future constitution.
8. Nothing in his Instrument affects the continuance of my Sovereignty in and over this State, or, save as provided by or under this Instrument, the exercise of any powers, authority and rights now enjoyed by me as Ruler of this State or the validity of any law at present in force in this State.
9. I hereby declare that I execute this Instrument on behalf of this State and that reference in this Instrument to me or to the Ruler of the State is to be construed as including a reference to my heiers and successors.

Given under my hand this twenty sixth day of October, nineteen hundred and forty seven.

Sd/-
Harri Singh
Maharajadhiraj of Jammu and Kashmir State

Acceptance of Accession by the Governor-General of India

I do hereby accept this Instrument of Accession.

Dated this twenty seventh day of October, nineteen hundred and forty seven.

Sd/-
Mountbatten of Burma
Governor-General of India

SCHEDULE

The matters with respect to which the Dominion Legislature may make laws for this State

A. *Defence*

1. The naval, military and air forces of the Dominion and any other armed forces raised or maintained by the Dominion, any armed forces, including forces rasied or maintained by an acceding State, which are attached to, or operating with, any of the armed forces of the Dominion.
2. Naval, military and air force works, administration of cantonment areas.
3. Arm, fire-arms, ammunition.
4. Explosives.

B. *External Affairs*

1. External affairs, the implementing of treaties and agreements with other countries; extradition, including the surrender of criminals and accused persons to parts of His Majesty's dominion outside India.
2. Admission into, and emigration and expulsion from, India including in relation thereto the regulation of the movements in India of persons who are not British subjects domiciled in India or subject of any acceding State, pilgrimages to place beyond India.

C. *Communications*

1. Posts and telegraphs, including telephones, wirless, broadcasting, and other like forms of communication.
2. Federal railways; the regulation of all railways other then minor railways in respect of safety, maximum and minimum rates and fare, station and services terminal charges, interchange of traffic and the re-

sponsibility of railways administrations as carriers of goods and passenger; the regulation of minor railways in respect of safety and the responsibility of the administration of such railways as carriers of goods and passengers.

3. Maritime shipping and navigation, including shipping and navigation on tidal waters; Admiralty jurisdiction.
4. Port quarantine.
5. Major ports, that is to say, the declaration and delimitation of such ports, and the constitution and powers of Port Authorities therein.
6. Aircraft and air navigation; the provision and aerodromes; regulation and organisation of air traffic and or aerodromes.
7. Lighthouse, including lightships, beacons and other provisions for the safety of shipping .
8. Carriage of passengers and goods by sea or by air.
9. Extension of the powers and Jurisdiction of members of the police force belonging to any unit to railway area outside that unit.

D. *Ancillary*

1. Elections to the Dominion Legislature, subject to the provisions of the Act and of any Order made thereunder.
2. Offences against laws with respect to any of the aforesaid matters.
3. Inquiries and statistics for the purposes of any of the aforesaid matters.
4. Jurisdiction and power of all courts with respect to any of the aforesaid matters but, except with the consent of the Ruler of the Acceding State, not so as to confer any jurisdiction or powers upon any courts other than ordinarily exercising jurisdiction in or in relation to that State.

Appendix II

LETTER OF OCTOBER 26, 1947 FROM MAHARAJADHIRAJA HARI SINGH TO LORD MOUNTBATTEN, REQUESTING THE ACCESSION OF THE STATE TO INDIA

My Dear Lord Mountbatten,

I have to inform Your Excellency that a grave emergency has arisen in my State and request immediate assistance of your Government.

As Your Excellency is aware, the State of Jammu and Kashmir has not acceded to either the Dominion of India or to Pakistan. Geographically, my State is contiguous to both the Dominions. It has vital economical and cultural links with both of them. Besides my State has a common boundary with the Soviet Republic and China. In their external relations the Dominions of India and Pakistan cannot ignore this fact.

I wanted to take time to decide to which Dominion I should accede, whether it is not in the best interest of both the Dominions and my State to stand independent, of course with friendly and cordial relation with both.

I, accordingly approached the Dominions of India and Pakistan to enter into a standstill agreement with my State. The Pakistan Government accepted this arrangement. The Dominion of India desired further discussion with representatives of my Government. I could not arrange this in view of the developments indicated below. In fact the Pakistan Government under the standstill agreement is operating the Post and Telegraph system inside the State.

Though we have got a standstill agreement with the Pakistan Government, that Government permitted and increasing strangulation of supplies like food, salt and petrol to my State.

Afridis, soldiers in plain cloth, and desperadoes, with modern weapons, have been allowed to infilter into the State at first in Poonch area, then from Sialkot and finally in mass in the area adjoining Hazara district on the Ramkote side. The result has been that the limited number of troops at the disposal of the State had to be despersed and thus had to face the enemy at several points simultaneously so that it has become difficult to stop the wanton destruction of life and property and lotting. The Mahoora Power House which supplies the electric current to the whole of Srinagar has been burnt. The number of women who have been kidnapped and raped makes my heart bleed. The wild forces thus let loose on the State are marching on with the aim of capturing Srinagar, the Summer Capital of my Government, as a first step to over running the whole State.

"The mass infiltration of tribesmen drawn from the distant areas of the North-West Frontier Province, coming regularly in moter trucks, using Manshera-Muzaffarabad road and fully armed with up-to-date weapons cannot possibly be done without the knowledge of the Provincial Government of the North-West Frontier Province and the Government of Pakistan. In spite of repeated appeals made by my Government no attempt has been made to check those raiders or stop them from coming into my State. In fact, both the Pakistan Radio and Press have reported thse occurrences. The Pakistan Radio even put out a story that a provisional Government has been set up in Kashmir. The people of my State both Muslims and non-Muslims, generally have taken no part at all.

With the conditions obtaining at present in my State and the great emergency of the situation as it exists I have no option but to ask for help from the Indian Dominion. Naturally they cannot send the help asked for by me without any State acceding to the Dominion of India. I have accordingly decided to do so. The other alternative is to leave my State and my people to free-booters. On this basis no civilised Government can exist or be maintained. The alternative I will never allow to happen so long as I am the Ruler of the State and I have life to defend my country.

I may also inform Your Excellency's Government that it is my intention at once to set up an Interim Government and ask Sheikh Abdullah to carry the responsibilities in this emergency with my Prime Minister.

If my State has to be saved, immediate assistance must be available at Srinagar. Mr. V.P. Menon is fully aware of the situation and he will explain to you, it further explanation is needed.

In haste and with kindest regards,

Yours sincerely,

Hari Singh

Appendix III

TEXT OF U.N. RESOLUTION

The Resolution of the U.N. Security Council of August 13,1948 to which Pakistan was a party but observed it only in its breach, reads:

The United Nations Commission for India and Pakistan.

Having given careful consideration to the points of view expressed by the representatives of India and Pakistan regarding the situation in the State of Jammu and Kashmir; and

Being of the opinion the prompt cessation of hostilities and the correction of condition the continuance of which is likely to endanger international peace and security are essential to implementation of its endeavours to assist the Governments of India and Pakistan in effecting a final settlement of the situation;

Resolves to submit simultaneously to the Governments of India and Pakistan the following proposal.

Part 1: Cease-Fire Order

A. The Government of India and Pakistan agree that their respective High Commands will issue separately and simultaneously a cease-fire order to apply to all forces under their control in the State of Jammu and Kashmir as of the earliest practicable date or dates to be mutually agreed upon within four days after these proposals have been accepted by both Governments.

B. The High Commands of Indian and Pakistani forces agree to refrain from taking any measures that might augment the military potential of the forces under their control in the State of Jammu and Kashmir.

(For the purpose of these proposals forces under their control shall be considered to include all forces, organized and unorganized, fighting or participating in hostilities on their respective sides.)

C. The Commanders-in-Chief of the forces of India and Pakistan shall promptly confer regarding any necessary local changes in present dispositions which may facilitate the cease-fire.

D. In its discretion and as the Commission may find practicable, the Commission will appoint military observers who under the authority of the Commission and with the cooperation of both Commands, will supervise the observance of the cease-fire order.

E. The Government of India and the Government of Pakistan agree to appeal to their respective peoples to assist in creating and maintaining and atmosphere favourable to the promotion of further negotiations.

Part II: Truce Agreement

Simultaneously with the acceptance of the proposal for the immediate cessation of the hostilities as outlined in

Part I, both Government accept the following principles as a basis for the formulation of a truce agreement, the details of which shall be worked out in discussion between their representatives and the Commission.

A

1. As the presence of troops of Pakistan in the territory of the State of Jammu and Kashmir constitutes a material change in the situation since it was represented by the Government of Pakistan before the Security Council, the Government of Pakistan agrees to withdraw its troops from that State.
2. The Government of Pakistan will use its best endeavour to secure the withdrawal from the State of Jammu and Kashmir of tribesmen and Pakistan nationals not normally resident therein who have entered the State for the purpose of fighting.
3. Pending a final solution, the territory evacuated by the Pakistani troops will be administered by the local authorities under the surveillance of the Commission.

B

1. When the Commission shall have notified the Government of India that the tribesmen and Pakistani nationals referred to in Part II-A-2 hereof have withdrawn, thereby terminating the situation which was represented by the Government of India to the Security Council as hiving occasioned the presence of Indian forces in the State of Jammu and Kashmir, and further, that the Pakistani forces are being withdrawn from the State of Jammu and Kashmir, the Government of India agrees to begin to withdraw the bulk of its forces from that State in stages to be agreed upon with the Commission.

2. Pending the acceptance of the conditions for the final settlement of the situation in the State of Jammu and Kashmir, the Indian Government will maintain within the lines existing at the moment of the cease-fire the minimum strength of its forces which in agreement with the Commission are considered necessary to assist local authorities in the observance of law and order. The Commission will have observers stationed where it deems necessary.
3. The Government of India will undertake to ensure that the Government of the State of Jammu and Kashmir will take all measures within its powers to make it publicly known that peace, law and order will be safeguarded and that all human and political rights will be guaranteed.
4. Upon signature the full text of the truce agreement or a communique containing the principles thereof as agreed upon between the two Governments and the Commission, will be made public.

Part III

The Government of India and the Government of Pakistan reaffirm their wish that the future status of the State of Jammu and Kashmir shall be determined in accordance with the will of the people and to that end, upon acceptance of the truce agreement, both Governments agree to enter into consultations with the Commission to determine fair and equitable conditions whereby such free expression will be assured.

Appendix IV

THE DIXON REPORT

Text of the summing up and concluding portion of the report of Sir Owen Dixon, UN Representative for India and

Pakistan on Kashmir, submitted to the Security Council in September, 1950

95. It will be seen that two main lines have been pursued in the attempt, which have been made to settle the dispute between the two countries about the State of Jammu and Kashmir. The attempt to find a solution by taking a plebiscite over the whole State and so decided by a majority to which country the entire State shall go has its origin in the first proceedings before the Security Council. It would be recalled that by the Resolution of 21 April 1948 the desire of both India and Pakistan that the question of accession of the State to one or other of them should be decided by and free and impartial plebiscite was noted with satisfaction. In the agreed resolution of the United Nations Commission for India and Pakistan January 5, 1949 there is recital of the acceptance by the Governments of both countries of the principle that the question of the accession of the State to India or Pakistan would be decided through the democratic method of a free and impartial plebiscite.

96. From the date of this resolution until the present there have been continual efforts to bring about conditions in which the preparations for taking a poll might go forward. No one has supposed that they could even begin while much of the respective territories on either side of the cease-fire line was occupied by opposed armies and their base units. There are in addition many other obstacles to the holding of a free and fair plebiscite which must be removed before the State would be ready for the organisation and machinery which the taking of a poll would make necessary. Unfortunately all this has been made to depend upon the agreement of the parties. It is enough to refer to paragraph 2, 6(a) and 10 of the Resolution of 5 January 1949 and to the provisions of the Resolution of 13 August 1948 upon which these paragraphs hang.

97. There is, I believe, on the side of India a conception of what ought to be done to ascertain the real will of the people which is not that tacitly assumed by me. Doubtless it is a conception which Pakistan does not share. The resolution of January 1949 contains some rather general provisions in relation to the holding of the plebiscite and the antecedent steps, and about, these more general provisions the parties were able to agree. But to apply propositions of this kind a programme of practical acts and physical events must be agreed upon. Without that it is impossible for the Plebiscite Administrator to begin the extensive and difficult work of organizing the taking of a poll. It is the practical measures which have proved the obstacle, not the mere general propositions.

98. Pakistan has complained of India's failure to agree on the practical measures which must precede the preparations for the actual taking of a poll, and has maintained that this failure is the result of a deliberate policy. But the fact remains that under the resolutions the agreement of India to the course to be pursued in these matters is a condition-precedent to carrying out a plebiscite of the State, and there is no such agreement, Moreover, the United Nations Commission failed in its efforts to secure an agreement upon them; I failed in mine; neither party put forward any other proposals and both appeared to concur in the view that the possibility of agreement has been exhausted.

99. The contention of Pakistan that it was incumbent on India to agree did not advance the matter practically. It was in these circumstances that I decided to turn away from a plebiscite of the whole State, an "over all" plebiscite, as a method of solving the problem of Kashmir. Partition of the whole State between the two countries is of course an obvious alternative. But unfortunately the Valley of Kashmir cannot itself be partitioned and it is an area claimed by each side. Pakistan claims it not only because it is

predominantly Muslim but also because the Jhelum river flows from it and Pakistan will not readily give up her claim. India is just as insistent upon her claim that has the advantage of possession. Some method of allocating the Kashmir Valley to one party or the other, is, therefore, essential to any plan of partition.

100. I am inclined to the view that no method of allocating the Valley to one or the other of the contending parties is available except a poll of the inhabitants. By the inhabitants I mean those of them who fulfil whatever may be fixed as the test of eligibility to vote. The difficulty of using the expedient of a plebiscite appears to lie entirely in the conflict between on the one hand the necessity of ensuring that the plebiscite is held in conditions which make it an effective means of ascertaining the real will of the people independently formed and freely expressed and, on the other hand, certain conceptions or preconceptions of the Indian Government. These are based, in part, on what India conceives to be the origin and course of the fighting in 1947 and 1948 and part on her unwillingness to have any interference to the civil administration. In addition, it may be, as I have suggested that a different conception exists of the process of ascertaining the will of the people. Although I myself found no reconciliation of this conflict possible, it may be that India's help some resolution of the conflict may be discovered. She may come to realize that the necessity of practical measures which will really secure the freedom and fairness of a plebiscite must be paramount over these conceptions. At all events I have formed the opinion that if there is any chance of settling the dispute over Kashmir by agreement between India and Pakistan it now lies in partition and in some means of allocating the Valley rather than in an overall plebiscite. The reasons for this may be shortly stated (emphasis added).

101. The State of Jammu and Kashmir is not really a unit

geographically, demographically or economically. It is an agglomeration of territories brought under the political power of One Maharaja. That is the unity it possesses. If as a result of an overall plebiscite the State as an entirety passed to India, there would be large movements of Muslims and another refugee problem would arise for Pakistan who would be expected to receive them in very great numbers. If the result favoured Pakistan a refugee problem, although not of such dimensions, would arise for India, because of the movement of Hindus and Sikhs. Almost all this would be avoided by partition. Great areas of the State are unequivocally Muslim. Other areas are predominantly Hindu. There is a further area which is Buddhist. No one doubts the sentiment of the great majority of the inhabitants of these areas. The interest of the people, the justice as well as the permanence of the settlement, and the imperative necessity of avoiding another refugee problem all point to the wisdom of adopting partition as the principle of settlement and of abandoning that of an overall plebiscite. But in addition the economic and geographic considerations point in the same direction. The difficulty in partitioning the State is to form a sound judgement where the line should be drawn.

102. While what I have said deals broadly with the State as a whole, it is by no means easy to fix the limits on each side. That is because it is necessary that the territory allocated to each side should continuous in itself and should be continuous with that country, because there are pockets of people whose faith and affiliations are different from those of people by whom they are cut off, because the changes in the distribution of population as the result of the troubles cannot be completely ignored and because geographical features remain important in fixing what may prove an international frontier.

103. I shall not deal with the matter with more particularity, and I say so much only in case the Security

Council should be of opinion that it should take further steps to effect a settlement between the parties. But for myself I doubt whether it may not be better to leave the parties to themselves in negotiating terms for settlement of the problem how to dispose of Jammu and Kashmir between them. So far the attitude of the parties has been to throw the whole responsibility upon the Security Council or its representatives of settling the dispute not withstanding that except by agreement between them there was no means of settling it.

104. When actual fighting was going on between them it was natural, if not necessary, that the Security Council and the Commission as its delegate should intervene between them and propose terms to stop the hostilities and the question came to be how to settle the rival claims to Kashmir, the initiative was still left with the Security Council and the Commission. The whole question has now been thoroughly discussed by the parties with the Security Council, the Commission and myself and the possible methods of settlement have been exhaustively investigated. It is perhaps best that the initiative should now pass back to the parties. At all events, I am not myself prepared to recommend any further course of action on the part of the Security Council for the purpose of assisting the parties to settle between them how the State of Jammu and Kashmir is to be disposed of.

105. The continued maintenance of two armies facing one another across a cease-fire line is another matter. A danger to peace must exist while this state of things continues. Except for mutual distrust and fear, one or another, there is no reason why the two countries should go on maintaining armies separated only by the cease-fire line. It is a boundary which might be kept by check posts and the like in the same way as any frontier between countries of peace. It is hard to believe that the Indian and Pakistan Chiefs of Staff would have any difficulty in arranging for a concur-

rent reduction of forces or in effecting the necessary changes in the manner in which the cease-fire line is held, if they were instructed by their respective Governments to meet for the purpose.

106. Before leaving the sub-continent I addressed to the Prime Ministers severally a request that this should be done. It is a matter in which the Security Council is directly concerned because it involves a proximate danger to peace.

107. I recommend that the Security Council should press the parties to reduce the military strength holding the cease-fire line to the normal protection of a peace-time frontier.

108. In the meantime it is my recommendation that the party of United Nations Military Observers be retained on the cease-fire line. They cannot continue there indefinitely but after a time the question of their withdrawal might be settled in consultation with two Governments.

Sd/-
Owen Dixon
United Nations Representative
for India and Pakistan

15 September, 1950

Appendix V

THE TASHKENT DECLARATION

The Prime Minister of India and the President of Pakistan, having met at Tashkent and having discussed the existing relations between India and Pakistan hereby declare their firm resolve to restore normal and peaceful relations between their countries and to promote understanding and friendly relations between their peoples. They consider the attainment of these objectives of vital importance for the welfare of the 600 million people of India and Pakistan.

(*i*) The Prime Minister of India and the President of Pakistan agree that both sides will exert all efforts to create good neighbourly relations between India and Pakistan in accordance with the United Nations Charter. They reaffirm their obligation under the Charter not to have recourse to force and to settle their disputes through peaceful means. They considered that the interests of peace in their region and particularly in the Indo-Pakistan sub-continent and, indeed, the interests of the peoples of India and Pakistan were not served by the continuance of tension between the two countries. It was against this background that Jammu and Kashmir was discussed and each of the sides set forth its respective position.

(*ii*) The Prime Minister of India and the President of Pakistan have agreed that all armed personnel of the two countries shall be withdrawn not later than 25 February, 1966, to the position they had prior to 5 August, 1965, and both sides shall observe the ceasefire terms on the ceasefire line.

(*iii*) The Prime Minister of India and the President of Pakistan have agreed that relations between India and Pakistan shall be based to the principle of non-interference in the internal affairs of each other.

(*iv*) The Prime Minister of India and the President of Pakistan have agreed that both sides will discourage any propaganda directed against the other country and will encourage propaganda which promotes the development of friendly relations between the two countries.

(*v*) The Prime Minister of India and the President of Pakistan have agreed that the High Commissioner of India to Pakistan and the High Commissioner of Pakistan to India will return to their posts and that the normal functioning of diplomatic missions of both countries will be resorted. Both government shall observe the Vienna Convention of 1961 on diplomatic intercourse.

(*vi*) The Prime Minister of India and the President of Pakistan have agreed to consider measures towards the restoration of economic and trade relations, communications as well as cultural exchanges between India and Pakistan and to take measures to implement the existing agreement between India and Pakistan.

(*vii*) The Prime Minister of India the President of Pakistan have agreed that they will give instructions to their respective authorities to carry out the repatriation of the prisoners of war.

(*viii*) The Prime Minister of India and the President of Pakistan have agreed that the two sides will continue the discussion of questions relating to the problems of refugees and evictions/illegal immigrations. They also agreed that both sides will create conditions which will prevent the exodus of people. They further agree to discuss the return of the property and assets taken over by either side in connection with the conflict.

(*ix*) The Prime Minister of India and the President of Pakistan have agreed that the two sides will continue meetings both at the highest and at other levels of matters of direct concern to both countries. Both sides have recognised the need to set up joint Indian-Pakistani bodies which will report to their government in order to decide what further steps should be taken.

The Prime Minister of India and the President of Pakistan record their feelings, deep appreciation and gratitude to the leaders of the Soviet Union, the Soviet Government and personally to the Chairman of the Council of

Ministers of the USSR for their constructive, friendly and noble part in bringing about the present meeting which has resulted in mutually satisfactory results. They also express to the Government and friendly people of Uzbekistan their thankfulness for their overwhelming reception and generous hospitality.

They invite the Chairman of the Council of Ministers of the USSR to witness this declaration.

Prime Minister of India	President of Pakistan
Lal Bahadur Shastri	Mohd. Ayub Khan

Tashkent, 10 January 1966

Appendix VI

SIMLA AGREEMENT

Simla Agreement on Bilateral Relations between India and Pakistan signed by Prime Minister Mrs. Indira Gandhi, and President of Pakistan, Mr. Z.A. Bhutto, in Simla on July 3, 1972.

1. The Government of India and the Government of Pakistan are resolved that the two countries put an end to the conflict and confrontation that have hitherto marred their relations and work for the promotion of a friendly and harmonious relationship and the establishment of durable peace in the sub-continent so that both countries may henceforth devote their resources and energies to the pressing task of advancing the welfare of their people. In order to achieve this objective, the Government of India and

the Government of Pakistan have agreed as follows:

(*i*) That the principles and purposes of the Charter of the United Nations shall govern the relations between the two countries.

(*ii*) That the two countries are resolved to settle their differences by peaceful means through bilateral negotiations or by any other peaceful means mutually agreed upon between them. Pending the final settlement of any of the problems between the two countries, neither side shall unilaterally after the situation and both shall prevent the organisation, assistance or encouragement of any acts detrimental to the maintenance of peace and harmonious relations.

(*iii*) That the prerequisite for reconciliation, good neighbourliness and durable peace between them is a commitment by both the countries to peaceful co-existence, respect for each other's territorial integrity and sovereignty and non-interference in each other's internal affairs, on the basis of equality and mutual benefit.

(*iv*) That the basic issues and causes of conflict which have bedevilled the relations between the two countries for the last 25 years shall be resolved by peaceful means.

(*v*) That they shall always respect each other's national unity, territorial integrity, political independence and sovereign equality.

(*vi*) That in accordance with the Charter of the United Nations, they will refrain from the threat or use of force against the territorial integrity or political independence of each other.

2. Both governments will take all steps within their power to prevent hostile propaganda directed against each other. Both countries will encourage the dissemination of such information as would promote the development of friendly relations between them.

3. In order progressively to restore and normalise relations between the two countries step by step, it was agreed that:

   (*i*) Steps shall be taken to resume communications, postal telegraphic, sea, land, including border posts, and air links, including over-flights.

   (*ii*) Appropriate steps shall be taken to promote travel facilities for the nationals of the other country.

   (*iii*) Trade and cooperation in economic and other agreed fields will be resumed as far as possible.

   (*iv*) Exchange in the fields of science and culture will be promoted.

   In this connection delegations from the two countries will meet from time to time to work out the necessary details.

4. In order to initiate the process of the establishment of durable peace, both the governments agree that:

   (*i*) Indian and Pakistani forces shall be withdrawn to their side of the international border.

   (*ii*) In Jammu and Kashmir, the line of control resulting from the cease-fire of December 17, 1971, shall be respected by both sides without prejudice to the recognised position of either side. Neither side shall seek to alter it unilaterally, irrespective or mutual differences and legal interpretations. Both sides further undertake to refrain from the threat or the use of force in violation of this line.

   (*iii*) The withdrawals shall commence upon entry into force of this agreement and shall be completed within a period of 30 days thereof.

5. This agreement will be subject to ratification by both countries in accordance with their respective constitutional procedures, and will come into force with effect from the date on which the instruments of ratification are exchanged.

6. Both governments agree that their respective heads will meet again at a mutually convenient time in the future and that in the meanwhile the representatives of the two sides will meet to discuss further the modalities and managements for the establishment of durable peace and normalisation of relations, including the questions of repatriation of prisoners of war and civilian internees, a final settlement of Jammu and Kashmir and the resumption of diplomatic relations.

Indira Gandhi	Zulfiqar Ali Bhutto
Prime Minister	Prime Minister
Republic of India	Islamic Republic of Pakistan

Simla, the 2nd July, 1972

Appendix VII

KASHMIR ACCORD (FEBRUARY 1975)

Agreed conclusions which led to Sheikh Mohammad Abdullah's accord with Mrs. Indira Gandhi, Prime Minister, and his subsequent assumption of office as Chief Minister in February, 1975.

1. The State of Jammu and Kashmir which is a constituent unit of the Union of India, shall, in its relations with the Union, continue to be governed by Article 370 of the Constitution on India.

2. The residuary powers of legislation shall remain with the State; however, Parliament will continue to have power to make laws relating to the prevention of activities directed towards disclaiming, questioning or disrupting the sovereignty and territorial integrity

of India or bringing about cession of a part of the territory of India or secession of a part of the territory of India from the Union or causing insult to the Indian National Flag, the Indian National Anthem and the Constitution.

3. Where any provision of the Constitution of India had been applied to the State of Jammu and Kashmir with adaptations and modifications, such adaptations and modifications can be altered or repealed by an Order of the President under Article 370, each individual proposal in this behalf being considered on its merits; but provisions of the Constitution of India already applied to the State of Jammu and Kashmir without adaptation on modification are unalterable.

4. With a view to assuring freedom to the State of Jammu and Kashmir to have its own legislation on matters like welfare measures, cultural matters, social security, personal law, and procedural laws, in a manner suited to the special conditions in the State, it is agreed that the State Government can review the laws made by Parliament or extended to the State after 1953 on any matter relatable to the Concurrent List and may decide which of them, in its opinion, needs amendment or repeal. Thereafter, appropriate steps may be taken under Article 254 of the Constitution of India. The grant of President's assent to such legislation would be sympathetically considered. The same approach would be adopted in regard to the laws to be made by Parliament in future under the proviso to Clause (2) of that Article. The State Government shall be consulted regarding the application of any such law to the State and the views of the State Government shall receive the fullest consideration.

5. As an arrangement reciprocal to what has been provided under Article 368, a suitable modification of that Article as applied to the State should be made by Presidential order to the effect that no law made

by Legislature of the State of Jammu and Kashmir, seeking to make any change in or to the effect of any provision of the Constitution of the State of Jammu and Kashmir, seeking to make any change in or in the effect of any provision of the Constitution of the State of Jammu and Kashmir relating to any of the under-mentioned matters shall take effect unless the bill, having been reserved for the consideration of the President, receives his assent, the matters are:

(*a*) the appointment, powers, functions, duties, privileges and immunities of the Governor; and

(*b*) the following matters relating to Elections, namely, the superintendence, direction and control of Elections by the Election Commission of India eligibility for enclusion in the electoral rolls without discrimination, adult suffrage, and composition of the Legislative Council, being matters specified in Sections 138, 139, 140 and 50 of the Constitution of the State of Jammu and Kashmir.

6. No agreement was possible on the question of nomenclature of the Governor and the Chief Minister and the matter is therefore remitted to the Principals.

Mirza Mohammad Afzal Beg G. Parthasarathi
New Delhi

Dated: November 13, 1974

PARLIAMENTARY ELECTIONS IN J AND K 1996

.Jammu

In Jammu constituency 5,81,307 people voted out of which 5,67,293 votes were valid. The winning Cong (I) candidate polled as many as 1,95,166 votes while his closest BJP rival got 1,47,494 votes. The break-up of the polling was as follows:

Votes polled	5,81,307
Valid votes	5,67,293
Mangat Ram Sharma (Cong -I)	1,95,166
Vaid Vishnu Dutt (BJP)	1,47,494
Abdul Rehman Sheikh (BSP)	91,480
Balwan Singh (JD)	88,072
Anil Sawhney (Cong-T)	2,145
Navin Bakshi (Panthers Party)	3,275

Ladakh

In Ladakh, the winning Cong. (I) candidate polled 54,592 votes while his close Independent rival polled 44,457 votes. The break-up of polling was as follows:

Votes polled	1,06,347
Valid votes	1,04,777
P. Namgyal (Cong. -I)	54,592
Qamar Ali Akhoon (Ind.)	44,457
Ms Spalzes Angnoo (BJP)	5,728

Baramulla

In Baramulla constituency, 3,05,740 votes were polled out of which 22,948 turned out to be invalid. The winning Cong. (I) candidate polled 1,10,331 while his close Independent rival got 45,350 votes. The break-up of the polling was as follows:

Votes polled	3,28,866
Valid votes	3,05,740
Ghulam Rasool Kar (Cong.-I)	1,10,331
Ghulm Nabi Mir (Ind.)	45,350
Daljit Singh	

Contd.

(Panthers Party)	21,038
Din Mohd. Cheeta (Ind.)	24,628
Giani Sant Singh (Ind.)	18,331
Abdul Ahad Yatoo (Ind.)	26,343
Sheikh Mohd. Sadiq (JD)	25,554
Mohd. Yasin (Ind.)	11,568
N.N Koul (BJP)	12,261
Wali Mohammed (Ind.)	10,336

Anantnag

In Anantnag, the votes polled were 3,83,861 and the winning Janata Dal candidate got 1,17,221 votes while his close Cong. (I) rival polled 59,137 votes. The break-up of the polling was as follows:

Votes polled	3,83,861
Valid votes	3,57,858
Mohd. Maqbool Dar (JD)	1,17,221
Taj Mohi-ud-Din (Cong.-I)	59,137
Mohd. Yusuf (PP)	15,445
Ghulam Nabi Shah (Ind.)	17,726
Abdul Rashid Misgar (Ind.)	29,076
Mohd. Rafiq (Ind)	19,519
Ghulam Nabi Wani (Ind.)	15,352
Ms. Sarla Taploo (BJP)	55,568
Dwarka Nath Raina (Ind.)	5,676
Bashir Ahmed (Ind.)	5,704
Ramzan Bangi (Ind.)	3,151
Mohd. Akbar (Cong.-I)	5,865
Abdul Qayoom Khan (Ind.)	1, 243
Shuban Krishen Tickoo (Ind.)	12,590
ALi Mohhd Dar (Ind.)	5,95

Srinagar

In Srinagar, 3,21,928 people voted out of a total electorate of 7,85,293. The winning Cong. (I) candidate polled 55,503 votes and won barely by 1600 votes against his Janata Dal rival who polled 53,904 votes. The break-up was as follows:

Votes polled	3,21,928
Valid votes	2,97,891
Ghulam Mohd. Mir (Cong.-I)	55,503
Farooq Ahmed Andrabi (JD)	53,904
Amar Nath Vaishnavi (BJP)	35,911
Bashir Ahmed Kathoo (Ind.)	16,863
Roshan Fayaz Rahat (Ind.)	17,230
Javed (Ind.)	38,834
Ghulam Mohammed (Ind.)	15,999
Mohammad Akbar (PP)	36,330
Mrs Mehbooba (Ind.)	18,369
Brij Nath Dhar (Ind.)	5,878
Nazeer Ahmed (Ind.)	3,070

Udhampur

In Udhampur,4,59,456 people exercised their franchise of which16,968 votes were declared invalid. The BJP candidate won the seat by defeating his close Cong. (I) rival.The break-up of the votes polled by major political parties is as under:

Votes polled	4,59,456
Valid votes	4,41,852
Prof. Chaman Lal Gupta (BJP)	1,66,206
Janak Raj Gupta (Cong.-I)	96,151
Devi Das Thakur (JD)	81,123
Prof Bhim Singh (Panthers Party)	23,611
Tulsi Dass (BSP)	32,011
Gulchain Singh Charak (Cong.-I)	9,269

Constituency wise Polling Stations and Electorate of Lok Sabha in J & K as on January, 1996

S. No.	Name Of The Constituency	Total No. Of Polling Stations	Total No. of Electorate
1.	Anantnag	991	7,65,571
2.	Baramulla	1,120	7,04,601
3.	Srinagar	939	7,85,293
4.	Ladakh	361	1,27,729
5.	Jammu	1,501	11,83,772
6.	Udhampur	1,279	8,53,460
	Total	6,191	44,20,426
	S..... Voters		30,836
	G. Total		44,51,262

Kupwara District

S. No.	Name of the Constituency	Total No. Of Polling Stations	Total No. Of Electorate	S. Vote
1.	Karnah	56	21193	102
2.	Kupwara	97	62479	40
3.	Lolab	86	55754	158
4.	Handwara	84	52962	9
5.	Langate	70	41408	3
	Total:-	393	2,33,796	312

Baramulla District

6.	Uri	80	44257	16
7.	Rafiabad	72	47245	-
8.	Sopore	87	63387	-
9.	Gurez	17	9846	-
10.	Bandipora	91	54217	14
11.	Sonawari	61	54422	-
12.	Sangrama	63	38925	-
13.	Baramulla	90	57544	-

Contd....

14.	Gulmarg	100	53765	-
15.	Pattan	66	52997	-
	Total:	727	4,70,805	30

Srinagar District

16.	Kangan	55	35910	1
17.	Ganderbal	62	47814	-
18.	Hazratbal	90	67147	-
19.	Zadibal	56	47370	-
20.	Idgah	65	55270	-
21.	Khanyar	76	58486	-
22.	Habakadal	68	55517	2
23	.Amirakadal	65	50417	-
24	.Sonawar	64	50863	3
25.	Batmaloo	84	73318	-
	Total:	685	5,42,112	6

Badgam District

26.	Chadura	38	40418	5
27.	Budgam	54	54492	-
28.	Beerwah	58	54892	13
29.	Khansahib	53	47538	29
30.	Charar-i-Sharief	51	45841	7
	Total:	254	2,43,181	54

Pulwama District

31.	Tral	82	53380	11
32.	Pampore	58	42104	2
33.	Pulwama	64	46199	-
34.	Rajpora	76	51332	3
35.	Wachi	63	45259	-
36.	Shopian	65	45406	2
	Total:	408	2,83,680	18

Anantnag District

37.	Noorabad	53	40140	17
38.	Kulgam	72	53857	6
39.	Homeshalibugh	54	41692	3
40.	Anantnag	66	52422	7
41.	Devsar	68	46765	12
42.	Doru	52	43895	21
43.	Kokernag	54	53208	13
44.	Shangus	51	44734	22
45.	Bijbehara	58	60655	9
46.	Pahalgam	55	44523	1
	Total:	583	4,81,891	111

Leh District

47.	Nobra	45	9587	446
48.	Leh	149	53518	3107
	Total:	194	63105	3553

Kargil District

49.	Kargil	110	47839	78
50.	Zanskar	57	16785	42
	Total:	167	64,624	120

Doda District

51.	Kishtwar	79	45793	153
52.	Inderwal	74	43793	155
53.	Doda	83	43999	102
54.	Bhaderwah	83	58012	331
55.	Ramban (SC)	71	42601	87
56.	Banihal	65	43600	59
	Total:	455	2,77,198	887

Udhampur District

57.	Gulabgarh	65	39908	29
58.	Reasi	115	64739	187
59.	Gool Arnas	64	35340	32
60.	Udhampur	82	63658	345
61.	Chenani (SC)	71	47747	467
62.	Ramnagar	80	62966	575
	Total:	477	3,14,358	1635

Kathua District

63.	Bani	41	24692	24
64.	Basohli	61	44507	826
65.	Kathua	80	70712	1292
66.	Billawar	80	54285	568
67.	Hiranagar (SC)	85	67708	1189
	Total:	347	2,61,904	3899

Jammu District

68.	Samba (SC)	73	55063	925
69.	Vijaypur	78	67085	3860
70.	Nagrota	55	38989	1050
71.	Gandhinagar	113	95453	779
72.	Jammu East	76	64633	95
73.	Jammu West	114	96423	307
74.	Bishnah	60	54122	307
75.	R.S.Pura (SC)	63	55575	1180
76.	Suchetgarh	46	42446	777
77.	Marh	51	45297	1409
78.	Raipur Domana (SC)	56	45669	900
79.	Akhnoor	85	55678	989
80.	Chhamb (SC)	64	48031	2003
	Total:	934	7,64,464	16,152

Rajouri District

81.	Nowshera	77	57768	2087
82.	Darhal	78	58773	323
83.	Rajouri	86	70587	335
84.	Kalakote	66	49221	568
	Total:-	307	2,36,349	3323

Poonch District

85.	Surankote	87	59448	145
86.	Mendhar	81	59844	252
87.	Poonch Haveli	92	63667	339
	Total:	260	1,82,959	736
	Grand Total:	619144,	44,20,426	30,836
	Including Service Votes		44,51,262	

Votes polled by Political Parties in Lok Sabha Elections

	1984	*1989*
Total Electorate	34,00,010	41,50,973
Total Votes Polled	20,65,489	10,46,121
INC	6,61,435	4,07,474
JKNC	9,07,627	71,194
BJP	37,309	74,732
JKNC (K)	1,60,148	-
PP	95,149	22,625
JKPC	646	-
Lok Dal	2,423	-
Janata Dal	-	3,14,357
Janata Party (JP)	-	11,049
BSP	-	42,453
Proutist Bloc India	-	1,718
Others	2,05,431	1,00,160

Votes polled by Political Parties in Lok Sabha Election

	1977	*1980*
Total Electorate	25,57,422	28,91,052
Total Votes Polled	14,24,324	13,77,988
INC (I)	2,33,144	2,49,760
BLD (Janata Party)	1,17,198	
National Conference	4,83,192	4,93,143
INC (U)	-	1,94,138
JP	-	1,15,503
Others	5,90,790	2,84,459

District-wise Population—1981

District	*Population 1981 Census*	*Scheduled Castes (persons) 1981 Census*
1	*2*	*3*
Anantnag	6,56,351	6
Pulwama	4,04,078	22
Srinagar	7,08,328	109
Badgam	3,67,262	39
Baramulla	6,70,142	92
Kupwara	3,28,743	29
Kargil	65,992	65
Ladakh-Leh	68,380	228
Doda	4,25,262	37,173
Udhampur	4,53,636	85,056
Kathua	3,69,123	84,308
Jammu	9,43,395	2,67,508
Rajpouri	,3,02,500	22,519
Poonch	2,24,197	209
Total:	59,87,389	4,97,363

Religion-wise Population in J&K 1981

District	Hindu	Sikh	Muslim	Christian	Buddhists	Jains	Other	Rg. not stated	Total
1	2	3	4	5	6	7	8	9	10
Anantnag	24731	3863	627721	36	.	.	.	.	656351
Pulwama	10096	6568	387414	.	.	.	.	.	404078
Srinagar	59449	6334	642106	209	176	54	.	.	708328
Badgam	9642	5158	352355	96	11	.	.	.	367262
Baramulla	13513	9806	646707	106	2	8	.	.	670142
Kupwara	6647	1448	320629	19	.	.	.	.	326743
Leh	2046	184	10475	156	55514	.	5	.	68380
Kargil	1492	150	51407	81	12862	.	.	.	65992
Jammu	824209	72034	40309	5413	11	1412	7	.	943395
Udhampur	327538	5741	118987	1283	.	81	.	6	453636
Doda	179538	847	243666	49	1113	17	32	.	425262
Kathua	336503	6082	25699	820	15	4	.	.	369123
Rajouri	118705	7326	176302	165	2	.	.	.	302500
Poonch	16339	8134	199674	48	.	.	.	2	224197
State	1930448	133675	3843451	8481	69706	1576	44	8	5987369

Scheduled Caste Population in J&K 1981 Census

District	*Scheduled Castes*		
	Rural	*Urban*	*Total*
1	*2*	*3*	*4*
Anantnag	6	-	6
Pulwama	22	-	22
Srinagar	1	108	109
Budgam	28	11	39
Baramulla	92	-	92
Kupwara	29	-	29
Leh	147	81	228
Kargil	65	-	65
Jammu	226043	41465	267508
Udhampur	80070	4986	85056

1	2	3	4
Doda	36517	656	37173
Kathua	75144	9164	84308
Rajouri	21648	871	22519
Poonch	205	4	209
State	440017	57346	497363

Source: Census Deptt.
Note: Census in J&K in 1991 have not been conducted.

Segment-wise Result of 1989 Lok Sabha Elections

(Note:- Result of only first three contestants given)

1. BARAMULLA

Assembly Segment	*Candidates with party affiliation & valid votes polled*			*Total valid votes*	*Votes rejected polled*	*Total votes polled*
	Prof. Saif-ud-Din Soz (JKNC)	*Sheikh Abdul Rehman (IND)*	*Sant Singh (IND)*			
1	2	3	4	5	6	7
1. Karnah	3,303	61	33	3,594	135	3,729
2. Handwara	11,119	331	29	11,595	186	11,781
3. Langate	2,938	41	18	3,041	85	3,126
4. Kupwara	1,469	20	9	1,519	46	1,565
5. Bandipore	1,711	118	135	2,256	89	2,345
6. Sonawari	1,494	9	15	1,548	28	1,576
7. Pattan	1	-	-	1	-	1
8. Gulmarg	142	2	2	150		150
9. Sangrama	59	-	-	60	-	60
10. Sopore	156	-	-	180	-	180
11. Rafiabad	585	1	5	599	6	605
12. Baramulla	1,097	5	195	1,308	14	1,322
13. Uri	11,029	127	171	11,543	172	11,715
Votes recorded on postal Ballots	36	4	8	72	8	80
Grand Total:	35,139	719	620	37,466	769	38,235

2. SRINAGAR PARLIAMENTARY CONSTITUENCIES MOHD. SHAFI BHAT OF JKNC DECLARED UNCONTESTED WINNER.

3. ANANTNAG

	P.L. Handoo (JKNC)	*Abdul Rashid Khan (IND)*	*Abdul Rashid Thokar (IND)*			
1	*2*	*3*	*4*	*5*	*6*	*7*
28. Pulwama	842	1	6	874	271	1,145
29. Pampore	4,404	8	14	4,505	18	4,523
30. Tral	36	-	1	118	1	119
31. Wachni	358	-	3	366	18	384
32. Shopian	3,470	3	30	3,583	45	3,628
33. Noorabad	4,962	9	26	5,097	44	5,142
34. Devsar	3,896	15	6	3,946	17	3,963
35. Kulgam	1,332	1	2	1,339	4	1,343
36. Homeshali-bugh	81	-	-	81	-	81
37. Pahalgam	3,034	1	7	3,066	10	3,076
38. Bijbehara	4,468	25	8	4,532	17	4,549
39. Anantnag	47	-	-	47	-	47
40. Shangag	1,193	1	2	1,200	-	1,200
41. Kokernag	937	91	15	1,057	10	1,067
42. Duroo	6,995	31	27	7,097	715	7,111
Votes recorded on postal ballots	-	-	-	-	-	-
Grand Total :	36,055	186	147	36,908	470	37,378

4. LADAKH

1	P. Namgiyal (INC) 2	Mohd. Hassan Commander (IND) 3	4	5	6
43. Leh	35,748	3,907	39,655	796	40,451
44. Kargil	4,495	41,241	45,736	459	46,195
Votes recorded on postal Ballots	369	3	372	845	1,217
Grand Total :	40,612	45,151	85,763	2100	87,863

5. UDHAMPUR

1	Dharam Paul (INC) 2	Abdul Rehman (JD) 3	Th. Baldev Singh (BJP) 4	5	6	7
45. Kishtwar	6,821	2,102	2,724	12,958	185	13,143
46. Inderwal	5,629	5,100	413	12,232	197	12,429
47. Bhaderwah (SC)	5,973	6,003	2,725	15,262	211	15,773
48. Doda	4,259	3,285	823	9,181	110	9,291
49. Ramban	5,314	5,272	955	12,849	135	12,984
50. Banihal	1,051	4,216	43	5,740	48	5,788
51. Gool Gulab Garh	2,528	16,899	113	22,687	373	23,062
52. Reasi	9,325	9,775	1,050	23,829	356	24,185
53. Udhampur	13,442	5,655	7,094	30,472	506	30,978
54. Chenani Ghordi	11,913	3,497	1,025	26,702	695	27,397
55. Ramnagar (SC)	8,957	4,127	1,552	20,936	380	21,316
56. Basohli	10,552	8,422	1,905	24,848	361	25,209
57. Billawar	11,946	8,354	3,000	27,231	1,126	28,357
58. Kathua (SC)	15,156	10,431	5,958	35,839	764	36,603
59. Hiranagar	14,295	3,213	10,120	31,696	536	32,232
Votes recorded on postal Ballots	-	-	-	-	581	581
Grand Total :	1,27,161	96,351	39,509	3,12,762	6,564	3,19,326

6. JAMMU

1	*Janak Raj Gupta (INC)* 2	*R.S. Chib (JD) (IND)* 3	*Girdhari Lal (BSP)* 4	5	6	7
56. Samba	12,449	15,639	5,340	39,414	896	40,310
57. Bari-Brahmana (S)	9,943	12,280	5,953	32,487	717	33,204
58. Bishnah (SC)	12,221	10,412	5,593	32,354	915	33,269
59. Ranbir Singh Pora	12,710	16,868	7,035	40,465	646	41,111
60. Jammu Contonment	13,917	17,860	3,411	39,895	967	40,862
61. Jammu West	14,627	9,821	1,857	31,998	541	32,539
62. Jammu East	9,687	6,654	251	23,929	334	24,263
63. Jandrah Gharota	14,842	14,216	3,429	37,698	748	38,446
64. Marh (SC)	16,033	11,522	2,304	33,180	980	34,160
65. Akhnoor	16,705	7,861	2,989	32,878	469	33,347
66. Chhamb	15,140	11,104	3,163	32,955	521	33,476
67. Nowshera	20,096	14,625	587	39,717	518	40,235
68. Darhal	11,097	18,878	151	34,184	454	34,638
69. Rajouri	20,830	15,093	118	39,691	605	40,376
70. Suran	11,877	14,207	80	28,354	322	28,676
71. Mendhar	14,243	13,466	62	29,479	838	30,317
72. Haveli	13,284	8,300	130	24,545	304	24,849
Grand Total :	2,39,701	2,18,006	42,453 ,	5,73223	10,855	5,84,078

Postal ballot papers have been included in 56-Samba Assembly Segments

GENERAL ELECTION ON LOK SABHA -1984

Assembly segment-wise valid votes polled by each contesting candidate

Constituency Parliamentary 1- Baramulla

Contd....

Name of the Assembly Segment	*Name of candidates with their party affiliation and valid votes polled*			*Total valid votes polled*
	Prof. Saif-ud-Din Soz. (JKNC)	*Ghulam Ahmed Ganai Wani. (IND.)*	*Mohi-ud-Din Wani (JKNC) (K)*	
1	2	3	4	5
Karnah	18,170	673	6,500	25,403
Handwara	25,927	901	5,870	32,698
Langate	13,573	603	5,830	20,006
Kupwara	17,621	618	4,284	22,523
Bandipora	22,542	918	6,420	29,880
Sonawari	22,057	673	10,136	32,866
Pattan	19,681	433	9,801	29,915
Gulamarg	16,244	521	7,518	24,283
Sangrama	15,062	509	5,162	20,733
Sopore	18,536	572	5,897	25,005
Rafiabad	16,897	652	7,274	24,823
Baramulla	15,280	387	6,532	22,199
Uri	12,586	451	12,551	25,588
Votes recorded on postal ballots	181	87	103	371
Grand Total :	2,34,357	7,998	93,958	3,36,293

Parliamentary Constituency 2- Srinagar

Name of the Assembly Segment	Name of candidates with their party affiliation and valid votes polled each of them.			Total Valid Votes polled
	P.N. Koul (IND)	*Vakil Abdul Rashid Kabli (JKNC)*	*Muzaffar Ahmed Shah (JKNC) (K)*	
1	2	3	4	5
Kangan	51	19,429	3,150	22,940
Ganderbal	42	20,004	2,547	22,837
Hazratbal	46	20,597	4,134	24,952
Amirakadal	85	23,587	7,691	31,649

1	2	3	4	5
Habakadal	57	21,581	3,895	25,840
Zainakadal	11	10,882	381	11,323
Idgah	21	20,767	1,133	22,066
Zadibal	17	25,201	3,562	28,970
Nagin	55	21,056	3,562	28,970
Beerwa	54	18,471	5,086	26,430
Khansahib	71	15,728	6,284	25,134
Budgam	53	15,857	7,567	23,699
Chadura	66	19,243	5,046	21,166
Chararisharif	43	12,210	4,781	24,440
Votes recorded on			6,248	18,763
postal ballots	8	20	26	60
Grand Total :	680	2,64,63	61,531	3,30,269

Parliamentary Constituency 3- Anantnag

	Akabar Jehan Begum (NC)	*Hissam-ud-Din (INC)*	*Total Valid Votes Polled*
1	2	3	4
Pulwama	22,207	9,849	32,906
Pampore	25,113	6,154	32,081
Tral	19,855	8,371	29,778
Wachi	19,533	8,691	28,832
Shopian	20,382	7,412	28,634
Noorabad	12,501	10,420	24,001
Devsar	13,836	12,531	27,328
Kulgam	14,114	11,201	20,583
Bijbehara	14,025	16,659	25,261
Anantnag	15,132	12,009	25,971
Shangas	13,833	11,321	31,287
Kokernag	12,632	14,264	27,595

1	2	3	4
Doru	12,079	11,114	25,872
Votes recorded on postal ballots	61	22	23,921 84
Total	2,40,973	1,58,963	4,11,826

Parliamentary Constituency 4- Ladakh

	P.Namgiyal (INC)	*Sonam Wangdus (Ind)*	*Qamar Ali (JKNC)*	*Total Votes*
1	2	3	4	5
Leh	18,019	591	3,776	22,386
Kargil	14,294	710	21,269	36,273
Votes recorded on postal ballots	724	30	15	769
Total	33,037	1,331	25,060	59,428

Parliamentary Constituency 5- Udhampur

	Baldev Singh (BJP)	*Bhim Singh (PP)*	*G.L. Dogra (INC)*	*Total Votes Polled*
1	2	3	4	5
Kishtwar	579	6,039	10,915	19,152
Inderwal	295	8,704	8,894	19,292
Bhaderwah (SC)	779	7,638	11,197	20,645
Doda	409	8,562	11,497	22,108
Ramban	555	6,940	11,076	19,889
Banihal	233	9,587	6,362	17,861
Gulabgarh	368	14,424	7,786	25,089
Reasi	2,933	6,069	16,912	28,819
Udhampur	4,509	3,245	20,363	30,035
Chenani Ghordi	1,249	5,329	16,597	25,199
Ramnagar (SC)	1,830	4,425	16,398	24,926
Basohli	2,668	4,464	13,571	22,922

1	2	3	4	5
Billawar	3,620	3,607	16,397	26,228
Kathua (SC)	6,998	3,460	19,387	33,342
Hiranagar	10,113	2,374	17,964	34,591
Votes recorded postal ballots	171	282	9	1,979
Total	37,309	95,149	2,06,689	3,72,077

Parliamentary Constituency 6. Jammu

	Janak Raj Gupta (INC)	*Ch. Shabir Ahmed Salaria (JKNC)*	*Dr. Karan Singh (Ind.)*	*Total Votes polled*
1	2	3	4	5
Samba	14,801	3,652	16,623	37,632
Bari-Brahmana (SC)	16,842	4,036	8,795	33,239
Bishnah (SC)	22,385	2,895	9,015	37,135
Ranbir Singh Pura	20,819	7,251	8,435	38,330
Jammu Cantonment	16,437	9,884	9,751	38,389
Jammu West	17,430	2,492	12,558	33,890
Jammu East	11,539	2,188	14,393	28,805
Jandrah Gharota	16,035	4,301	13,576	36,832
Marh (SC)	19,972	3,065	9,500	34,884
Akhnoor	16,316	3,232	9,559	30,917
Chhamb	14,121	863	12,741	29,105
Nowshera	21,410	6,609	7,892	37,945
Darhal	13,350	18,661	2,795	36,011
Rajouri	9,022	24,025	1,931	36,190
Suran	10,781	15,439	129	27,138
Mendhar	11,382	18,209	406	30,660
Haveli	8,751	15,673	462	26,193
Votes recorded on postal ballots	1,403	133	1,360	3,095
Total:	2,62,796	1,42,604	1,39,913	5,76,390

ANALYSIS OF LEGISLATIVE ASSEMBLY ELECTIONS (DISTRICT WISE)

Abstract (Electorate and Votes Polled) (1972) ASSEMBLY ELECTIONS

District	Electorate			Electorate voted		
	Men	*Women*	*Total*	*Men*	*Women*	*Total*
1	*2*	*3*	*4*	*5*	*6*	*7*
Baramulla	2,27,474	1,85,396	4,12,869	1,66,784	1,09,783	2,76,567
Srinagar	2,14,675	1,74,437	3,89,112	1,58,026	97,696	2,55,722
Anantnag	2,07724	1,70,493	3,78,217	1,74,660	1,02,889	2,77,149
Ladakh	14,539	15,032	29,571	11,348	11,052	22,400
Doda	73,485	64,013	1,37,498	43,894	19,572	63,392
Udhampur	87,458	77,102	1,64,560	60,070	43,196	1,03,266
Kathua	67,907	62,897	1,30,804	48,653	38,678	87,331
Jammu	1,64,623	1,57,942	3,22,565	1,18239	1,09721	2,27,960
Rajouri	54,028	49,501	1,03,529	40,579	23,385	63,964
Poonch	45,279	41,726	87,005	33,553	16,991	50,544
Total:	11,57,191	9,98,539	21,55,730	8,55,732	5,72,963	14,28,695

(1977) ASEMBLY ELECTIONS

District	Electorate			Electorate voted		
	Men	Women	Total	Men	Women	Total
1	2	3	4	5	6	7
Baramulla	2,53,803	2,04,121	4,57,924	2,05,085	1,35,572	3,40,651
Srinagar	2,85,641	2,40,787	5,26,428	2,30,487	1,80,975	4,11,462
Anantnag	2,62,299	2,16,812	4,79,111	2,19,186	1,56,601	3,75,787
Ladakh	34,558	32,079	66,637	24,757	21,272	46,029
Doda	94,661	83,452	1,78,113	54,585	25,395	79,980
Udhampur	92,941	84,805	1,77,746	55,131	29,832	84,963
Kathua	80,640	72,456	1,53,096	48,803	39,552	88,355
Jammu	2,07,344	1,89,729	3,97,073	1,28,190	1,16,827	2,45,027
Rajouri	65,522	60,799	1,26,321	42.150	27,863	70,013
Poonch	54,281	48,262	1,02,543	38,832	23,009	61,841
Total:	14,31,690	12,33,302	26,64,992	10,47,206	7,56,898	18,04,104

1983 ASSEMBLY ELECTIONS

Name of the District	Electorate			Voted Polled		
	Men	Women	Total	Men	Women	Total
1	2	3	4	5	6	7
Kupwara	98,235	81,394	1,79,629	79,753	51,666	1,31,419
Baramulla	1,94,657	1,54,494	3,49,151	1,57,641	1,14,641	2,72,009
Srinagar	2,27,569	1,78,798	4,06,367	1,88,662	1,45,769	3,34,431
Budgam	1,06,278	83,401	1,89,697	83,497	56,300	1,39,797
Pulwama	1,04,995	90,422	1,95,417	91,767	70,354	1,62,121
Anantnag	2,10,448	1,50,715	3,61,163	1,60,965	1,32,989	2,93,954
Ladakh	19,335	18,431	37,766	13,335	12,007	25,342
Kargi 1	24,489	24,795	49,284	20,206	17,643	37,849
Doda	96,560	82,380	1,78,940	71,009	46,894	1,17,903
Udhampur	1,08,542	99,789	2,08,331	72,268	50,425	1,22,693
Kathua	96,889	89,818	186,707	63,547	53,834	1,17,381
Jammu	2,48,313	2,28,610	4,76,923	1,67,800	1,52,276	3,20,076
Rajouri	81,289	73,182	1,54,471	55,623	49,768	1,05,391
Poonch	68,335	59,502	1,27,837	51,226	40,217	91,443
Total:	16,85,934	14,15,731	31,01,665	12,79,135	9,92,674	22,71,809

1987 ASSEMBLY ELECTIONS

District	*Electorate*	*Voted Polled*	*Valid Votes*
1	*2*	*53*	*4*
Kupwara	1,94,179	1,49,656	1,64,292
Baramulla	4,06,305	3,21,880	3,13,846
Srinagar	4,64,364	3,33,998	3,25,373
Budgam	2,22,425	1,76,603	1,71,544
Pulwama	2,35,553	1,95,519	1,90,275
Anantnag	4,20,185	3,42,105	3,31,650
Ladakh	43,455	29,658	28,624
Kargil	51,646	40,614	39,986
Doda	2,44,485	1,60,930	1,58,386
Udhampur	2,44,505	1,55,243	1,52,993
Jammu	5,29,691	3,80,351	3,73,340
Kathua	1,98,468	1,31,523	1,29,590
Rajouri	1,75,697	1,32,858	1,30,807
Poonch	1,46,423	1,11,417	1,10,119
Total:	35,77,381	26,62,355	26,00,765

NO. AND NAME OF THE ASSEMBLY CONSTITUENCY

KUPWARA DISTRICT

1. Karnah	2. Kupwara	3. Lolab
4. Handwara	5. Langate	

BARAMULLA DISTRICT

6. Uri	7. Rafiabad	8. Sopore
9. Gurez	10. Bandipora	11. Sonawari
12. Sangrama	13. Baramulla	14 Gulmarg
15. Pattan		

SRINAGAR DISTRICT

16. Kangan	17. Ganderbal	18. Hazratbal
19. Zadibal	20. Idgah	21. Khanyar

22. Habbakadal
23. Amirakadal
24. Sonawar
25. Batamaloo

BUDGAM DISTRICT

26. Chadoora
27. Badgam
28. Beerwah
29. Khansahib
30. Chrar-i-Sharief

PULWAMA DISTRICT

31. Tral
32. Pampora
33. Pulwama
34. Rajpora
35. Wachi
36. Shopian

ANANTNAG DISTRICT

37. Noorabad
38. Kulgam
39. Devsar
40. Homeshalibugh
41. Anantnag
42. Doru
43. Kokernag
44. Shangus
45. Bijbehara
46. Pahalgam

LEH DISTRICT

47. Nobra
48. Leh

KARGIL DISTRICT

49. Kargil
50. Zanskar

DODA DISTRICT

51. Kishtwar
52. Inderwal
53. Doda
54. Bhaderwah
55. Ramban (SC)
56. Baniha

UDHAMPUR DISTRICT

57. Gulabgarh
58. Reasi
59. Gool Arnas
60. Udhampur
61. Chanani (SC)
62. Ramnagar

KATHUA DISTRICT

63. Bani
64. Basohli
65. Kathua
66. Billawar
67. Hiranagar (SC)

JAMMU DISTRICT

68. Samba (SC)
69. Vijaypur
70. Nagrota
71. Gandhinagat
72. Jammu East.
73. Jammu West.
74. Bishnah
75. R.S. Pura (SC)
76. Suchetgarh
77. Marh
78. Raipur Domana (SC)
79. Akhnoor
80. Chhamb (SC)

RAJOURI DISTRICT

81. Nowshara
82. Darhal
83. Rajouri
84. Kalakote

POONCH DISTRICT

85. Surankote
86. Mendhar
87. PoonchHaveli